This document is geared towards providing exact and reliable information regarding the topic and issue covered. The publication is sold because the publisher is not required to render officially permitted or otherwise qualified accounting services. If advice is necessary, legal or professional, it should be obtained.

From a Declaration of Principles, which was accepted and approved equally by a Committee of the American Bar Association and a Committee of Publishers and Associations.

It is not legal to reproduce, duplicate, or transmit any part of this document electronically or in printed format. Recording this publication is strictly prohibited, and any storage of this document is prohibited unless the publisher gives written permission. All rights reserved.

The information provided herein is truthful and consistent in that any liability, in terms of inattention or otherwise, by any usage or abuse of any policies, processes, or directions contained within is the sole and utter responsibility of the recipient reader. Under no circumstances will any legal obligation or blame be held against the publisher for any reparation, damages, or monetary loss due to the information herein, either directly or indirectly.

Respective authors own all copyrights not held by the publisher.

The information herein is offered solely for informational purposes and is universal. It is presented without a contract or any guaranteed assurance.

The trademarks used are without consent, and the trademark publication is without permission or backing from the trademark owner. All trademarks and brands within this book are for clarifying purposes only and are owned by the owners and not affiliated with this document.

I have recreated events, locales, and conversations for my memories of them. In some instances, I have changed the names of individuals and places to maintain their anonymity. I may have changed some identifying characteristics and details, such as physical properties, occupations, and areas of residence.

This book or parts thereof may not be reproduced in any form, stored in any retrieval system, or transmitted in any way by any means—electronic, mechanical, photocopy, recording, or otherwise—without prior written permission of the publisher, except as provided by United States of America copyright law. For permission requests, write to the publisher at "Attention: Permissions Coordinator" at the address below.

This memoir is a work of nonfiction. Names, characters, places, public or private institutions, corporations, towns, and incidents are a product of the author's life based on actual events. Some names and identifying details have been changed.

All rights reserved following the U.S. Copyright Act of 1976; the scanning, uploading, and electronic sharing of any part of this book without the publisher's permission is unlawful piracy and theft of the author's intellectual property. If you would like to use material from the book (other than for review purposes), prior written permission must be obtained by contacting the publisher at email atlife@yahoo.com

I appreciate your support of the author's rights. 1st edition: Fighting Hell Headed to Israel © Copyright 2024 by Cheryl Remington – All rights reserved.

Contents

1. Introduction
2. The Day Faith Died
3. Headed to the Casino
4. Reservations
5. Tel Aviv
6. Why Jerusalem?
7. Jerusalem-The Old City
8. Idolatry Destroyed
9. Western Wall
10. Ark of the Covenant
11. Singing in the Streets
12. Prayer Tower
13. Return to Dallas
14. Leap Year-February 29, 2020
15. Endora the Witch
16. Arrested Mexican Jail
17. Marie Arrives in Mexico May 19, 2020
18. Kris was Murdered on May 28, 2020
19. Justice for Kris
20. Does ObamaCare?
21. Dream School
22. One Big Swoosh
23. The Exodus Escape
24. Miracle in the Plaza

25. Medical Emergency
26. Critical Mission

Chapter One
Introduction

To my cherished son JD,

From the moment you entered this world as my firstborn, you became a radiant light in my life, filling my heart with an indescribable love that grows deeper with each passing day. Your very presence is a remarkable gift that astonishes me continually. Even in infancy, you showcased a gentle spirit, radiating love, compassion, and kindness that seemed to transcend your tender years. As you matured, I watched you embrace the role of protector, exhibiting a profound loyalty that enveloped Kris and me, a trait I hold close to my heart.

Together, we have journeyed through the many intricate twists and turns that life has brought us. In the wake of your Dad's heartbreaking death, our family dynamic underwent a drastic transformation. It became a sacred trio—just you, me, and Kris—leaning on one another as we navigated the depths of grief and its accompanying challenges. As time moved, our world shifted again, narrowing to just the two of us, facing the vast landscape of life with unwavering resilience and an indomitable spirit.

The timeless song "You and Me Against the World" by Helen Reddy encapsulates our shared journey, perfectly mirroring the unbreakable bond we have forged through the trials we faced. Each note and lyric serves as a reminder of the strength we've drawn from one another, intertwined with the support we've received through our faith. With God's unwavering strength guiding our steps, we have faced and overcome life's challenges, emerging intact and more robust.

Your heartfelt words often echo in my mind, reminding me of my significance in your life: "Mom, I am proud of you. Now go get 'em, tiger." Those profound yet straightforward phrases resonate deeply, inspiring me to keep moving forward while constantly reminding me of the love that binds us together.

Thank you for being such an incredible son. My love for you knows no bounds, and I cherish every moment we share on this beautiful journey together. The most heartwarming words a single mother could ever hear echo in your young voice when you tell me, "You are my hero, and I want to be just like you." In those precious moments, I am reminded that I must have done something right as you shower me with profound love and respect.

Kris, you have always believed that I could perform miracles and move mountains, but it was not I who accomplished those amazing feats; it was God. You, JD, and Adonai have been my entire world and purpose. Your unwavering support has given me the strength to persevere through life's challenges. You left this world on May 28th to be with the Lord, leaving behind the most incredible treasure: your son. Although he was absent from my life for three years, he recently returned on November 14th, 2024, during a time when he committed his life to God.

You asked me to write my life's stories so you would know how I made it through the nightmares. This series will guide your son on his new journey as he takes your place by my side.

What seemed impossible became within reach as Adonai blessed me with the two of you. Disappointing you was never an option, which fueled my determination to stay focused and never give up, no matter the obstacles in my path.

I am profoundly grateful for your encouragement throughout this exhausting journey of writing my memoirs. I know the world will one day thank you for urging me to bring this series to life and complete the books I've meant to share.

I remember first picking up Robert Munsch's poignant book, "Love You Forever." As I read the heartfelt story, I was flooded with thoughts of you boys, and when you later gifted me a copy, it became a cherished keepsake. I cannot hold back the tears whenever I attempt to read it. My love for you is eternal—forever and always; as long as I have breath, you will always be my baby.

Kris, my beloved son, you have meant the world to me. Over the years, you have asked me to recount my life's story, yearning to know how I triumphed over pain, heartache, trials, and disappointments. I have sat down many times to fulfill your request, yet each day seemed to bring another unexpected twist that overwhelmed me.

One of my last attempts was made a daunting fourteen years ago, and that draft bore the title "Down Memory Lane." Though my efforts were cut short, I eventually completed the manuscript, yet the weight of daily struggles loomed heavily over me. Writing that book would have evolved into an expansive series if I pressed on.

In an ironic twist of fate, this narrative blossomed into what is now known as the "Victorious" series. Each page is rich with the layers of trauma and drama that have marked my life. Readers can dive deep into the pages or listen to the audiobooks. As each chapter unfolds, many will discover resonant echoes of their own life experiences woven into mine.

Let me state emphatically: none of this journey would have been possible without Adonai, the master of the Universe and the essence of my soul. I will show you how to trust Him, for it is essential to understand that He has never been the source of our pain or heartache. Those burdens belong solely to the wicked who roam this Earth.

The adventures chronicled in this series arrived like sudden storms, without any warning or hazard signs; challenges emerged unexpectedly, reshaping the very fabric of who I am today.

Within each story lies a profound revelation of the secrets that led to my survival and success against the odds. You will discover how Adonai, the omnipotent creator of the Universe, steadily guided my vessel, steering me through waves of pain and turmoil. My unwavering dedication to Him is like an unshakable lighthouse in the storm, illuminating my path with love and grace.

Some may scoff and insist that no one could endure the trials I have faced, dismissing my tales as mere fabrications or the fantasies of an overactive imagination. They might wonder aloud how anyone could traverse such harrowing experiences without succumbing to despair, isolation, or the confines of a mental health institution.

Through the tapestry of my life stories, I will unveil a testament to the divine truth that only Adonai's immense wisdom and boundless strength preserved my mental clarity and kept me whole amidst the chaos.

Sometimes, it felt like a vivid bullseye was drawn around me, marked with the daunting command to destroy, no matter the cost.

Kris, I am honoring your memory by fulfilling your request. As I type with tears cascading down my cheeks, I am pouring out every painful detail of our shared journey. I embark on this narrative with the memories of our profound trip to Israel in 2019 and will weave through the tapestry of our experiences until 2023. No book can encapsulate every facet of my life, so I have dedicated this series to my beloved family.

In penning this series, my deepest desire is to offer hope and inspiration to those who feel lost, adrift without navigational stars, living in an oppressive darkness of defeat, choked by overwhelming challenges. I aim for this collection of writings to serve as a navigational map, guiding readers through life's winding paths and unforeseen turns.

To my children and grandchildren, I want you to understand that when life delivers its harshest blows, you do not have to succumb to being a victim of your circumstances.

Never, under any circumstances, relinquish control of your life to others simply because they are struggling with their own. You possess the power to choose; no one else can dictate your actions or compel you to stray from your moral compass—you can always walk away. Peer pressure may create a façade of excuses for poor choices, and it is vital to distance yourself from those who lack integrity. Remember, you do not need social media validation; those lurking in those digital corners will never honestly care for your well-being. Chasing likes or shares through posts will not nurture your self-esteem.

Genuine confidence is not cultivated by the number of friends you accrue online but is forged through the obstacles you overcome and the endeavors you see to completion.

In this life, you may find yourself pursuing fortune and fame while desperately seeking the approval of others, risking the loss of your true identity. Be wary of flattery; it can be a double-edged sword.

Pleading for acceptance through compromises can erode your character. Your reputation is a precious commodity that must be protected and valued.

The wisdom found in Proverbs 24:16 from the New King James Version of the Bible perfectly encapsulates the essence of the human experience: "For a righteous man may fall seven times and rise again, but the wicked shall fall by calamity." This scripture eloquently conveys the reality of our nature.

We will stumble along the way; when you do, face your mistakes head-on and rectify them promptly.

I hope this series of books transforms into a treasured guide, imparting invaluable lessons on leading a victorious life. I sincerely hope these words endure long after I have departed.

To my family, honor my legacy by passing down your heritage and the steadfast legacy of faith to others. The pain I have endured was not inflicted by God but rather by those with evil intentions whose sole purpose was to undermine my faith, extinguish my dreams, and shatter my hope.

Expressing my heartfelt gratitude is a formidable challenge, given the profound support and unwavering love the following individuals have shown me.

They became the family I never knew I needed. When many chose to walk away, they remained steadfast by my side.

I want to extend a special acknowledgment to my Private Secretary, Stacey. Your Mom first stepped into my church in July 1994 while I was in El Paso, Texas, a moment charged with emotion and significant personal resonance for me.

During a peaceful visit to my grandmother's home in Skiatook, Oklahoma, my cousin and I planned an exciting adventure with our children. We decided to take a drive to Carthage, Missouri, with the primary goal of exploring the enchanting Precious Moments Museum.

When we arrived at the museum, we were greeted by the serene beauty of the grounds, which included a charming Chapel. The Chapel's interior was a visual feast, adorned with vibrant wall paintings by Sam Butcher, the talented artist behind the Precious Moments figures.

One mural, in particular, captivated my attention. It portrayed a scene of people entering the glorious gates of heaven, bathed in soft, ethereal light. I found myself utterly enchanted, my eyes drawn to the delicate brushstrokes and the emotional depth captured in the artwork. I stood there, entranced, unable to pull myself away as I contemplated its meaning.

Little did I know that within the next 24 hours, I would understand why this mural had struck such a deep chord within me. It felt like Adonai was gently preparing my heart for the storm ahead.

On July 4th, my younger brother, David, was making his way home from a festive gathering when tragedy struck. As he approached an intersection, a drunk driver barreled into his car without warning, sending shockwaves through our family. David was rushed by life flight to a military trauma center, his condition critical.

That night, the Lord stirred me awake around 3 a.m., an urgency prickling at my consciousness, compelling me to reach out to my Dad. Knowing he would likely be asleep at that hour, I waited until the sun rose and the clock struck 7 a.m.

When I called my Dad on the morning of July 5th, his words brought me to a halt: David had been in a terrible accident. I listened, my heart racing, as he informed me that they were boarding a flight from Houston to El Paso—an ominous journey that signified the gravity of the situation.

He promised to check David's condition and let me know if it was urgent enough for me to fly to El Paso. The entire day unfolded as I sat in my grandmother's cozy apartment, filled with memories but burdened with worry. As the sun set, I realized that I would have to return to my home in Dallas and catch a flight from there—a decision that weighed heavily on my heart.

I finally boarded a plane and left Dallas on July 6th with hope and dread swirling within me. Sadly, just a day later, on July 7th, I received the devastating news that he had passed away. This brief narrative contains only the essentials, as the intricate details are woven into another book. Yet, in sharing this story, I want to highlight the miraculous and mysterious ways the Lord operates.

Even amidst such sorrow, unexpected beauty can emerge—small glimpses revealing a grander design. Unbeknownst to me, this was when your family would unexpectedly enter my life.

While I was in El Paso, your mother graced my church with her presence, a moment that felt serendipitous amid my grief. Once I returned to my desk, I began sorting through the accumulated mail, and at the very bottom of the stack, a visitor's card caught my eye.

When visitors came to the church, I would typically send two staff members to check if they had a specific request or need. They would report back to me with the details of their visit, and life would carry on. However, something unusual about that card—perhaps the weight of my emotions or a gentle nudge from above—compelled me to break tradition. I accompanied one of my staff members to meet your mother this time.

When we finally arrived at your apartment, I approached the door with eagerness and trepidation. I knocked gently, but the silence that followed suggested no one was home. With a deep breath and a hint of impatience, I knocked again, this time with a sharper rap that echoed in the stillness. When you opened the door, the coolness of your reception took me by surprise. You rolled your eyes, a gesture that seemed almost theatrical, and quipped, "Mom, a white lady is at the door. I think she is a Jehovah's Witness."

The moment your Mom stepped into the room, there was an undeniable spark—a connection that seemed to bridge years and experiences. After our initial meeting, she felt inspired to rekindle her ties to the church, embracing faith in a way I had never anticipated. This decision, however, was met with a frown from you. With your Mom not driving, you were now the designated chauffeur, trapped in taking her to services. You would drop her off and spend the hours sitting in the parking lot, where the vibrant sounds of worship mingled with your quiet discontent. Church was never a place you felt called to, but your loyalty to your mother was unwavering; abandoning her was not an option.

Although I can't pinpoint exactly how our paths intertwined, it all started with your mother reaching out to me about your struggles in math. Given my history as an exceptional student, particularly in Algebra, I offer to be your tutor, eager to help. Yet, as we began our sessions, reality struck. The math I once excelled at had transformed into something completely unfamiliar. The sophisticated equations and methods you were learning bore little resemblance to my schooling—it was as if I had stepped into a foreign land, and I had to concede that I was not equipped to guide you humbly.

What began as a mere academic endeavor became a profound, thirty-year journey. You became woven into the fabric of my daily life, punctuating the chapters of the many books I have written. To some, you may appear as my secretary, assistant, or co-conspirator in my schemes. Yet in the depths of my heart, you occupy a far more sacred role; you are my daughter, bound to me with the most substantial ties imaginable—duct tape and zip ties, if you will.

In the aftermath of my son's tragic murder, when my own family turned their backs on me, I found myself engulfed in a profound desolation that seemed to consume every part of my being. This act of betrayal cut more deeply than any knife, leaving me isolated and abandoned in a world that suddenly felt cold and unwelcoming. For what felt like an eternity, the shadows of grief and loneliness wrapped around me, making it hard to see any glimmer of hope.

Yet, amid that overwhelming darkness, a revelation began to dawn on me—an important truth that helped light my path. The very individuals God had placed in my life more than two decades ago, who stood by me with unwavering support, had not abandoned me. Their steadfast presence became an anchor, offering solace amidst the chaos that enveloped my life.

Everyone I mention in this heartfelt acknowledgment has showered me with love and encouragement, becoming the family I desperately needed. When the dust finally settled, I realized I had gained an immeasurable gift: a profound connection with these beautiful souls who never considered walking away.

Out of respect and a desire to safeguard the true identities of those who have remained faithfully by my side on this challenging journey, I have chosen to alter their names for their privacy.

My heart overflows with love for my family and special friends. I am eternally grateful to Adonai for meaningfully intertwining our lives. There is no group like them—dedicated first to Adonai and then to me. As you read my books, you'll discover more about their remarkable presence and indelible impact on my life.

In this series, you will embark on a journey that chronicles how diverse individuals came together, each driven by a shared purpose and vision. You will meet remarkable figures like Julian Martinez, Olivia Ashley, Ali Jacobson, Samantha Jade, Joi Brazille, America Summers, Phillipe Giavante, and Allen Dale. Each extraordinary person plays an essential role in my life, navigating existence's murky and often tumultuous swamps.

To my dearest friend Katherine Homan, words fall short of encapsulating the depth and uniqueness of our friendship. I can vividly recall the first time our paths crossed at a city meeting. Your fierce determination and unwavering tenacity in addressing city council issues left me in awe. Armed with facts and an indomitable spirit, you stood your ground, embodying a strength that inspired me and everyone in the room. Your passion ignited a spark within me, and I found myself captivated by your commitment to making a difference.

Our bond deepened when you invited me to join the League of Women Voters in Dallas.

Our monthly meetings transformed into a cherished ritual, where we would update each other on the whirlwind of our lives. Your curiosity about my chaotic existence often prompted you to ask, "Cheryl, why don't you write a book?" Before I could respond, you'd chuckle and add, "Because no one could make this stuff up."

Fifteen years later, the weight of sorrow consumed me as I picked up the phone to share the heart-wrenching news: my son Kris was gone. With tremors in my voice, I struggled to articulate the tragedy. "His estranged wife...she murdered him," I finally managed, the reality of the words leaving an unbearable ache in my chest.

Though I was miles away in Mexico, overseeing the opening of a learning center, I could feel your unwavering love and support enveloping me. Unlike many who merely extended their condolences before quickly returning to their lives, you remained steadfast, checking in with heartfelt phone calls filled with genuine interest and encouragement.

As the weeks passed and new developments unfolded, you became my anchor—someone I could lean on through the emotional storm. During one of our long, cathartic conversations, you once again urged me, "Cheryl, you have to write a book." A thought struck me: this could be the first time in history that the anointed Prophetess of God shares her insights on surviving the complex tapestry of life. More importantly, it would guide others on how to serve Adonai, imparting wisdom that could help change lives.

My dear, sweet Katherine, I hold you personally accountable for this series. Thank you for being an unwavering friend during my darkest hours. Because of your relentless encouragement, I now have the opportunity to impact the lives of others.

This book is part of a series that offers readers an intimate glimpse into the tapestry of my life, where every detail, no matter how painful, is laid bare before you.

It illuminates the journey of the First Woman Prophetess, revealing her story as a guiding light for those who seek to navigate their paths.

The individuals in this book are real, though their names are slightly altered to protect their identities. The events recounted herein are factual, yet time has muddled some specifics, making presenting this narrative in a strict chronological order challenging.

Every page of this series is a testament to the truth of my experiences—nothing has been enhanced or embellished. I stand here today as a survivor, shaped by my relationship and love for Adonai, the Creator of the Universe. Without His guiding presence, I know I would not have endured.

To all who read this and place their trust in God (Adonai), may you come to understand who He is and what He represents. Reflect His love and compassion through your actions and words, embodying His essence and the profound experiences He desires for humanity.

Chapter Two
The Day Faith Died

In life's journey, each individual eventually encounters a profound and transformative moment that brings the weighty notion of mortality to our minds. Realization often emerges from the gut-wrenching sorrow of bidding farewell to a beloved family member, a loss that leaves an indelible mark on our hearts.

Alternatively, it may arrive unbidden, heralded by the calm yet sorrowful words of a doctor who gently breaks the news that our time on this earth is limited. This truth crashes into us like a tidal wave, sweeping away the veil of invincibility we so often cling to, forcing us to confront the fragility of our existence.

Death is a topic that many people find profoundly unsettling and challenging to discuss. In our family, it lingers like a silent storm cloud overhead, wrapped in layers of discomfort and swirling unarticulated fears, like a ghost haunting the joyous gatherings of our lives. Much like unknowing travelers, our little ones stand vulnerable and unprepared amid the emotional chaos that such a monumental shift unfolds. Their eyes widen with innocence and confusion as they confront the jagged realities of grief, struggling to navigate the intricate maze of sorrow and loss. Each moment feels disorienting as they wrestle to understand the weight of absence and the profound void it creates in their young hearts.

For centuries, the enigma surrounding the final moments of life has captivated the human imagination, stirring a deep-seated curiosity about what lies beyond our last breath. The subject of death remains an intricate puzzle, cloaked in uncertainty and mystery, a veil that no one can pierce fully. It wasn't until the pivotal year of 1975 that near-death experiences emerged as a compelling phenomenon, capturing the public's fascination and igniting spirited debates. These extraordinary accounts of individuals hovering between life and death have provoked profound questions and wonder about the nature of the afterlife, the essence of consciousness, and the boundaries of human experience that we have yet to explore.

On a momentous day, November 13th, 1789, Benjamin Franklin—a revered figure among the Founding Fathers of America—composed a profoundly insightful letter addressed to the distinguished French scientist Jean-Baptiste Le Roy. Within the elegant folds of this correspondence lay a line that would resonate across centuries, encapsulating the immutable truths of the human experience. Franklin penned the immortal words, "Our new Constitution is now established; everything seems to promise it will be durable; but, in this world, nothing is certain except death and taxes." This striking declaration is a timeless reminder of the unavoidable nature of mortality that we must confront.

Reflecting on my upbringing, I have come to realize that the subject of death remained largely unexamined during my formative years. Memories of my early childhood are marked by a conspicuous absence of discussions surrounding loss or the finality of life. I cannot recall attending any funerals for friends or family before I reached the tender age of twelve, creating a considerable void in my understanding of grief, sorrow, and the profound impact that loss can have on the human heart.

In our household, children were gently ushered away from the room where adults engaged in serious discussions, their voices low and sad, like a distant thunderstorm approaching the horizon. As I wandered past those gatherings, snippets of conversation would occasionally float through the air, the words weaving in and out like ghostly whispers—hints of someone's passing punctuating the atmosphere with a sense of gravity. Yet, the substantial distance of over a thousand miles from our extended family meant that we rarely participated in mourning rituals. Funerals remained an abstract concept to me, a distant event that felt almost like a scene from a storybook, far removed from the realities of my young life.

Death presents us with an unyielding truth: a loved one will no longer occupy a space in our lives, their absence leaving a palpable void. This harrowing realization can descend like a suffocating blanket, stealing the breath from those left behind and enveloping them in a profound, aching sense of loss that lingers in the silence. It is a heavyweight that colors the world around you, a muted reminder of what once was and can never be again.

As a child, the concept of separation felt like an insurmountable wall that loomed over me. I can still picture that day with stunning clarity—the first time my oldest brother, Ronnie, left to spend the summer with our grandparents in Oklahoma. When David and I stepped inside our home, a wave of urgency propelled us to seek out our Mom. Our hearts raced wildly in our chests, pounding like drums in a tense symphony of anticipation.

David and I inquired about Ronnie's whereabouts, and after a long pause, Momma informed us that Ronnie had left with Grandma and Grandpa. This news was difficult for us to accept; it felt like we had experienced a loss similar to that of a death in the family.

In an instant, devastation crashed over us like a relentless tidal wave. It was as if the very ground beneath our feet had given way. David and I sank to the floor, our despair crushing us. Tears poured from our eyes, each drop a testament to the profound sense of loss that enveloped us.

At that moment, the world felt vast and hollow, carving out an emptiness that seemed impossible to fill—our big brother, our protector, was gone.

The following summer, our parents deemed us old enough for a long-awaited journey to Oklahoma to visit our grandparents. Initially, our hearts danced excitedly, visions of grand adventures swirling in our minds like fireflies in the dusk. Yet, as the departure date grew closer, that bubbling anticipation morphed into a heavy cloud of anxiety that loomed over us.

Finally, the day came when we piled into the car for the Shawnee, Oklahoma journey. As I strapped myself into the worn back seat, a strange mix of eagerness and a deep-seated dread coiled within me. The familiar weight of apprehension settled onto my shoulders like a heavy blanket. I pressed my forehead against the cool glass of the side window, watching as the home I knew slowly retreated into the distance, fading into a patchwork of vibrant colors and hazy outlines.

As each mile unfurled like an endless ribbon between us and the sanctuary we once called home, I found myself kneeling on the seat, my heart heavy with the bittersweet ache of separation. I turned, my gaze fixating on the back window, and felt my breath catch. The familiar landscape that once embraced us began to fade away, dissolving into a watercolor blur of cherished memories and wistfulness.

Tears, silent and unyielding, carved delicate paths down my cheeks, glistening in the dim light like liquid crystal. They pooled in the corners of my mouth, where their salty taste mingled with the profound emptiness that consumed my insides. My body trembled, quivering with the raw intensity of sorrow, each tremor a poignant echo of the deep longing that overwhelmed me—a visceral reminder of all the cherished moments and memories I was leaving behind, now overshadowed by the weight of my heartache.

Fear gripped me tightly; what if Grandma sensed my inner turmoil? What if she could read the longing in my heart, the pleading desire to turn back and retreat from this emotional chess game? A deep ache resonated within me, amplified by the knowledge that our family ties stretched thin, leaving me wrestling with the weight of goodbyes that tugged at my soul with each passing moment. I longed for a closeness that could shatter these bittersweet farewells, a solution to this heart-wrenching dilemma that fractured my spirit with every mile we traveled away from home.

My grandparents were extraordinary figures, giving us unconditional love and warmth that felt like a haven. However, I often felt trapped in a tug-of-war between the clashing dynamics of two worlds. From the time I was a curious five-year-old until I reached the stirring age of fourteen, my Dad's parents would embark on long drives that seemed to stretch across miles and memories, no matter if we were nestled in the sunbaked deserts of New Mexico or surrounded by the sprawling, green landscapes of Texas.

My Grandma, with her soft-spoken wisdom and nurturing touch, intuitively sensed my Mom's challenges managing three energetic children. Despite our boundless energy, we were raised to be well-behaved, a reflection of my Dad's strict parenting style, which often left a mark, both figuratively and literally, through the harsh lashes of a heavy leather belt. The echoes of that tension reverberated through our minds, leaving a lasting imprint.

Seeing our strain, my grandparents stood as unwavering support pillars, firmly disapproving of my Dad's stern disciplinary ways. They became our sanctuary, stepping in as guardians who sought to shield us from the anxiety and frustration that loomed like dark clouds over our home. The oppressive atmosphere he created enveloped us in dread, so as soon as the final school bell rang to signal the beginning of summer, we found ourselves bursting with anticipation. We longed for the bright escape at their home, where security and love would envelop us like a warm blanket on a chilly night.

Their influence on our lives was profound. Unlike our parents, my grandparents offered us unconditional love and comfort, creating a sanctuary where we felt free to express ourselves. We could share our thoughts and worries with them without fear, finding solace in their understanding. It starkly contrasted the silence we often maintained around our parents; in them, we found refuge and the confidence to be who we were.

During a particularly enchanting phase of my childhood, I was blessed to be surrounded by the loving presence of two remarkable great-grandmothers, each embodying her unique essence and charm. My family playfully adopted gentle identifiers to navigate our conversations and distinguish between them. My great-grandma Prather, a robust and nurturing figure, resided on a vast, picturesque farm, where the air echoed with the sweet melodies of chirping birds and the rustle of leaves. She was fondly referred to as the Grandma who lives on the farm, a title that perfectly captured her earthy spirit and the warmth that radiated from her home.

In contrast, my great-grandma Eller was a delicate yet vibrant soul. Her soft-spoken nature was infused with a radiant energy that drew everyone in. She was affectionately known as Ole Granny, a name that reflected her gentle demeanor and the wisdom that came with her years.

As my cousin Lea and I grew older and embraced the thrill of childhood adventures, our family dynamic was beautifully shaped by the distances between our grandparents. My paternal and maternal grandparents lived about 130 miles apart, creating a tapestry of experience that colored our summers. My Grandpa Prather would excitedly load the car, his energy infectious as he packed up my siblings and Grandma for our journey. With eager anticipation, I would settle into the back seat, the scent of adventure filling the air as we drove from Shawnee to Skiatook, where I would joyfully immerse myself in a month-long stay with the Ellers, ready to create cherished memories under their loving guidance.

Ole Granny's home was nestled just a stone's throw away—less than two miles—from my grandparents' charming little abode in Skiatook. Every visit to her felt like an adventure waiting to unfold, and after just a few days of my arrival, my heart ached with anticipation to see her again.

The thrill of heading to her house always filled the air with a special kind of magic. I could vividly envision her perched by the window, her warm, kind eyes sparkling with joy as she eagerly tracked our approach down the winding road. When we finally arrived, she would sweep me up in a giant, enveloping hug, her soft arms feeling like a cozy blanket around me. The familiar scent of lavender wafted through the air, wrapping around us as she settled me into her lap.

Her gentle fingers would lovingly stroke my hair, weaving through the strands in a rhythmic motion that instantly calmed me. Her well-worn Bible rested nearby as she sang sweet, melodic hymns about Jesus. Its pages were frayed and creased from years of devoted reading, each marked with loving annotations that spoke of her faith.

Although Lea often caught glimpses of Ole Granny at church, her indifference to those brief encounters couldn't overshadow the magic of my visits. Each moment spent with her was a precious highlight of my summer in Skiatook. In those quiet yet profound instances, enveloped in her love, I felt a connection that resonated deep within my heart, unlike anything I had ever known.

In the stifling embrace of an Oklahoma summer, our visits typically began within the calm sanctuary of her home, where the walls seemed to cradle us in a comforting stillness. But soon enough, we would make our way to her charming country porch swing, perched beneath the shade of towering oak trees. The gentle rocking motion of the swing created a soothing rhythm, its creaking punctuating our conversations with a nostalgic melody. She listened with an intensity that made her eyes glisten like stars illuminated by warm, golden light. With every question she asked about my life, I felt like I was the center of her universe, the most critical person in the world. Those moments, simple yet profound, became treasured memories I tucked away in the recesses of my heart.

Parting from her company always felt like a heavy burden. Her enveloping embrace accompanied each goodbye, her warmth wrapping around me like a cozy blanket. She held me tight, whispering prayers filled with boundless hope and unwavering love, infusing me with a surge of strength I carried with me long after I left. Every visit was a gentle reminder of the unbreakable bond we shared.

In our family, conversations about health issues were shrouded in an unspoken silence, a topic we all avoided when my siblings and I were gathered. Yet, one fateful day stands out vividly in my memory, a Saturday etched into my mind forever: April 1st, 1967.

The previous night, the phone rang long after twilight had settled in, shattering the usual stillness of our home with a jarring urgency that sent chills down my spine. Lying in bed, I could hear my parents' hushed voices mingling with the sounds of the night—whispers thick with concern and lingering anxiety. When the call finally concluded and silence blanketed the house again, I called out to my Momma, my curiosity piqued, desperate to know who had disturbed our evening.

My Dad, adopting an air of feigned composure, offered up a lie that fell from his lips like a fragile leaf suspended in the air. "It was your Grandpa Eller," he said, the tremor in his voice betraying the calm he sought to project. "He wanted to know about some tires he needed to pick up." Even as I listened, unease coiled tightly in my gut, whispering that something was amiss. I brushed off the nagging doubt and fell asleep, blissfully unaware of the storm poised to sweep our lives.

The dawn of April 1st crept in with a sharp chill that sliced through the cocoon of warmth provided by my blankets. Momma glided into my room, her silhouette framed by the soft, golden light seeping through the barely parted curtains. She settled on the edge of my bed, her eyes shadowed with an unsettling solemnity, taking my hand in hers—a gesture that felt like a delicate lifeline. "Sweetheart," she murmured, her voice trembling on the edge of breaking, "Grandpa wasn't calling about tires."

A heavy stone dropped in my stomach as her words landed with the force of a thunderclap: Ole Granny had passed away. The reality of her announcement struck me like an unexpected wave, forcing tears to spill from my eyes, cascading down my cheeks like rivers of grief flowing into the very depths of my soul. In that instant, my heart felt like an invisible weight was crushing it, and as Momma quickly gathered my clothes—her movements charged with urgency—I heard her whispering, "We need to go to Oklahoma."

An unsettling thought began to grip me like a vice, a flicker of hope that perhaps this was all just some elaborate, cruel joke. After all, it was April Fools' Day—surely someone would burst into my room at any moment, laughter bubbling from their lips, joyously declaring, "April Fool!" But in the suffocating silence that enveloped me, no one came to shatter my disbelief.

As we made our way to the airport, a sense of dread coiled tightly in my stomach, more constricting than any roller coaster ride. While soaring through the skies toward Oklahoma, I pressed my forehead against the excellent, scratched window. I watched the patchwork quilt of fields and towns blur beneath us, each fleeting glimpse of earth invoking a whirlpool of thoughts and emotions. How could all of this be real? Wasn't Jesus supposed to listen to our desperate prayers? Wasn't He meant to cradle our hearts with the comfort we yearned for? If that were true, then why did grief wrench my heart with such brutal ferocity?

I felt as if I were suspended in a vast, dark abyss, overwhelmed by the shock that gripped my heart. Though I had been painfully aware of Granny's declining health, a flicker of hope resided deep within me—an unwavering belief that she would not leave me. In the weeks leading up to this moment, I had poured my soul into fervent prayers, praying for her healing with every ounce of my being. How could this sorrowful reality feel so absolute? The love of Jesus was meant to be a protective shield, or so I had always believed. If that love were genuine, how could He allow the woman who had filled my life with warmth and wisdom to slip away from me?

Our family was fortunate to own an airplane, a small luxury that spared us the stress of commercial travel. After hastily packing our bags—shoes, clothes, and a few cherished mementos—we would drive to the hangar where our aircraft awaited, gleaming under the sunlight, ready to carry us into the endless sky. The journey to Skiatook, Oklahoma, would stretch out before us like an endless road of uncertainties—four long hours filled with the suffocating weight of grief, a barrage of swirling thoughts, unanswerable questions, and an ever-deepening sense of loss that settled heavily on my chest.

Skiatook was a quaint and unassuming town, devoid of an airport, where I had woven countless cherished memories during my visits to my grandparents' warm and welcoming home. My father had struck a unique arrangement with a rancher who owned a vast expanse of land just across from my grandparents' residence, granting us the privilege of transforming his open pasture into a makeshift runway for our small aircraft.

My Dad had an extraordinary way of heralding our family's arrival; his spirit was imbued with unmistakable pride and uncontainable joy. He would take to the sky with a flourish that we all lovingly called the "buzzing" maneuver.

As we soared into the dazzling expanse of the sky, the aircraft dipped low, gliding effortlessly just above my grandparents' charming, sun-kissed home. Its formidable engine roared like a majestic beast unleashed, shattering the tranquil ambiance of the countryside with a resounding crescendo. The sound reverberated across the rolling hills and sprawling fields, cascading through the peaceful landscape—a thunderous declaration of our return that reverberated in every nook and cranny of the surrounding area, wrapping the familiar sights in a vibrant embrace of sound.

With the skill of a seasoned pilot, my father would deftly pull back on the control wheel, sending the aircraft climbing into the vast expanse of the sky. The mighty roar of the engines filled the air, announcing our ascent with an unmistakable authority. Every inch of altitude gained ignited a thrilling rush that coursed through me, mingling with the tingle of anticipation as we edged closer to reuniting with the loved ones waiting below.

The atmosphere around us buzzed with an electrifying energy as if the air was charged with joy. It felt like the entire neighborhood could sense our impending arrival, sharing in the collective excitement that rippled outward like waves. The harmonious symphony of roaring engines and the whispering winds danced together, creating a breathtaking melody that resonated through the heavens.

At this moment, the sky became our grand stage, showcasing a spectacular display of power and emotion. This jubilant celebration heralded our triumphant homecoming, drawing the gazes and hearts of those below, exhilarated by our return.

As the unmistakable rumble of thunder echoed in the distance, our family members scrambled outside, their figures frantic and animated against the oppressive sky. They waved their arms wildly, desperate signals that they were en route to pick us up.

Uncle Hermon arrived promptly to gather us from the expansive, sun-baked pasture, his vehicle a cherished refuge amidst the turmoil of our emotions. An unsettling silence marked the journey to the funeral home, each poignant moment amplifying the rising awareness of our harsh reality. The realization that Granny was no longer a part of our lives began to seep through the comforting layers of disbelief I'd wrapped around myself.

Crossing the threshold of the funeral home felt like stepping into a different realm, one heavy with sorrow and finality. A profound weight pressed against my chest, the ache in my heart growing deeper with each hesitant step. The muted hues of the building's entrance drained vibrancy from the world, casting everything into a shadowed palette of grief. Then, my gaze landed on my Grandpa as if I had been struck by a runaway train.

His face, a map of lines etched by time and sorrow, glistened with tears that flowed freely down his weathered cheeks—a silent testament to the unimaginable grief he bore. In that instant, the gravity of our situation rushed over me like an overwhelming tide. It wasn't just a loss; it was the profound absence of his beloved Mother-a—matriarch whose life had been a wellspring of love and warmth and whose departure left behind an emotional void that felt impossibly vast and insurmountable.

Despite the tumultuous wave of emotions urging me toward acceptance, a stubborn disbelief coiled tightly in my chest, refusing to yield. Part of me clung desperately to the notion that this must be some intricate prank, a cruel jest played by fate. As I approached the casket, my heart raced erratically, each beat echoing the question: Was Granny genuinely going to be lying there, still and silent?

Absurd as it seemed, hope lingered like a flickering candle in the depths of my soul. A tiny ember of faith remained, refusing to be extinguished. If she was indeed in that coffin, I promised myself I would summon the courage to step forward, lean close, and urgently whisper, "Wake up, Granny, I am here." I drew strength from the tales I cherished from the Bible, imagining Jesus calling her forth, just as He had for Lazarus after those agonizing four days. Indeed, He could do the same for my beloved Granny.

With each hesitant step, I made my way to the casket, peering inside with trepidation. There lay Granny, serene and untouched, as if in a peaceful slumber. At that moment, the overwhelming urge to wake her surged within me. Tears cascaded down my cheeks as I fought against the irresistible temptation to cry, "Come on, Granny, wake up!"

Eventually, the family stepped outside to confer in hushed voices, leaving me alone with my thoughts. It was now or never, I reasoned. I leaned closer to the casket and whispered, "Granny, wake up." The silence that followed was deafening. Perhaps she hadn't heard me, I thought, so I raised my voice, pleading again. Still, there was yet to be a response. A whirlwind of confusion swirled within me; how could this be? I believed in Jesus wholeheartedly and was always told that faith could move mountains.

Why wasn't this working?

Granny knew the depth of my love for her. Desperation clawed at my insides, and I struggled to suppress the urge to shake her awake, to scream for her to return to me.

Then, in a moment of clarity, it struck me: if Jesus couldn't answer my prayers, perhaps Granny would. From that point forward, I resolved to turn away from Jesus and seek comfort in my beloved Granny.

I remember vividly a moment when my cousin confided in me about the fear that washed over her when she heard me pray aloud, invoking the spirit of Granny. Granny had always been more than just family; she was my sanctuary, the one to whom I would lay bare my deepest thoughts and worries in heartfelt prayers. How my cousin described her discomfort made me reflect on the weight of those words, echoing in the cozy corners of our childhood home, as I sought solace and guidance from the very essence of my beloved Granny.

It was merely a month shy of my 12th birthday when my belief system unraveled, torn apart by the weight of loss. I was resolute in dedicating my prayers to the one person I knew had loved me unconditionally.

My Ole Granny had been my anchor for as long as I could remember, declaring her love for me since I drew my first breath. It was a love I had clung to, especially since my love experiences with my parents felt distant and uncertain. My understanding of affection was shaped entirely by her big heart. My mother had been just 19 when my older brother was born, and a mere 13 months later, I emerged into this bustling world.

Following me, 18 months later, came my little brother.

I held on dearly to the moment my mother finally told me she loved me. It was a vivid scene; I was 21 years old, nestled in the vibrant chaos of Houston, Texas, when she visited from the quieter landscape of El Paso. As we drove through the thrumming streets of downtown, my mother turned to me, her eyes reflecting an emotion I had longed to see, and softly said, "Sherry, I think I love you." The shock of those words reverberated within me, a revelation that startled and awakened me to the complexities of love.

Granny's love has been a constant, a warmth I can always rely on throughout my life. I accepted, through faith, that Jesus loved me, too. Still, that belief began to unravel the day I lost Granny—the pivotal moment on November 16th, 1969, when an unexpected chain of events transformed my perception of Jesus forever.

Chapter Three
Headed to the Casino

For all my years serving God, I never desired to go to Jerusalem, Israel.

From everything I had observed on television, in various travel videos, and through countless promotional presentations, the place seemed like nothing more than a carefully crafted commercial trap designed to lure unsuspecting tourists. I found myself questioning the authenticity of the locations being promoted. Just how credible are these sites that claim historical significance?

As I gazed at pictures depicting the revered paths Jesus once walked, my skeptical mind ignited with curiosity and skepticism, propelling my thoughts to dizzying heights. I was bombarded with questions: How can we be sure that these remarkable events unfolded in the very locations they boast about? What evidence supports these grand claims?

On May 21st, 2019, my son JD approached me with a sparkle of excitement in his eyes, brimming with the idea of embarking on a journey to Jerusalem. Instantly, I felt a wave of reluctance wash over me, and I promptly voiced my disinterest in visiting Israel.

However, JD was undeterred. He leaned in closer, his voice filled with passion as he implored, "Just think about it, Mom. This November marks 50 years since you dedicated your life to serving the Lord; what could be a more meaningful way to celebrate than for our family to experience this together?" His enthusiasm was infectious, and I could see how deeply he believed in the significance of this pilgrimage.

As he spoke, I realized he had been captivated by the allure of Christian television and the vibrant promotions from various TV evangelists, which had painted Jerusalem as a place of profound spiritual importance. His excitement revealed how powerful and persuasive the media can be in shaping our desires and aspirations.

He understood perfectly that my vulnerability lay within the bonds of family. My immediate family had shattered following my father's betrayal, leaving me to pick up the pieces of a fractured past. In the wake of that heartache, I redirected my love and attention toward my children and grandchildren, who became my greatest treasures.

The joy they brought me was immeasurable, but it also highlighted my sacrifices; we had never been able to take a vacation together, often constrained by our tight finances. As fate would have it, my sons had successfully established their businesses.

Their hard work had finally afforded them the means to plan a trip—a much-anticipated escape that would allow us to create cherished memories together.

I wanted to respond with an enthusiastic yes, yet the reality of my financial situation loomed large in my mind. The idea of taking a family vacation felt like an elusive dream, especially considering celebrating such a significant occasion together. The vision of traveling abroad with my children and grandchildren was both exhilarating and daunting.

JD had mentioned that he had spoken with Kris, and they were both convinced that this was the perfect way to commemorate the event. His words resonated with me, stirring a mix of excitement and hesitation. I hesitantly told JD I would need to see if I could save enough money over the next four to five months. Just as I spoke, he interjected, reassuring me with a bright smile that the best part was that they would cover all the expenses. All I had to do was figure out the details and let them know how much was needed.

With that generous offer, my heart raced with joy and relief. It felt like a weight had been lifted, and suddenly, the dream was within reach. We were all set for an unforgettable journey to Israel, and I could hardly believe the adventure ahead.

The trip was still a work in progress, with many details yet to be finalized, especially regarding the flight and hotel accommodations. I pondered how long we would linger in the enchanting city of Jerusalem, a place steeped in history and culture. As I crunched the numbers in my mind, it dawned on me that the airline tickets alone would set us back a staggering $10,000. When I factored in the cost of meals and lodging, the total shot up to over $15,000. The boys, with their youthful dreams and aspirations, didn't have that kind of money at their disposal. While the idea of wandering through the ancient streets together felt incredibly heartwarming, the reality of the situation weighed heavily on my mind; it was a beautiful thought, but utterly impractical.

A few days later, JD suggested I invite my Staff to the celebration. He suggested they bring their families along, turning our gathering into one big, happy family affair.

"Mom," JD said enthusiastically, "this would make your anniversary momentous.

Everyone who loves and respects you will be there to celebrate your special day on November 16th."

I felt a twinge of uncertainty as I replied, expressing my concerns about whether everyone could attend. Considering various work schedules, the question of vacation time might be challenging. Nevertheless, it didn't hurt to ask.

Curiosity buzzed in my mind about how this gathering would unfold, but it seemed worth discussing with the team. I called for a Staff meeting and shared what JD and Kris had proposed for my 50th anniversary celebration. As I spoke, I could see the excitement grow in their faces; they thought it was a fantastic idea. I conveyed that my children were eager for them to join us, and they wholeheartedly agreed.

We may not be bound by blood, but we share a profound connection that feels just as strong. Each team member is devoted to God, pouring their heart and soul into serving Him with unwavering strength and dedication. Their loyalty and unique talents shine brightly, contributing to the rich tapestry of our group.

Having worked together for over twenty years, we've forged an incredibly tight bond, more akin to family than colleagues. In that moment, we turned what would have been a simple gathering of my children and grandchildren into a joyful extended family celebration, promising to create memories that would last a lifetime.

As I looked at the growing list of names eager to embark on our trip to Israel, a wave of anticipation washed over me. The prospect of organizing a journey for such a more extensive group filled me with both excitement and a sense of responsibility. I knew each family's financial situation; some were well-prepared, while others struggled with tighter budgets. If we wanted this dream to materialize, we needed to rally together and hustle hard.

Our team quickly set to work brainstorming effective fundraising strategies. Seeing those with a more secure financial footing step up to lend a hand was heartening. They didn't hesitate to offer their support, working alongside struggling people, determined to make this trip possible for everyone.

Before long, news of our planned journey to Israel spread like wildfire through our congregation, igniting excitement and anticipation. Members approached me with bright, eager smiles, their eyes sparkling with the thrill of the awaited adventure. Each shared heartfelt, personal stories about why this journey held profound significance for them, often recounting how this opportunity might be a rare chance in their lives. Their enthusiasm was infectious; it breathed new life into our planning efforts and made us acutely aware of this trip's potential impact on many lives.

I've always believed in inclusivity, encouraging everyone to join us if they could afford the trip or assist in fundraising efforts. Yet, as I reflected on this philosophy, I began to wonder if that decision might end up being the most significant error of the entire experience.

It soon became apparent that the three ladies who pledged to assist with fundraising had contributed very little. Initially, I was hesitant to jump to conclusions; I tried to give them the benefit of the doubt, convincing myself that maybe they had the means to pay for the trip after all, and I had misjudged their financial situations.

Despite my apprehensions, it was crucial to prepare for the possibility that some individuals, burdened by their pride, might not readily disclose their actual situations. A nagging doubt lingered in my mind, suggesting it was not entirely the case.

I gathered everyone together, emphasizing that this adventure would demand our entire group's commitment and teamwork to complete the project. My dedicated Staff understood how significant this trip was for me, a rare opportunity to create lasting memories with my children and grandchildren. They stepped up admirably, working tirelessly to balance their responsibilities at home while finding ways to contribute financially to our cause.

The funds flowed painfully slowly, each dollar seeming to take its time, deepening a sense of desperation that quietly took root in my heart. In a moment filled with deep conviction, I voiced my belief that if the Lord truly wanted me to embark on a journey to Israel, He would undoubtedly pave the way and unlock the necessary opportunities ahead of me. As I reflected on earlier struggles, vivid memories surfaced of times when I had sought refuge in the dimly lit halls of Indian casinos. There, amidst the flickering lights and the cacophony of hopeful voices, I often turned to the one-armed bandits—the slot machines that seemed to promise a much-needed fortune with each lever pull.

When I share this chapter of my life, I can feel the gasps of disbelief from those listening. It's a stark reminder that when you find yourself in a precarious position, your life lies bare like an open book, exposed to the scrutiny and judgment of those around you.

WinStar and Choctaw Casinos, nestled in the heart of Oklahoma, are just over an hour's drive from the bustling Dallas-Fort Worth area in Texas. The journey would take me through scenic landscapes, and anticipation would build with each passing mile. Once I arrived at those sprawling entertainment complexes, the air would be thick with excitement, and the sounds of jingling coins and electrifying slot machines would envelop me.

As I stepped inside, I carried a crisp $100 bill, my only stake in this gamble of fate. I approached the slot machines with hope and trepidation, believing that if divine intervention were on my side, I'd leave as a winner, paving my way to the sacred lands of Israel. However, if luck wasn't on my side, I was prepared to accept my defeat and return home, reflecting on my loss with no intention of ever stepping foot in a casino again.

Gambling isn't a pastime; I wouldn't say I like the thought of frivolously throwing away money. This trip was more of a test than a thrill, a deep-seated belief guiding my every decision as I awaited my fortune to unfold.

We had only been in the Casino for about 30 minutes when I won some money, but I didn't count it. I would put the money in my waist purse in a particular location so I wouldn't use it, and then I would keep a close eye on where my $100 was. I would play for hours until exhausted, then tell the team I was tired, it was late, and I wanted to go home.

When I entered my bedroom, I would open my wallet and see how much I had won for the evening. I counted the money I had won, over a thousand dollars, and put it in the safe.

The following week, we went back with the same plan. I would take with me another one-hundred-dollar bill and say, "If I lose it all, we go home; if not, great, I am walking out ahead." And we went home. For several months, I kept going to the Casino every week, putting the money in the safe for the trip. After about three months, I had a nice nest egg to put on the trip.

I want to take a moment to clarify my feelings about casinos and gambling. I wouldn't say it's something I particularly enjoy, and I would have never considered going if it hadn't been for the powerful and overwhelming urge to support my colleagues on Staff who were in need.

Here's a word of caution for anyone reading this: It's wise to step away from the Casino if you want to raise money. Although it turned out favorably for me, many of my companions who joined me in this venture felt discouraged, either breaking even or losing money altogether.

So, how did I find myself at a casino? It's tricky to locate the exact year, but it was 2003.

I was invited to be a guest speaker at a ladies' conference in Atlanta, Georgia. While there, I met a lovely couple who were local church pastors. They graciously invited me to extend my stay to speak at their congregation.

This remarkable family welcomed us into their home, treating us with kindness and hospitality. As we settled into their warm atmosphere, the Pastor shared fascinating stories about his roots in Jamaica, adding a rich layer to our conversations and making me feel even more connected to them.

I shared with them my long-held dream of exploring the country, a journey that I found utterly fascinating. To my delight, they invited my Staff and me to join them in June, just a few short months away.

I mentioned that accommodating my Staff and their families would require at least ten people. While I expressed my gratitude for their generous offer, I also conveyed my concern about raising enough funds in six weeks to embark on this adventure. They quickly reassured me, saying there was no need to worry about arrangements for lodging or meals—our gracious hosts would ensure everything was taken care of. They even offered to provide transportation, which made the prospect of the trip seem much more attainable.

As we contemplated the details of our upcoming journey, the notion of transforming this venture into a mission trip began to take root in our minds. The idea blossomed further when they suggested I could share my message with the community we would be visiting, which filled me with a renewed sense of purpose and excitement. Everything aligned as I left their warm, inviting home, the anticipation of our adventure swirling in my heart. We had officially committed to this thrilling experience set for June.

Upon returning to Texas, I gathered the rest of the Staff to share the fantastic news about our trip to Jamaica. Their enthusiasm was contagious, and I could see the spark of excitement in their eyes as they rallied around the idea, eagerly beginning to map out preparations. With just a few short weeks left before our departure, I felt a rush of urgency. Traditionally, I was not one to make special requests for offerings from the church, but the thought of this mission ignited my determination to seek support for our noble cause.

Over 14 years, I had never taken a penny from the church's funds for personal use.

Every dollar that came in was reinvested into the community and the church. I supplemented my income through other means, which allowed me to focus on the church's mission without financial worries. Our congregation was modest, so we often had to roll up our sleeves and get creative to fund our initiatives.

To raise money, we organized sales of various personal items, baked goods, and anything else we thought might entice donations. However, we faced a daunting challenge: we had no clear idea of how much the airfare would cost, and since covering the flight was solely our responsibility, we turned to prayer, hoping for a miracle to guide us.

Eventually, we discovered the ticket prices, and I was confronted with a seemingly impossible task: How could we generate enough funds through our sales to afford the airfare? During this critical moment, a staff member proposed an unconventional idea—why not try our luck at the Casino? I dismissed the suggestion immediately, concerned that it wasn't the right path for us.

As a single mother, life often felt like a relentless uphill battle. Financial struggles were a constant companion, and luxuries were simply out of reach. Yet, through it all, I clung to my faith, trusting that God would provide for my needs. Now, with my children grown and out of the house, I find myself with a bit of savings, though not enough to consider myself comfortable.

The idea of spending any of that hard-earned money at a casino sparked a deep inner conflict in me. In my Christian faith, gambling was often labeled as a sin, and as a spiritual leader, I felt an overwhelming weight of responsibility. The thought of stepping through those casino doors filled me with anxiety; I imagined the judgmental glances from others in my community and the potential backlash that could follow.

I voiced my concerns to the Staff, sharing my uncertainty about whether indulging in such an act would offend God. They listened attentively before outlining their perspectives. Then someone suggested, "Let's go. We can leave if you feel uncomfortable before we enter or even after we're inside." Their invitation seemed fair and reasonable, especially since I knew why churches discouraged such activities.

Curiosity tugged at me, and despite my reservations, I agreed to the venture.

What transpired next was nothing short of comical. Picture this: a group of mismatched friends walking into a casino, each of us clutching a bank bag overflowing with pennies. I had diligently saved for an extended period, and $100 worth of this forgotten change was in my possession. The excitement was palpable; it felt like a spontaneous adventure.

As we entered the Casino, I could almost hear the collective gasp of astonishment from those around us. The sight of eager faces soon turned to confusion when we discovered none of the machines accepted pennies. It was a crushing blow to our naive expectations, and nervous laughter bubbled among us. None of us dared approach the cashier, fearing the ridicule we might face for our rookie mistake. Instead, we dispatched one brave soul, a man determined to turn our stash into dollar bills.

We were all anxious to see what this new realm held for us. The gleaming lights, the sounds of spinning reels, and the atmosphere that thrived on hope and luck intoxicated us. None of us had ever imagined this experience would be so thrilling. To our utter astonishment, we walked out that night with enough cash to spark the urge to return.

Over several weeks, I won thousands, which ignited our group's excitement. The funds flowed in, and suddenly, it became evident that this could be our fastest route to raising money for our upcoming mission trip.

As the date of our journey approached and the flights were locked in and non-refundable, the Pastor and his family shared unexpected news: they would not be joining us after all. This abrupt change left us scrambling, our plans thrown into disarray. I recount more of this unexpected adventure in Book 4, "Navigating the Storm."

And so began my journey to the casinos of Oklahoma—a journey that ignited a wild thrill in me. Until that point, the slot machines were my only experience with games of chance, and little did I know how this would lead to a series of unforgettable escapades.

CHAPTER FOUR
Reservations

The air crackled with excitement and a palpable sense of anticipation as our group engaged in lively conversations, every word infused with the thrill of the adventure that awaited us.

With only a few months left until our long-anticipated flight to Israel, the energy in the room felt electric, as if we could almost touch the distant shores we would soon explore.

In our pursuit of the best travel deals, we had chosen to depart from the bustling Dallas-Fort Worth International Airport with a planned layover at the iconic John F. Kennedy Airport. The layover promised to stretch on for ten long hours, which could be a dull wait or an opportunity for spontaneous exploration. After that, we would embark on the final leg of our journey, a grueling 14-hour flight that felt like a marathon ahead of us, testing our endurance and excitement for future adventures.

I couldn't shake the sensation of looming stress that settled over me like a heavy fog—the night before our departure loomed like a storm, promising to be a chaotic frenzy of packing and frenzied last-minute adjustments. I envisioned us stumbling through our preparations, bleary-eyed and weary, as fatigue crept in before it was even time to board the plane. The pressure of meticulously checking our luggage loomed large in my mind, simmering with the urgency of adhering to strict baggage limits to circumvent any potential hiccups at the airport.

As I buried myself in the details of our itinerary, a significant anxiety began to bubble to the surface—one that had the power to reshape our entire family's plans.

We all shared an unspoken understanding of JD's paralyzing fear of flying, a heavy gray cloud that loomed over his spirit during our travel discussions. A wave of concern washed over me as I contemplated the significance of the situation; breaking the news of our travel arrangements to him felt like standing at the edge of a precipice. It wasn't just a trivial update—it was a pivotal moment that could shape the entire landscape of our adventure together.

JD's apprehension about flying was almost tangible, a knot of anxiety that seemed to tighten around him when the subject arose. Knowing this, I approached the topic of our upcoming trip with the utmost care, like treading on fragile ground. He reassured me when I finally mustered the courage to bring it up. "My mom can get us first-class tickets," he proposed confidently. "With more room," he continued, his voice steady, "I won't feel so claustrophobic. I'll be fine." While his optimistic tone provided a sliver of comfort, I still planned to pack Dramamine, an ally against my anxious tendencies.

Caught in a whirlwind of curiosity, I dove into the depths of the internet, searching for airfare prices for two first-class tickets. The staggering numbers that blinked back at me were enough to steal my breath—how could they be so unreasonable? I took a moment to ground myself, reminding my racing thoughts that we still had a month before needing to finalize our travel plans. I held onto a flicker of hope that, as time passed, those punishing prices might soften, allowing our journey to take flight more affordably.

As I sat down to plan the upcoming trip, a thought crossed my mind that I could not ignore. Excitedly, I asked JD if my two granddaughters could accompany us, even if he and his wife decided to stay behind. With a reassuring smile, he responded, "Absolutely!

I'm still in for the journey, so don't worry." Yet, despite his confident tone, a nagging doubt lingered in my mind—what if JD decided to back out at the last moment?

As the departure date for our adventure to Israel approached, I dove into the preparations with a sense of purpose. I meticulously selected each item my granddaughters would need for the journey. Clothes were neatly folded and packed, chargers were checked for functionality, sturdy water bottles were gathered, and countless other essentials were collected. I wanted to ensure they had everything necessary for a memorable and hassle-free experience.

Although I often found myself in a whirlwind of "what-ifs," I consciously tried to focus on the bright side. There were 14 spirited individuals wholly committed to our mission, and nearly 90% were fervently engaged in fundraising efforts. It was hard to ignore the buzz of excitement building around our trip, a promising prelude to the unforgettable experiences that awaited us.

Among our group was Rachael, a spirited woman in her 70s, known for her vibrant personality and unfiltered opinions. She carried an air of confidence, a glimmer of defiance in her eyes, as she easily navigated discussions. Our past was intricately woven together; over three decades ago, Rachael had been a staff member at my church. Her sudden disappearance had left me in a state of turmoil, grappling with an ache of guilt that echoed through the years. I revisited our last conversations countless times, replaying them in my mind, convinced that I must have inadvertently done something to drive her away.

When Rachael reappeared after all those years, the truth unraveled before me like a sad tale I had long feared. She had become entangled in a tumultuous relationship with a married man, drawn to the financial security he offered—a beacon of stability she had desperately craved. Her story was a poignant reminder of life's intricate complexities and the choices that shape our paths.

Rachael knew of my firm beliefs regarding issues like adultery and fornication, values that had guided my spiritual journey. In hindsight, given my moral convictions, I realized that her departure had been her preemptive escape, a way to sidestep the inevitable confrontation that would have arisen. Now, three decades later, our paths had crossed again, and to my astonishment, she expressed a deep yearning to reclaim her place within the church community.

As someone who holds the Ten Commandments close to my heart, adhering to these timeless principles is essential for a righteous existence. Among them, the commandment against adultery resonates profoundly with me. As a spiritual leader, I am acutely aware of the weight of my responsibilities; we are called to embody and uphold God's commandments throughout our lives.

When Rachael stepped back through the church doors, her presence ignited a mixture of emotions within me—joy, disbelief, and a flicker of uncertainty. At that moment, I was utterly oblivious to the reasons behind her long-ago departure. I embraced her warmly, welcoming the chance for reconciliation with open arms. My heartfelt reception seemed to signal that she could glide back into her former role as if the passage of time had melted away.

With confidence, Rachael quickly positioned herself, once again sharing her opinions and insights as if she had never left the Staff. It was as though she believed she still wielded influence and authority over our community, seamlessly assuming her previous standing amidst an ever-evolving landscape.

Occasionally, we gathered after church, a tight-knit circle of dedicated individuals, to delve into the status of our fundraising efforts. These assemblies were not just meetings; they were pivotal moments for reflection and strategy, where the pulse of our mission beat strongest. With her vibrant enthusiasm, Rachael often added a spark of energy to our discussions, her passion infectious as we sought to forge ahead.

I can still vividly picture one particular gathering, the atmosphere charged with anticipation. Rachael stood before us, her gaze steady, and her voice sliced through the air with an unexpected sharpness. "We are not going on a vacation; this is a mission trip. If you were considering sightseeing, you might as well stay in the States," she declared with conviction. The weight of her words hung heavily, creating a ripple of discomfort that settled over the room like a thick fog. I watched closely, noting the various expressions on my teammates' faces — a mix of surprise, discomfort, and unease as her blunt honesty reverberated in the silence.

Over the years, I have come to know my Staff deeply, and each member is a thread in the intricate fabric of our community. Eventually, Stacey confided in me, her voice barely above a whisper, revealing how deeply unsettled she felt by Rachael's harsh remarks. As I later discovered, many within our group were reluctant to express their frustrations, fearful of offending me, given my long-standing ties with Rachael, Kim, and Toni. Our relationship stretched back three decades, laden with shared experiences and history. However, Rachael uniquely exuded an air of superiority since her return. In contrast, Kim and Toni brought a refreshing spirit of warmth and humility, their faces bright with gratitude for the chance to reconnect.

Their absence had been felt keenly during the years they were away, so when they returned, I was genuinely pleased, ready to embrace the friendship and familiarity we had once shared. Yet, reflecting on their reintegration into our community, I realized I had evolved significantly.

Fear and uncertainty often engulfed me in my past, leaving me adrift in a world that sometimes seemed relentlessly hostile. But through a journey marked by perseverance and self-discovery, I emerged from that shadow as a woman of conviction, solid in my beliefs and unwavering in my faith. My path as a female pastor was undeniably challenging, littered with battles that arose from every corner, often ignited by deeply entrenched biases related to my gender.

As I pondered over those who had left our church, a familiar ache surfaced in my heart — a blend of guilt and responsibility for their spiritual journeys. The weight of wishing things had turned out differently felt like a heavy stone in my chest, especially when I thought of the deep bonds we had once forged. I often reminisced about the two sisters who entered our doors, bringing a youthful vibrancy that transformed our budding community. Their unwavering support during those early, fragile weeks created a shared mission charged with enthusiasm. Years later, a new woman joined our ranks, weaving her threads into the rich tapestry of our collective experience. The intricate tales of our church's beginnings and the myriad adventures we embarked upon together have found a home in the pages of my previous work, Book 3, *Wounded Soldier*.

Since their departure, the church has experienced profound spiritual transformations that have left me with a heavy heart, weighed down by a longing to reconnect. I deeply yearn for them to grasp the full extent of my remorse for leading them astray, for my decision to disregard the Sabbath and instead embrace worship on Sundays. This choice, I now recognize, strayed from a path I once believed to be justifiable.

For the past three decades, I have immersed myself in extensive research, delving deep into the shadows where Satan has ensnared numerous Christian churches, diverting them from their righteous course. This unsettling revelation has ignited a fire within me, spurring me to find ways to share my discoveries and earnestly invite those who departed back into the welcoming embrace of our faith community.

Throughout this tumultuous journey, my assistant, Stacey, has taken on the role of a steadfast guardian, operating with a sense of vigilance that borders stealth. Her unwavering resolve to protect our cherished anniversary celebration from any potential disruption is palpable; she will accept no interference in our carefully laid plans.

At the same time, while a staggering 90% of our church community diligently generated much-needed funds, my regular trips to Oklahoma began to bear fruit, resulting in a steady trickle of financial support. Progress came gradually, yet the weight of a pressing question loomed over me like a storm cloud: What was happening with the remaining 10%? Why were they seemingly idle, content to stay on the sidelines while the rest of us toiled?

In my frustration, I weaved justifications for those who had not stepped forward. I speculated that they had secured their funding through other means or that savings were accumulating in their accounts. I was aware of at least two individuals supporting the church financially. Still, we remained firmly committed to a principle—our church funds would never be used for personal expenses. Our responsibilities stretched far beyond mere financial support; they extended to the well-being of our community and its future.

Stacey has consistently been my voice of reason, a guiding luminary in the often-murky waters we navigate. "People can be vastly different from how they present themselves," she frequently reminds me, her words resonating with wisdom that serves as a gentle nudge, urging me to keep my expectations in check. With time, I have come to appreciate her insight more deeply. I know she will be there, ready to help me decipher the true intentions of others, assisting me in navigating the unexpected twists and turns that lie ahead.

With only a month remaining before our long-anticipated trip to Israel, the reality of our plans began to crystallize, urging us to address the looming financial logistics. I gathered everyone for a meeting, excitement bubbling as we prepared to dive into the details. The room pulsed with energy as we shared our dreams of young voices echoing through the ancient streets of Jerusalem—a poignant tribute to my 50 years of faithful service.

As the discussion unfolded, enthusiasm permeated the atmosphere, revealing those genuinely committed to our cause. The individuals who had taken the initiative to set aside funds for airfare radiated a sense of camaraderie, their heads synchronously nodding in agreement as we laid out our ambitions. Joy danced in their eyes, reflecting a shared determination and a deep, collective investment in our mission. However, one person stood out amid this united front as a stark contrast. Known for their vocal dissent, they cast a shadow over the otherwise uplifting energy, their body language radiating tension. Their presence hinted at an impending disruption, a potential source of conflict that threatened to unravel the harmonious spirit we had worked tirelessly to nurture.

I've always believed in respecting others' finances. Intrusiveness feels like crossing an invisible boundary, like prying into private matters better left undisturbed. My role has typically been that of a listener who offers advice only when solicited. Yet, an unsettling feeling churned in my gut—a warning signal that signaled trouble ahead, beginning within my own family and potentially rippling outward. I recognized that I needed to brace myself for the challenges that loomed on the horizon.

With a sense of urgency, I knew it was crucial to lock in our flights while prices remained reasonable. I decided to bring each family member into my office individually, where the soft glow of the computer screen awaited us, ready to facilitate our online booking. One by one, they entered, their expressions shifting to a mix of excitement and apprehension as we prepared to embark on this journey from Dallas to the vibrant landscapes of Israel.

With meticulous care, I navigated to the airline's website, determined to create an organized space for each individual to enter their details. The digital interface responded effortlessly, with each click and keystroke bringing the process to life as I moved through the required steps. However, as the three ladies approached, ready to finalize their flights, an electric tension filled the air—a mixture of excitement and apprehension that seemed almost tangible. Their footsteps whispered against the floor, and I noticed the glimmer of hope and uncertainty in their eyes, signaling the beginning of a pivotal new chapter in our lives.

Yet beneath my surface calm, a weighty suspicion settled heavily in my chest, like a stone stirring a tide of frustration. I confronted a stark reality: Rachael, Kim, and Toni lacked the funds necessary for their flight. My fingers curled into tight fists, clenching against the surging wave of anger threatening to break free. I leaned in slightly, taking a deliberate, steadying breath. With a voice that betrayed none of my inner turmoil, I inquired, "How much money do you have to contribute toward the flight?"

Their responses came out haltingly, tinged with hesitation. "I don't have all of it today; I need to make payment arrangements," one of them stumbled, their eyes darting away like a guilty child. Did I look like a loan officer?

Then, the reassurance came, albeit weakly: they promised to have the remaining money before our departure.

As those half-hearted words washed over me, they landed like a frigid wave crashing against my resolve, stirring a volatile mix of irritation and disappointment within. While others might have shrugged it off with a mere sympathetic nod, I grappled with an overwhelming compulsion to include everyone in this journey, no matter the cost to myself.

Taking a steadying breath, I fought back the simmering anger that threatened to boil over and reached for my debit card. The cold, hard plastic felt like a weighty anchor in my hand, a stark reminder of the choice I was about to make. Against my better judgment, I used my card, officially jeopardizing my financial stability.

Not long after, Rachael, Kim, and Toni approached me, their faces painted with expressions of regret that seemed to cast long shadows in the bright room. They gathered around me, each recounting how they had scraped a few coins, each promising to repay me in small, manageable installments. While I recognized their efforts, a nagging irritation festered within me, like an itch I couldn't reach.

What left me bewildered was their blatant assumption that I would bear the entire financial burden, especially after our team had worked tirelessly to fundraise for accommodations over the past several weeks. The ordeal left me feeling undervalued for my generosity and suffocated under the weight of responsibilities that had now been thrust upon me.

I felt trapped in a maze of expectations, thrust into a role I never signed up for, and forced to shoulder some of their flight expenses. What were they expecting from me? It became painfully clear that a decision had been made in my absence, and the frustration bubbled within me like a simmering pot ready to boil over. As I reflected more on the situation, my anger morphed into a dark cloud hanging heavily over me. I couldn't shake off the disappointment that gnawed at me—how little they had contributed to our fundraisers, especially when this moment felt pivotal for my journey.

The weight of my family's upcoming trip hung over me like a storm cloud, amplifying my inner turmoil. Time and again, I had pressed Kris for clarity, eager to know if he and Jason intended to join us as a pair. Each time I posed the question, he responded with unrestrained enthusiasm, his voice brimming with excitement as he confirmed their plans. Yet, amidst his cheerful assurances, there was a glaring omission—never once did he offer to help cover the costs associated with their adventure. Instead, the financial burden fell on me as I scrambled to fill the monetary gaps for the three women involved. Meanwhile, Kris seemed blissfully indifferent, fully absorbed in his excitement, without considering the expenses looming over him and his family.

When I mentioned JD's assurance that they would cover the costs for our family, Kris's response was curt and dismissive. He casually suggested I discuss it with JD instead. But deep down, I knew that come what may, I would bear the financial weight of this trip, a realization that only fueled my resentment.

The thought of having to inform Jason that his father was contributing nothing towards his future weighed heavily on my heart, like a stone pressing down on my chest. The possibility that this lack of support could rob him of precious opportunities made the decision even more unbearable. Instead of breaking the disheartening news, I remained silent, burying my feelings beneath layers of resolve. Once again, I resolved to dip into my savings—those hard-earned dollars that I had hoped would remain untouched—to cover the costs for another while I silently bore the burden of disappointment on my shoulders.

As I embarked on this celebratory journey, I felt a profound sense of unease, manifesting as an emotional and financial burden—an invisible weight that clung to my spirit. It gnawed at me relentlessly, casting a shadow over what should have been a time of excitement and reflection. Why did I grapple with an unseen darkness, an unpleasant sensation that coiled tightly in my gut? This upcoming trip to Israel was meant to be an enriching experience steeped in meaning and discovery. Yet, I wrestled with the nebulous sense of its significance in my life, longing for divine insight to illuminate my path.

In hindsight, I felt a surge of gratitude for the previous three months spent diligently fulfilling my commitments in Oklahoma. Those efforts carved out a slice of stability amidst the surrounding chaos. Without that structure, I would have been easily overwhelmed by the constant stress of financial worries that loomed like storm clouds, filled with endless uncertainties.

Rather than letting anxiety dictate my choices and actions, I resolved to trust God's hands regarding the trip. It became a leap of faith, a surrendering of control that stirred within me a blend of hope and trepidation—a delicate balancing act between aspiration and fear.

Years have slipped away since those early days. Yet, my promise to navigate life without debt, especially in serving our beloved church community's needs, remains steadfast. The members of our congregation are a tapestry of devotion and loyalty, each thread woven with care and commitment. However, we all traverse the treacherous terrain of financial fragility, living paycheck to paycheck, our thin safety nets barely holding us above the surging tide of our everyday struggles.

Throughout my ministry, I have opened my heart and resources broadly to support the members of our congregation during their times of need. Whether it involved providing food to a family struggling to put a warm meal on the table, offering clothing to someone in despair and desperate need of comfort, assisting with car repairs to ensure they could reach their jobs, or stepping in to manage unexpected emergencies, I have always stood ready to lend a helping hand. I never asked for donations from the church members; instead, I relied on my funds, drawn from the depths of my savings, to support those who needed it the most.

Between May and November, I dedicated myself to weekly trips to Oklahoma. By the end of October, I had saved an impressive $30,000.

The unexpected windfall washed over me like a refreshing tide, igniting excitement and hope in my heart. I suddenly realized I had the means to offer tangible support to those in my congregation who were struggling to save for their much-anticipated trips. With this newfound financial cushion, a wave of eagerness surged through me to extend my hand in assistance, aiming to alleviate the burdens that weighed down my fellow church members and bring some relief into their lives.

I held a steadfast commitment to ensure that my philanthropic endeavors remained shrouded in a cloak of secrecy, a precious confidentiality known only to the Staff. They were aware of my routine escapades to the glittering casinos of Oklahoma every week but blissfully oblivious to the impressive scale of my winnings. As I departed those vibrant halls filled with the intoxicating scent of chance and excitement, my pockets felt undeniably heavier, as though they were brimming with the very essence of my carefully constructed backup plan, flourishing just as I had envisioned. Each departure enveloped me in a warm glow of satisfaction, reaffirming that amid the exhilarating dance of chance, I was not merely accumulating wealth—I was harnessing the power to uplift those around me.

At this juncture in my life, I need to voice my profound gratitude to the tribes of Oklahoma, whose generosity has cast a significant light on my journey. This sentiment could invite sharp criticism, yet honesty triumphs above all. In truth, I wouldn't label myself as a gambling enthusiast; instead, I take pride in my frugal nature, particularly in shopping. My purchases are always pragmatic, eschewing the unnecessary luxuries that might tempt others. Throughout my life, I have wrestled with the concept of treating myself; spending money for mere enjoyment has often felt as alien as stepping onto another planet. While this surface may have intricate psychological depths, this is my essence.

With unwavering discipline, I would step into the lively and bustling casino, where the sounds of jingling coins and spirited chatter, a symphony of hope and thrill, electrified the air. I meticulously allocated a modest sum of $50 to $100 as my seed money, the crisp bills nestled in my pocket like carefully laid plans. If, for some reason, I didn't win, I would not stay. I would cash out with a steely resolve and make my way home, leaving the alluring kaleidoscope of flashing lights behind, my heart calm and my mind clear.

Time after time, as financial pressures loomed large, I would begrudgingly face that long drive, the gentle hum of the engine echoing my anxieties. Most often, I was accompanied by a few steadfast friends, each exchanging hopeful glances as we looked forward to a bountiful outcome. As I pulled the lever on the slot machines during those trying periods, I often stumbled upon unexpected victories, usually when I needed them most. The thrilling rush of each spin would momentarily wash over me, offering a respite from the uncertainty that life often brings, a fleeting sense of relief amid the swirling chaos of my responsibilities.

On several occasions, after completing the long and grueling journey to Oklahoma, I would return home with a substantial amount of cash, sometimes more than $1,000. Although I can't endorse this fundraising method, there's no denying that it proved to be a much quicker and more efficient way to gather resources compared to the often sluggish and unpredictable process of launching a GoFundMe campaign. The excitement of the trip, the hustle and bustle that accompanied it, and the immediate financial rewards were hard to resist, even if it wasn't the most conventional route. The adrenaline rush of each adventure left a lasting impression, making me momentarily forget the ethical dilemmas of my choices.

I had the most challenging time believing people needed to be more sincere. My daughters-in-law were two of the most deceptive individuals I had ever met. I stayed out of their business regarding their relationships with my sons. My opinion could have been more critical. It was essential to keep peace in the family for the sake of my grandchildren. Three weeks before the trip, the Lord had spoken to me and told me that one daughter-in-law could not make the trip. I couldn't figure out why. Later, I would find out that she was having an affair with another man.

I floated through life in blissful ignorance, wrapped in a warm cocoon of my honesty and trustworthiness. I genuinely believed that everyone around me possessed the same noble qualities. When I received a divine message, I chose not to share it with Lee, opting for silence as I allowed the events around me to unfold in their own time. My mind often wandered to my granddaughters, who had expressed their heartfelt desire to embark on a journey to Israel with us. Their unbridled enthusiasm and bright-eyed excitement sparked a deep sense of hope, illuminating my thoughts with dreams of shared adventures.

Everything began to unravel in a shocking twist of fate, sending ripples through the fabric of my existence. As I meticulously peeled back the layers of my reality, I was suddenly confronted with a brutal truth that shattered the illusions I had carefully constructed; what I had always relied upon as unwavering trust turned out to be nothing more than a delicate façade, crumbling before my eyes. The world, once familiar and stable, collapsed around me like a fragile house of cards, leaving me wrestling with the deep-seated pain of betrayal and a heavy, aching heart.

The atmosphere was tense as the clock loomed ominously, counting down to the final moment. My son, JD, sat across from me, his eyes wide with apprehension and fierce determination. The silence in the room was almost palpable until he finally broke it, his voice trembling as he asked, "Are you going to Israel?" A heavy pause hung in the air, and I could see his inner struggle reflected on his face. After what felt like an eternity, he shook his head firmly as if trying to dispel the uncertainty that weighed so heavily on us.

The weight of his decision hung in the air like a thick fog, shrouding his thoughts in uncertainty. JD could feel the unsettling echoes of the news he had inadvertently overheard—Kris was planning to invite his estranged wife on the trip. The mere notion of confronting that complicated relationship sent a chill racing down his spine, tightening his chest in a vise of anxiety. As vivid memories of their tumultuous past surged, a wave of dread washed over him, each pulling him deeper into the emotional vortex he desperately wished to avoid. At that moment, amidst the swirling memories and rising apprehension, JD's resolve crystallized with a fierce clarity—he wanted nothing to do with it. The prospect of being dragged back into that chaotic mess was intolerable, and he dismissed any thought of connection with swift finality.

I called Kris and asked if he was taking his wife, and he said yes. I told him I won't pay for her trip. She had been unfaithful. She abandoned her nine-year-old son along with my son to be an online porn star. I had seen the evidence when this happened, and was civil only because of my grandson.

He spoke to me with a gravitas that seemed to thicken the air around us, a weightiness that made it hard to breathe. "If Marie can't go, then neither will I," he declared, his voice steady yet laden with conviction—" and Jason will stay behind too." His words hung heavily between us, a stark reminder of how intricately woven our lives had become. He grasped the depth of the connection I shared with Jason, fully aware of the heartbreak that had shadowed his young life. Abandoned by his mother at the tender age of nine, Jason had endured a journey filled with more loss and sorrow than any child should bear. In the wake of his pain, I had stepped into the roles of both grandmother and mother, wrapping him in the warmth and love he so desperately craved, offering him the safety and support he needed to heal.

The image of Jason's eager face, his eyes sparkling with anticipation at the mere thought of traveling to Jerusalem, was etched deeply in my mind. I could vividly picture him wandering through the lively streets, where the air thrummed with laughter and music, harmonizing with the rich tapestry of cultures surrounding him. The idea of letting him down hung heavily in the air, a suffocating weight of disappointment that churned a storm of conflicting emotions within me. I found myself standing at a treacherous crossroads, acutely aware that the choice I faced would leave a profound imprint on my heart, shaping our future in unspoken ways.

With unwavering faith, Kris understood my firm opposition to her attending. Yet, he wore a hopeful expression, his eyes shimmering with dreams of a family journey that he believed could mend the rifts in their relationship. He envisioned how this sacred pilgrimage could breathe new life into their bond, igniting a shared passion for faith and community service that they had long neglected.

A profound sense of unease settled over me like a heavy fog as I reflected on Kris's heartfelt words. Each phrase replayed in my mind, filled with emotion and vulnerability.

As I anxiously awaited JD's final thoughts on our impending trip, a gnawing doubt took root in my stomach. I questioned whether he was subtly seeking reasons to back out or if a more complicated, tangled web of issues lurked beneath the surface, clouding our group dynamics in ways I couldn't yet interpret.

I was well aware of the deep bond between JD and Kris. Perhaps, in the quiet moments shared only between them, Kris had opened up about his struggles with his estranged wife, revealing layers of pain and complexity that could be influencing our plans in ways I hadn't considered.

I engaged in an open and heartfelt conversation with JD, clarifying that if Marie genuinely aimed to foster a positive transformation, her involvement in our plans would likely be productive. With a sense of responsibility, I gave Kris space to ponder whether Jason should be part of our group. My limited interactions with Marie left me wondering about her present circumstances. Still, I remained aware that she might have fundamentally changed her outlook or intentions.

As I meticulously worked through the final arrangements for our upcoming trip, I found myself once again standing before JD, a mixture of hope and anxiety swirling in my chest. "Are you planning to join us on this trip?" I asked, my voice laced with anticipation. JD looked up at me, serious and contemplative, and answered, "Mom, I can't, and it has nothing to do with Marie." In that poignant moment, it hit me: He had unconsciously used her as a convenient scapegoat, a veil to conceal the more profound truth of his feelings.

JD continued, his voice steady but tinged with a deep, palpable regret that hung in the air. "To be honest, I thought I could make the flight, but as the date drew nearer, it became clearer that I couldn't." His words carried a heavy weight, each syllable sinking like a stone dropped into still water, sending me ripples of disappointment mingled with understanding.

Deep inside, I longed to confide in JD about the gnawing intuition that had taken root in my gut—a whisper, a warning that they wouldn't go after all. Yet, some invisible force held me back, stifling the urge to voice my concerns. I desperately hoped that my instincts would prove false, that they would again consider the journey. The last thing I wanted was for JD to be caught off guard, blindsided by the bitter blow of unexpected news, when they ultimately chose not to embark on this adventure. I wished for this moment—the fragile exchange between us—to pass quietly, without the sharp sting of surprise.

JD had assured me that his daughters were excited at the thought of joining us on the trip, but when I approached them with the invitation, their response felt like a sudden chill. They politely declined, their voices soft yet resolute, expressing their longing to stay with their parents. A heavy weight settled upon my chest, an almost suffocating disappointment that wrapped around me like a shroud. I had poured my heart into preparing for this journey, purchasing everything they would need—from travel gear to snacks for the road—only to have them turn away from what I had envisioned as a shared, joyful experience. It felt like the entire family had woven a tapestry of plans without including me in the intricate design, leaving me standing on the fringes with unacknowledged feelings.

What had begun as a beautiful dream, laden with the promise of shared memories and joyous experiences, had morphed into a bittersweet nightmare. This heart-wrenching blow shattered my once-bright hopes into countless fragments. I cast my gaze around, desperately seeking a silver lining amidst the darkening clouds of disappointment. My heart swelled with gratitude as I observed my precious grandson, who was full of vigor and enthusiasm and still eager to embark on the trip. His bright, shimmering eyes sparkled with an infectious excitement, serving as a refreshing reminder of the joy that can bubble up even in the most trying circumstances.

I was fortunate enough to possess the financial means to cover the expenses of our journey. Yet, I was acutely aware that it would unfold with its own set of unexpected challenges. As we readied ourselves for departure, the sheer enthusiasm of my grandson began to envelop me, helping me focus on the positive facets of our situation rather than dwelling on the shadows of disappointment that loomed nearby.

He had dedicated countless hours to practicing with his youth group, earnestly learning the vibrant songs they planned to sing on the bustling streets of Jerusalem. His unyielding energy propelled me forward, reassuring me that moments of joy could be found even amidst heartache.

On the day we had eagerly anticipated for so long, the stark reality of JD's decision to back out hit me like a cold wave. I had learned from Kris that his wife, once trapped by the fatal grip of addiction, had managed to turn her life around, fully embracing sobriety. He hoped their pilgrimage to Jerusalem would become a turning point, a chance to heal old wounds and breathe new life into their relationship.

With determination, I gathered the group together, emphasizing the importance of bringing their passports and funds by the specified day so we could finalize our flights and accommodations. As the moment of departure approached, I felt an exhilarating rush mingled with a knot of anxiety in my stomach. Would everyone have enough money to make this cherished dream tangible?

As the moment approached to finalize their flight, tension filled the air when it came time to select seats and process payments for luggage and extra carry-ons. Rachael, Kim, Toni, and another group member exchanged nervous glances, their faces reflecting a mix of disbelief and anxiety. The flicker of worry in their eyes grew more pronounced, revealing an unsettling realization: the funds in their accounts wouldn't stretch to cover the cost of their tickets. In that charged atmosphere, it was painfully apparent that they were silently searching for a financial lifeline, unsure of how they would navigate their current predicament.

Faced with their silent yet desperate plea, I struggled with an intense dilemma. I drew in a deep, shaky breath, feeling the moment's gravity settle heavily on my shoulders.

Finally, I decided to cover those costs, a choice that felt like lifting a boulder from my chest. However, I made my intentions crystal clear—I expected them to repay me immediately. A palpable tension hung in the air, thick with unspoken understandings, as they exchanged hesitant glances, ultimately nodding in reluctant agreement.

If the decision had been mine alone, I would have forgone the trip to Jerusalem entirely; the city's deep-rooted historical and cultural allure held little charm for me.

Yet, as I observed the radiant excitement among the young people, I felt a surge of guilt creeping in. Their enthusiasm was contagious; an electric current seemed to pulse through the group. The thought of quashing their hunger with a somber refusal was unbearable. I couldn't bring myself to be the one who dampened their spirits, extinguishing the bright flame of their eager anticipation.

As our departure drew near, an overwhelming weariness settled deep within my bones, profound emotional exhaustion clinging heavily to my thoughts. The past two days had turned into a whirlwind of frantic preparations, a tiresome ballet of meticulously arranging and weighing our suitcases, each piece a small mountain of worry as I tried desperately to comply with the airline's rigid weight regulations.

With only two hours left before our flight was set to take off, an unsettling unease began to gnaw at me from the inside, amplified by the eerie silence that enveloped Kris. When his voice finally shattered the stillness, it carried an edge of raw panic that sent a cold shiver racing down my spine. His wife had vanished the night before, leaving no trace behind, and he had been left in the frustrating limbo of unanswered calls and unanswered questions. The air around us seemed to thrum with unsettling chaos, filling my mind with apprehension about the unpredictable challenges ahead.

I asked Kris if he had packed for our trip, and he assured me with a self-satisfied grin that everything was taken care of. However, as we arrived in the historic heart of Jerusalem, I stumbled upon the disheartening reality: his suitcase was nothing more than a chaotic jumble of wrinkled, dirty clothes hastily tossed together. Luckily, I had prepared beforehand, ensuring that Jason, who had traveled with me, had all the essentials for the journey ahead.

As we navigated the winding roads to the airport, Kris's wife's absence loomed heavily over us. A sense of dread settled in my chest as I slowly relayed the news that we had no choice but to leave without her. Just as despair threatened to tighten its grip, her voice cracked on our phones, announcing that she would meet us at the airport. I felt an immense wave of exhaustion wash over me; the turmoil we had already encountered felt like just the beginning.

When she finally appeared, it was clear she had been through her chaos. Her hair was unkempt, and her clothes askew, giving off an unsettling aura that hinted at a night of reckless indulgence, perhaps fueled by a spirit that was more than just poor decisions. At that moment, the day felt irreparably flawed.

After successfully navigating the chaotic maze of security checks after security check, Kris and his wife advanced toward the terminal gate. Still, tension crackled in the air between them like a live wire. I urgently implored them to settle down, a growing concern gnawing at me that their hatred would escalate to the point of attracting unwanted attention, potentially getting us kicked out of the airport before we boarded our flight.

I could never have imagined that this journey would soon transform into one of the most harrowing experiences of my life. As we settled into our cramped airplane seats, the tension in the cabin became palpable.

Kris and Marie erupted into a heated argument, their voices rising in a chaotic clash of accusations that filled the air with hostility. Each sharp word and bitter retort cut through the usual calming hum of the airplane, creating a jarring cacophony that left me feeling trapped in a storm of discomfort. The once serene atmosphere turned into a tumultuous whirlwind, and I anxiously glanced around, hoping for the storm to pass.

When we finally landed in New York, Kris's face was one of sheer panic; his eyes darted as if searching for something he had lost. In a frantic hush, he leaned toward me, barely able to suppress his fear, and asked if I had his passport. A wave of icy dread washed over me as I shook my head, the knot in my stomach tightening. The realization hit me like a cold slap: this situation was serious.

"Why on earth would I be responsible for your passport?" I exclaimed, incredulous at the suggestion. "You must have left it on the plane." Kris was insistent, vehemently arguing that it was safe and sound with him. The loudspeaker crackled with an announcement as the tension climbed to a boiling point: Kris's name echoed through the terminal, directing him back to the gate. In that moment of rising horror, we learned he had indeed forgotten his passport on the airplane.

Our lengthy 12-hour New York layover stretched like a never-ending marathon, weighing heavily on my shoulders. The time felt infinite as we waited for our connecting flight to Israel. Thankfully, the couple's vocal skirmishes began to fade, their energy waning as exhaustion overtook them, granting me a fleeting moment of solace amid the bustling crowd of the airport.

Traveling through such chaotic surroundings can be an actual test of patience. People from our group approached me incessantly with inquiries about departure times, flight destinations, and many other details, clamoring for my attention.

I had been promised that this adventure would etch itself into my memory—a quest to capture the essence of our momentous 50-year celebration. With each reflection penned in this book, I hoped to immortalize the chaos of our experiences.

When it became time to board the airplane, we reconvened, creeping through security again before taking our seats. In the aftermath of the airport's frenzy, a brief calm seemed to wash over Kris and his wife. Yet, deep down, I knew that once we were airborne, their arguments would reignite like a struck match.

Seated just behind them, Stacey leaned forward, her expression urgent as she warned them to temper their quarrel before the air marshals intervened, threatening to escort them off the flight in handcuffs.

Did they heed her warning? Not in the least. Their argument persisted, undeterred, for most of our journey to Israel. Fortunately, my grandson nestled beside me, blissfully unaware of the emotional upheaval swarming just a few seats away. He turned me into his pillow, drifting off into a peaceful slumber while I remained tangled in the storm of discord surrounding us.

The day stretched into an endless emotional turmoil, leaving me drained and utterly frustrated. As night enveloped the airplane, a blanket of fatigue settled over the passengers, many of whom had succumbed to sleep, their faces illuminated faintly by the dim cabin lights. I, however, felt anything but at ease. My legs ached, cramped in the confined space, an unwelcome reminder of the lengthy journey.

All I could muster at that moment was a silent prayer, a desperate plea for direction, and the strength to endure. Faced with chaos swirling around me, focusing on worship was a challenge. I drifted in and out of a restless sleep, caught between dreams and the stark reality of my surroundings.

Suddenly, a shift in the atmosphere pulled me from my haze. The unmistakable energy of devotion filled the cabin, and I realized we must be nearing Tel Aviv. I opened my eyes to see several Jewish men standing in the aisles, their voices softly rising in prayer, embodying a profound sense of faith amidst the confines of the aircraft. Their purposeful and serene movements drew the entire plane into a moment of unity, if only for a heartbeat.

The pilot's voice resonated through the cabin, signaling that we were commencing our descent toward Ben Gurion Airport. He provided essential details about the estimated arrival time and current weather conditions, painting a picture of the scene awaiting us. Moments later, a gentle jolt ran through the aircraft as the landing gear extended, locking into place with a reassuring click, preparing us for a smooth touchdown.

Chapter Five
Tel Aviv

On Monday, November 11th, 2019, our adventure commenced in Texas, teeming with excitement as we set our sights on the enchanting land of Israel. Our hearts were full of anticipation for the vibrant culture, rich history, and stunning landscapes we hoped to explore during our stay, which was set to extend until Friday, December 6th.

However, chaos erupted almost immediately upon our arrival. The atmosphere grew tense after we collected our luggage and weaved through the crowded customs area.

Kris and Marie were once cheerful companions. Now, they unleashed unpredictable outbursts that sliced through the bustling ambiance. Their quarrels hung heavy in the air, creating an awkward and profoundly disheartening atmosphere. I felt a wave of overwhelm wash over me; my patience was stretched thin as I tried to decipher the emotional storm swirling around us.

At first, I was blissfully unaware of the complexities of their conflicts, but it soon became apparent that their arguments were not just fleeting disagreements. They were intense and relentless, echoing the unresolved issues that had begun to bleed into our shared experience, amplifying my sense of unease amidst the excitement of our journey.

The moment we touched down, Marie inexplicably disappeared into the airport crowds.

Kris, fraught with anxiety, searched desperately for her, his face etched with concern. I took a moment to gather my thoughts before stepping in. I offered Kris the hotel address, urging him calmly, "Just head there when you can."

Unbeknownst to Kris, Marie had different plans entirely. While he navigated the airport searching for her, she was going to the U.S. Embassy. With a sense of purpose, she intended to claim that we had forced her to leave the United States against her will. Still in the dark, Kris grappled with the chaos of finding his wife. It was becoming increasingly clear why JD had hesitated to join us on this trip—her presence added a layer of complexity and tension that none of us had anticipated.

Jason had made a heartfelt promise to his dad, vowing to spend quality time together despite their whirlwind family dynamics. However, as tensions rose between his parents, that promise became increasingly out of reach.

Amid a particularly heated moment, Jason chose to sidestep the uncomfortable situation. Instead of getting drawn into the fray, he immersed himself in the vibrant energy of the lively young people around him, seeking the laughter and camaraderie that offered a welcome escape from the familial discord.

Everyone was exhausted and wanted to find the Hotel in the heart of Tel Aviv, where we intended to unwind and immerse ourselves in the city's infectious energy for at least two days. After enduring 48 hours without a wink of sleep, I could only think about sinking into a plush, inviting bed. The anticipation of a good night's rest was gradually overshadowed by the nagging threat of jet lag, creeping in like an unwelcome shadow, ready to take us down just when we were ready to explore.

When we finally arrived at the Hotel, disappointment washed over us—the reality of the accommodations starkly contrasted with the glossy images we had seen online. I huddled with Stacey and Julian to discuss our options. I proposed that, given our exhaustion, we should make do with what we had rather than seek a different place, especially since everyone was too tired to search anymore. To our relief, we soon discovered that we were just a stone's throw from the beach, which lifted everyone's spirits.

However, securing reservations for 15 people across two cities took a lot of work. While arranging lodging for smaller groups might be a breeze, coordinating this large number required careful planning, mainly because we were working with a tight budget.

When we initially booked the Hotel, we requested three rooms, each with at least two beds. Everything sounded beautiful in the online description, but we quickly learned that appearances can be deceiving. The Hotel was far smaller than we had anticipated, and I had to tell the group that we would need to make some adjustments and share the space closely. Maintaining a positive attitude was crucial, and I urged everyone to work together. The young people, showing remarkable resilience, assured me they were okay with sleeping on the floor or finding any available resting spot.

By evening, the atmosphere was heavy with exhaustion. When Kris and Marie finally arrived at the Hotel, they wore expressions that belied the day's turmoil, acting as if nothing was amiss. They strolled into my room, their bodies visibly drained, and without a word, collapsed onto my bed, intertwining in each other's arms, quickly succumbing to the sweet embrace of sleep.

Yet, their erratic behavior puzzled me. I couldn't quite discern if it stemmed from sheer sleep deprivation or the intense pressure lurking beneath the surface. Little did I know that Marie was still under the influence, grappling with her cravings for drugs and alcohol, her desperation hidden beneath a veneer of calm.

The following day, a palpable change swept over Marie as I reached for my purse, which lay nestled beside hers like a forgotten secret. Suddenly, she sprang forward, a whirlwind of fury, her expression twisting into a mask of rage that sent a shiver down my spine. Her eyes blazed with a fierce, almost primal intensity, and in that moment, she grabbed me and pushed me down.

That moment marked a turning point; she should never have trespassed.

As chaos erupted around us, Kris's frustrations, simmering beneath the surface, suddenly boiled over. In a blind fit of misguided anger, he lunged toward her with reckless intent, his face contorted in rage. Julian, my assistant, reacted swiftly; his instincts kicked in, and he leaped into the fray, grappling with Kris amidst the swirling chaos. Their struggle was tense, a raw display of desperation as Julian maneuvered to pull Kris away, eventually managing to push him into an adjoining room where he could no longer harm anyone.

Amid this turmoil, one of the women in our group—her expression fierce and resolute—intervened just in time to restrain Marie. Her grip was firm as she prevented Marie from unleashing the storm of fury building inside her, ready to be directed at me. The atmosphere was thick with tension, a palpable mixture of fear and confusion, creating a snapshot of turmoil that would linger heavily in the air long after the dust had settled.

It wasn't until much later that I unearthed the unsettling truth: Marie had been concealing a hidden cache of beer and drugs nestled deep within her purse. The moment she vanished from our lives, it began to make sense; she had embarked on a desperate quest, eager to find someone who could supply her with the substances she craved. It was a revelation that painted her struggle in a harsh new light, transforming my memories of her into a haunting reflection of her hidden battles.

When I reached for my purse, fear caused her to react violently to discovery, manifesting in her sudden, explosive reaction. The thought of me unveiling her concealed vice had sent her over the edge, transforming our shared space into a battlefield of suppressed anxieties and raw emotions.

Someone hurried into the hotel room where my grandson was mingling with his friends, concern etched on their faces as they reported that his mother had attacked me.

Without a moment's pause, he sprang into action, darting towards the exit with an urgency born from instinct. But his path was swiftly blocked by Kim, who stood firm as a sentinel, her presence an unyielding barrier that kept him from escaping. Anger surged within him, rage igniting a fierce, protective fire as he grappled against her impassable stance.

As the surrounding chaos gradually dissipated, the swirling dust settled around us like a heavy, suffocating blanket, wrapping the world in an unexpected, tranquil stillness that felt almost surreal. I turned my gaze back to Jason, and there Jason stood—determination carved into every youthful feature, a fierce resolve emanating from his very being. His eyes gleamed with an inner fire, a vibrant blaze of conviction that ebbed and flowed like a living force, illuminating the depths of his commitment.

"Grandma," he declared, his voice steady and unwavering, slicing through the heavy silence like a beacon of hope in the encroaching gloom. His sincerity resonated deeply within my heart, stirring a whirlwind of emotions that filled me with pride and gratitude.

"I refuse to let anyone," he continued, his expression unyielding and relentless, "not even my mom, hurt you." In that pivotal moment, the tender innocence of his youth seemed to dissipate, giving way to an unshakeable commitment that charged the air around us with a palpable sense of loyalty and purpose.

Overwhelmed by the moment's weight, I nodded vigorously, my heart swelling with raw emotion as I promised him I would cherish his heartfelt message and carry it into the world. I vowed to make it known that he would face no obstacle in his brave endeavor to protect me—his steadfast resolve would serve as my shield against lurking threats.

After two whirlwind days immersed in the vibrant energy of Tel Aviv, filled with both wonder and uncertainty, our eyes turned toward the historic skyline of Jerusalem, beckoning us for our next adventure. Our extensive research has determined that the train would be our best option. As we arrived at the bustling train station, the dusky twilight enveloped us, casting long shadows that danced whimsically across the crowded platform, alive with the din of chatter and movement. Although the exact duration of the train journey remained a mystery, a wave of relief washed over us as we settled into our seats, temporarily escaping the stresses of our new and unfamiliar surroundings.

The journey from Tel Aviv to Jerusalem unfolded aboard a sleek, high-speed train that whisked us along the tracks with remarkable speed. November's days fade quickly into twilight, draping the landscape in shadows and making it hard to catch glimpses of the scenery outside the windows as night falls.

I had heard tales of sections of the route where the train would plunge into the depths of the earth, veiled from view in pitch-black tunnels that would conceal any hint of the outside world. It would be several years before I boarded the train again, and even then, the mystery of those underground passages would linger in my mind—something I yearned to experience.

The train's interior was impressively modern and inviting, with plush chairs interspersed with spacious bench seats that beckoned for relaxation. Convenient charging plugs were thoughtfully provided for our devices, though a cautionary note played in my mind; without the proper adapter, I would be left without a lifeline to my electronics. The electrical system here differed significantly from what I was accustomed to in the United States, as a reminder of the journey into a different world.

The train ride captivated me in ways I hadn't anticipated. My only other rail experience was on the New York Subway, a bustling and chaotic underground system that paled compared to our serene journey. This train was spacious, gliding through stunning landscapes that whispered stories of ancient times.

However, my enjoyment was slightly overshadowed by a foggy haze that clung to my mind; I felt like a walking zombie, mechanically moving from one moment to the next, my thoughts lingering back in Texas like an unheeded echo.

Upon our arrival in Jerusalem, an unexpected maze unfolded before us. The vibrant signs, inscribed in three languages—Hebrew, Arabic, and English—created a facsimile of an intricate puzzle. Yet, the descriptions left much to be desired; terms familiar to us in the United States were veiled in layers of foreign terminology here, leaving us lost in translation.

It was suggested that we leave some of our baggage in the train station lockers, a practical way to lighten our load as we navigated the city in search of our Hotel. This foresight would ease our movements through the bustling streets.

Hailing a taxi made our hearts flutter with excitement and apprehension as we sped toward the address of our next accommodation. We had chosen an inviting apartment boasting three spacious bedrooms, a kitchen brimming with possibilities for culinary exploits, two bathrooms, and a cozy living room—all at a surprisingly reasonable rate that seemed almost too good to be true.

However, a disturbing silence greeted us upon our arrival, starkly contrasting with the bustling fervor just moments before. We stood there waiting for someone to usher us inside. Minutes stretched into what felt like an agonizing hour as our anticipation morphed into anxiety, hoping against hope for anyone to appear. After what felt like an eternity and countless fruitless phone calls to the Hotel, the disheartening news finally came: they had overbooked, leaving us stranded without a place to lay our heads.

Though sympathetic, the voice on the line could only assure us they would do their utmost to find an alternative, but unease lingered in the air.

Frustration seeped into my bones like a chilling wind, and I closed my eyes, praying fervently for guidance. Then I felt led to look online, and my eyes fell on the advertisement for Holy Suites. I called the facility and inquired if they had an apartment available.

Divine providence seemed at work as we secured the new accommodation. Although it was pricier, we were welcomed into a spacious two-bedroom apartment with a kitchen, a washer, and a dryer. However, the single bathroom for our group of 15 posed a logistical challenge; managing that would require patience, communication, and negotiation as we orchestrated bathroom schedules.

Just as we were about to set off for the Hotel, panic struck when Toni realized that her cherished donut pillow—a necessity following a car accident years ago—was missing.

The pillow was crucial to her comfort, and she was determined to discover whether she had left it behind in the terminal. She insisted that everyone wait while she retraced her steps.

Hours had passed since we first touched down in Jerusalem, and our group faced the monumental task of directing ourselves to the Hotel amidst the bustling chaos. The reality of traveling with at least 40 pieces of luggage—laptops, backpacks, and various bags—loomed over us like an insurmountable challenge.

With time ticking down and pressure mounting, our only option was to split into groups of four and hail taxis—a somewhat cramped arrangement, given the small size of the vehicles. As the urgency of our situation set in, Stacey stepped up as the organizer, her calm demeanor becoming the anchor that would help everyone settle amidst the chaos. Together, we would navigate this new city, united in our determination to make this journey successful.

Once we had the address to the new apartment, it was time to move toward the final destination.

Stacey and Julian swiftly escorted me to the Hotel. Their concern was palpable; they recognized the emotional and physical toll I had endured. "Get comfortable," they urged gently. We'll take care of everything." With a sense of relief, I complied without protest.

Upon arriving at the Hotel, I spotted a sturdy kitchen chair in the dimly lit foyer and sank into it, grateful for the brief moment of respite. The soothing silence was interrupted by a rhythmic knocking on the entrance door. Curiosity piqued, I rose to let Rachael, Kim, and Toni inside. They entered, each hauling their luggage and promptly leaving the remaining suitcases in the capable hands of the other team members. "Can you listen for the others?" I asked them, hoping they would keep an ear out for any returning comrades.

Feeling the need to carve out some solitude, I excused myself and went to my room. I commenced organizing my belongings there: locating device chargers amid the chaos and pulling out my night clothes. I resolved to tackle the search for my laptop and recording equipment the following day.

As Stacey and Julian managed the group's logistics, they realized that the Hotel was conveniently just a few blocks away. They decided everyone should walk a short distance to save on taxi fare.

I was bewildered by Kris and Marie's mysterious arrival at the apartment. They seemed to drop off their luggage hastily and dissipate into thin air as if swallowed by the night.

As the clock ticked past midnight, a soothing calm enveloped the Hotel, wrapping me in a stillness that contrasted sharply with the day's turbulence. Curiosity nudged at me, prompting me to reach out to Kris, who was concerned about his well-being. When I finally connected with him, he assured me he was perfectly fine and would join me shortly. However, a flicker of unease nestled in the back of my mind, growing with each passing moment as I pondered the meaning of that vague "later."

Jason stayed behind with the other young people, and I took solace in knowing he found safety in their company. The familiar tumult of his parents' constant arguments had always left him frazzled, prompting him to seek solace away from the chaos of home.

I quickly claimed the quieter of the two rooms, strategically positioned away from the constant foot traffic that would inevitably fill the space. My room would be shared with Kris, Marie, and Jason. There was only a full-sized bed, creating a tight-knit arrangement—we would have two people sleeping on the floor and two in the bed, all nestled together like sardines.

The second room, smaller than my selected one, would accommodate Julian, Stacey, and another family member.

The living room and kitchen would be transformed into a makeshift sleeping area for the rest of the group.

The pull-out sofa in the living room morphed into Rachael, Kim, and Toni's bed for the night. Their laughter danced through the air, mingling with the soft rustle of bed sheets, but it soon devolved into a playful yet heated negotiation over who would claim the coveted middle spot. Meanwhile, the younger ones settled quietly onto the cold, hard floor, fatigue wrapping around them like a comforting, albeit unwelcome, blanket.

As the evening wore on, I grew increasingly weary of the complaints wafting through the apartment like an uninvited guest. Finally, I couldn't hold back any longer. "You didn't pay for any of this trip, so just accept what you have and deal with it!" I exclaimed, a mix of frustration and exasperation seeping into my voice.

It was becoming increasingly evident that the three older women had caught wind of my recent casino win and were now harboring expectations of lavish treatment. I knew I had to monitor my finances closely with unexpected expenses piling up.

Our extended stay promised to consume a substantial amount of money since we would be away for almost a month. I was using what I had saved to fund this trip, initially planned as a special event but had morphed into more of an endurance test of patience and logistical juggling.

The morning after our arrival, the team eagerly investigated our surroundings.

Surprisingly, I realized the Lord had led us to the perfect location. The light rail and bus system were conveniently located just outside our apartment, making it incredibly easy to navigate the enchanting streets of Jerusalem.

CHAPTER SIX
Why Jerusalem?

As dawn broke on November 14th, 2017, sunlight poured into my room, bringing a renewed sense of purpose that stirred my spirit. The day ahead was woven with intention: I would dedicate time to prayer, seeking divine guidance and clarity regarding the path that led me to Israel. My challenges felt insurmountable, yet they hinted at a deeper spiritual battle, hinting that my journey held profound significance.

With the soft rustling of others beginning to greet the day, I turned to Stacey and Julian, my trusted companions. I asked them to scout our surroundings, mainly focusing on how we could navigate the intriguing sites that beckoned us. My occasional reliance on a wheelchair naturally limited my exploration abilities, but couldn't dampen my yearning for discovery.

As I considered my plans, the attentive staff approached, inquiring about my intentions for the day. "I plan to pray and seek the Lord's direction," I responded, my heart already drawn towards the City of David and the majestic Western Wall, steeped in rich history and profound spirituality.

The staff welcomed my aspirations without hesitation, ready to assist me in any way possible. I wanted my companions to relish this unique experience, so I encouraged them to wander the vibrant streets to immerse themselves in the lively cultural tapestry beyond our doorstep. With excitement coursing through them, they departed alongside the younger participants, eager to soak up every vibrant detail the city had to offer.

In parallel, I enlisted the staff to delve deeper into our new environment, ensuring we would uncover our treasures.

Eventually, Kris and Marie reemerged, but to my astonishment, they lingered briefly before vanishing again. Their erratic behavior stirred a peculiar indifference within me; at that moment, I lacked the energy to invest my thoughts in their unpredictability.

A profound sense of tranquility enveloped my room, accentuated by the heavy blackout curtains that hung like dark sentinels, blocking the chaotic world outside. I savored this rare moment of peace, knowing it was a precious opportunity for rest. As I allowed the soothing waves of slumber to wash over me, I drifted into a deep sleep, only to be abruptly jolted awake by the stormy tempest that stormed through the door without warning.

The atmosphere shifted dramatically, a palpable mix of tension and hostility returning like an unwelcome guest.

By this time, I had indeed reached my breaking point. My voice erupted in a desperate scream of fear and frustration, urging Kris and Marie to leave my sanctuary of solitude and take their unresolved issues elsewhere. Deep down, I sensed the enemy was intent on keeping me blind to the storm brewing around me and on the deeper reasons why Adonai had led me to Israel in the first place.

To flee the spiraling chaos that consumed our family, my grandson made the heart-wrenching yet wise choice to remove himself from the turmoil created by his parents.

Instead, he found solace within the embrace of a youth group and the nurturing staff members who radiated understanding and compassion. It was a decision steeped in sadness yet brimming with the wisdom of a young soul longing for peace amid the madness that enveloped us.

You might question why God seemed silent amid such distressing circumstances. I, however, was painfully aware of the demons haunting my two sons and their wives.

These specters were powered by drugs and heavy drinking, casting dark shadows over their lives and the lives of my grandchildren.

Despite their assurances that they had turned their lives around for their children's sake, I realized that true transformation was an elusive dream, requiring divine intervention to become a reality. The stark truth remained that I had never witnessed a genuine change in their behavior; my suspicions lingered like a heavy fog, yet I lacked any tangible proof. Their realities were cloaked in secrecy, hidden from my sight, and I often wondered how this veil of concealment was possible. The answer was painfully simple: I hardly ever had the opportunity to see them.

My spiritual presence tended to instill a quiet fear in others—a silent apprehension that God might choose to unveil their hidden struggles. I felt as if I could sense the weight of their burdens, knowing that the entire family seemed trapped in the relentless grip of substance abuse. Yet, confronting them was never in my nature; I couldn't bring myself to storm into their lives with accusations.

In 2004, after enduring the crushing waves of loss and isolation, I slowly pried open my heart once more, ultimately remarrying a gentle widower named Karlton. Our union felt like a fragile bloom emerging after a harsh winter. Yet, by 2013, the vibrant colors of our newfound happiness were muted beneath the heavy shadow of adversity when Karlton received the devastating diagnosis of kidney failure. His health crisis enveloped my existence in a consuming whirlwind, necessitating round-the-clock care and specialized home dialysis. Each day became a delicate balancing act, demanding my unwavering devotion and love as I navigated the complexities of his illness.

Meanwhile, my two sons had transitioned into adulthood, but I became acutely aware of the invisible chains that bound me. I felt powerless, realizing that unless I could provide irrefutable evidence of abuse or neglect surrounding my precious grandchildren, my hands remained shackled, unable to intervene on their behalf.

My daughters-in-law were like chameleons, their true intentions cleverly disguised beneath layers of deceit and malice. Marie's past was a tapestry woven with dark threads; she had emerged from a harrowing background entwined with the notorious Oak Cliff Cartel, a life where she had been manipulated for years, a helpless pawn in their treacherous drug trafficking operations that spanned the nation. One could delve into the pages of my earlier book to grasp the full extent of her twisted nature.

Then, there was Lee, embodying a different kind of deceit. Her demeanor was slick and insidious, artfully crafted to ensnare unsuspecting souls. Engaging in conversation with her required immense wisdom and caution as if one were delicately maneuvering through a treacherous minefield. Each interaction felt like a tightrope, with the ever-present risk that a single misstep could lead to disastrous consequences.

My mission was unambiguous: to shield my grandchildren from the toxic environment that trapped them and serve as a steady beacon in their tumultuous lives. They were innocent victims thrust into the maelstrom of chaos, and I yearned to keep the door ajar for them, a haven where they could confide in me during their darkest moments. My love for them burned bright and unwavering; I endured years of turmoil and hardship, steadfast in my commitment to be a source of strength and comfort amidst the relentless storms that raged around us.

These malicious women manipulated my love for my grandchildren, using them as mere excuses for me to purchase necessities for their families—food, clothing, and even cash. My sons remained oblivious, ignorant of the sinister truth about their wives, unaware of the darkness that lurked beneath their lives.

I prided myself on being the quintessential mother-in-law, embodying the ideals of patience and understanding. I never felt the need to intrude on their family matters; instead, I took on the calming role of mediator during disputes, effortlessly fostering peace and harmony among them. My interactions were always infused with kindness, love, and unwavering respect, creating an atmosphere where my children and their partners felt valued.

No matter the challenges that came my way, I stood firm in my commitment to high moral principles, ensuring that no one could ever label me as disrespectful or unkind. I was acutely aware of the underlying tensions within the family dynamics, but lacking concrete evidence, I chose to remain steadfast, deeply embedded in Adonai's teachings. My focus was squarely on expressing love and support for what was right and just.

Above all, my heart brimmed with a singular desire: to keep the door to my home open for my children and grandchildren, a haven where they could escape whenever they needed solace. I envisioned a strategic game plan rooted in wisdom, navigating each situation with divine guidance and prioritizing peace without yielding to compromise.

The family was well aware of my firm stance against drugs and alcohol, understanding that I viewed these temptations as tools through which darkness, personified by Satan, wreaked havoc on families. Rather than constantly lamenting this truth, I preferred to let my presence speak volumes.

Unbeknownst to them, I carried the weight of God's presence, a palpable energy that often left others feeling a sense of conviction. There was no need for harsh words; my being there invoked a quiet unease in those engaged in darker pursuits, as they feared the inevitable exposure of their actions.

Little did they realize that Adonai had already seen their truths and was extending an open invitation for redemption, keeping the door ajar for their eternal future. In light of this, I consciously chose to set aside my grievances, instead demonstrating the boundless love of God in every interaction.

When my son, Kris, was diagnosed with attention-deficit hyperactivity disorder (ADHD) in elementary school, it would have been easy for doctors to prescribe medication as a quick fix. However, I was determined to take a different approach. I extensively researched the side effects of the recommended drugs, weighing the risks and benefits carefully.

The best way to address Kris's challenges was to nurture diet adjustments, promote a lifestyle rich in physical activity, and provide as much structure as possible in our home environment. While he thrived under my care, I understood that maintaining this regimen would be crucial once he stepped into the world beyond our doors.

Kris's greatest struggle lay in his unyielding inclination to help others, a trait that often clouded his judgment and prevented him from recognizing the darker aspects of humanity – a quality not unlike mine. As I walked alongside him, guiding him toward understanding and insight, I remained acutely aware that everything changed as a young boy matured into adulthood. Any trauma he faced could send his thoughts spiraling, highlighting the delicate balance I had to maintain in supporting him effectively.

Despite the challenges, Kris's IQ test results revealed his brilliance, placing him in the top percent of intelligence globally.

I learned that panic can be an overwhelming force—a surge of fear so intense that it paralyzes reason and logical thinking, replacing them with an all-consuming wave of anxiety, uncertainty, and frenetic urgency. This classic fight-or-flight response can grip anyone unexpectedly.

The word panic best describes how Kris came to my house. He had called and was on his way over. I could tell by his voice that it was an emergency. When he opened the door, I looked into Kris's eyes; I immediately knew his state of mind.

Jason was engulfed in an overwhelming wave of anxiety, his tiny body trembling as panic attacks washed over him like a relentless storm. Without hesitation, I gathered him into my lap, enveloping him in a warm embrace. I held him tightly, feeling the rapid beat of his little heart against me, my whispers of comfort gently breaking through his fear. "You're safe," I assured him softly, my voice steady and soothing, as I prayed fervently for his peace. To calm his racing thoughts, I even began to sing softly, rocking him back and forth in my well-loved rocking chair, the familiar creak providing a sense of stability in that chaotic moment.

He was only nine, yet he was burdened with emotions that seemed too heavy for such a young soul. His father, Kris, brought him to me. Once Jason's breaths became more profound and rhythmic, a sign that he was starting to settle, Kris sank into the recliner beside mine, his expression a mix of worry and heartache.

It was then that he hesitantly shared the devastating news: Marie had vanished in the dead of night. Initially, he struggled to find the words, the weight of the situation hanging heavily in the air, clinging to us like a dense fog.

Kris, filled with a father's love and concern, kept glancing at Jason, his eyes reflecting both fear and hope. "Is he going to be OK?" he implored, his voice tinged with desperation. The bond they shared was palpable—he referred to Jason as "my love," a name laced with affection that spoke volumes of the depth of his feelings. At that moment, as I cradled Jason close, we all felt the shadows of uncertainty looming over us.

Kris approached me with a look of worry etched on his face, asking if I could keep an eye on his son Jason while he searched for his estranged wife. Deep down, Kris understood that Jason would be safest in my care during this tumultuous time. Within a few days, he and Jason moved in with me, their belongings hastily packed into boxes containing remnants of a chaotic life.

As the week unfolded, the layers of their reality began to unravel—a veritable can of worms. I soon discovered that drugs and alcohol were inextricably woven into the fabric of their daily existence, casting shadows over their every interaction. The shocking revelation that

Marie had abandoned her family to pursue a career as an online porn star hit me hard; at first, I dismissed it as outrageous gossip until undeniable evidence surfaced, confirming the heartbreaking truth.

Amidst this turmoil, Kris found himself overwhelmed and in desperate need of help for Jason, who was struggling with debilitating panic attacks. He turned to me, fully aware of the tranquility his son experienced in my presence. With a steadfast belief in my ability to support Jason through this chaos, Kris trusted me, hoping I could offer the guidance and stability his son desperately needed.

He could see the profound impact Jason was experiencing by simply being in my presence. The tranquil peace of God enveloped us like a warm blanket, creating a sanctuary amid the chaos of life. Kris, who was well aware of my journey and the values I held dear, believed that if anyone could guide Jason through his struggles, it would be me.

On several occasions, Kris earnestly turned to me, asking me to watch over Jason and be his support system, mainly in case anything happened to him. I solemnly promised Kris I would be there for Jason, no matter the circumstances. Then, with a heavy heart, he implored me never to let Marie have custody of his son. His concern was palpable as he emphasized my need to ensure that Jason was cared for and protected.

After uncovering the harrowing extent of drug and alcohol abuse that had plagued their family, I made a firm commitment always to keep a watchful eye on Jason and to take care of him.

When Jason and Kris moved into my home, it was as if a veil of stability and peace descended upon us. Friends and visitors would comment on the serene atmosphere that filled my house, remarking on the remarkable calm in the air. I felt the unmistakable presence of

God walking alongside me; I prayed earnestly within those walls, determined to keep chaos at bay.

It had been nearly four long years since that fateful night when Kris's wife chose to walk away. Kris held onto the hope that bringing his family to Israel would offer them a chance at renewal, a fresh start where they could serve the Lord together. Yet one insurmountable obstacle loomed over his dreams—he was the only one who envisioned that possibility.

In Israel, the atmosphere was often charged with tension. There were moments when I could barely glimpse their lives, like shadows darting through doorways, voices rising amid chaotic arguments, or the desperate scuffle for food that seemed to vanish as quickly as it appeared.

I had invested everything into this trip, fueled by the hope that it would transform their lives, bringing them closer together as a family once more. Yet, amidst the swirling emotions and chaos, I grappled with a bitter realization: my generosity seemed to go unnoticed, overshadowed by an unsettling lack of appreciation for the sacrifices I had made to make this journey possible.

We were due to return home on December 6th, and with just under a month remaining, an overwhelming sense of dread settled in my chest. How would we navigate this encroaching turmoil, punctuated by the almost palpable sense of a demonic presence looming over us all?

During this fraught time, Marie stormed into my apartment, her frustration palpable as she demanded that I pay her way back to Texas. I calmly explained that the airline had strict policies regarding refunds and adjustments and that she would have to adapt to the circumstances. I urged her to seek distraction from the travel group and explore the sights, but my proposal fell flat—it was far from satisfactory for her. Defeated, she left the apartment, anger trailing behind her like a dark cloud.

Later, in a desperate attempt to resolve the situation, Stacey called my financial director, Samantha. Her voice held an urgency as she asked Samantha to find a way to get rid of Marie before her presence took a toll on my health; she feared that I might have a heart attack. Samantha, resourceful and determined, sprang into action. She contacted the airlines, framing the situation as an emergency with extenuating circumstances necessitating Marie's immediate return to the United States.

When Marie finally returned to the apartment, her demeanor was different. She recounted a dramatic tale of seeking help at the U.S. embassy, claiming that she had reported being kidnapped and arranged for an urgent ride home. I was taken aback, assuring her that such drastic measures were unnecessary, as Samantha had already petitioned the airline for a solution. The airline had agreed to adjust her ticket for a mere $300, allowing her the chance to leave without further complications.

Yet, Marie's grandstanding about contacting the embassy felt like just another web of lies, particularly given that the situation had been resolved before her dramatic return. I offered her two choices: she could accept the embassy's offer or wait until the following day to fly home. She chose the latter, remaining in this turbulent chapter a little longer.

I recently took the time to research the location of the U.S. Embassy in Israel. My curiosity stemmed from the possibility of two embassies— one in Tel Aviv and another in Jerusalem. To my surprise, I learned that the U.S. Embassy has resided on HaYarkon Street in the vibrant city of Tel Aviv since the late 1960s. However, on May 14th, 2018, a significant change occurred when the embassy was officially relocated to Jerusalem, a city of profound historical and political significance. The previous building in Tel Aviv has since transitioned to serving as an Embassy Branch Office. It was a revelation for me, especially since I recalled traveling to Israel in 2019, leading me to question the accuracy of earlier statements made by someone I know.

CHAPTER SEVEN
Jerusalem-The Old City

It had been a long, tumultuous week, and finally, Marie was about to board her flight. A wave of relief washed over me, knowing that we could now embrace the freedom of our trip. The extra $300 spent to ensure her departure felt justified; it was a small price to pay to rid ourselves of what seemed like a haunting specter. I couldn't help but think that perhaps one day, Israel might express gratitude for having freed itself from this tormented soul.

Time had slipped through our fingers like sand for that momentous occasion—the elusive 50th anniversary. The day came and went amidst the chaos, and in the haze of turmoil, I struggled to remember if there had been a special dinner or a heartfelt acknowledgment. It felt as though survival had taken precedence over celebration.

Historical accounts narrate that the Ark of the Covenant, a sacred symbol of divine presence, was once temporarily sheltered within the ancient walls of the City of David. After King David triumphantly returned the Ark from Kiriath-Jearim, he carefully placed it in a tent he had skillfully constructed in the heart of Jerusalem.

However, this sanctuary was meant to be temporary. King David cherished the ambition of building a lasting temple for the Ark, a vision he held dear but was ultimately not granted to fulfill. His son, King Solomon, later realized this dream, dedicating monumental efforts to construct the first temple in Jerusalem, where the revered Ark would finally find its rightful home.

I was drawn to the storied City of David, eager to explore the ancient Gihon Springs. This historical site, as recounted by countless archaeologists and researchers, was believed to be the final temporary resting place of the Ark of the Covenant. This sacred vessel symbolized the very presence and power of God on earth. Gihon Springs, the region's sole source of fresh water, held immense significance; it was essential for the sacrificial rituals that permeated the spiritual life of the ancient Israelites, providing the purity needed for their offerings.

Although I had never been particularly fascinated by artifacts from the temple periods, the lure of the Ark captivated me. Countless seekers had embarked on arduous quests to uncover its whereabouts, yet all had failed in their pursuit of this elusive relic.

Deep in my heart, I believed that as one chosen by God, there lay a possibility that He might reveal the Ark's hidden location to me. I thought that if someone claimed to have discovered it, I would possess the discernment to recognize the truth in their words.

In reflection, I turned my thoughts to Adonai, asking if He would communicate with me and guide my understanding of whether the Ark of the Covenant had ever graced that sacred site. I pondered the significance of this ancient artifact, wondering why it was so pivotal to Judaism. It dawned on me that the Ark was crucial for constructing the third temple, where many believed the long-awaited Messiah would come and where Adonai would reign once more on earth.

I felt the weight of revelation pressing upon me: whoever held this sacred object would possess immense spiritual authority and extraordinary power capable of influencing the world. Throughout history, the Ark had been a beacon of divine strength, and the prospect of its discovery ignited a mixture of excitement and caution within me.

About two months before my journey to Jerusalem, I felt a deep yearning to seek confirmation from the Lord regarding a matter that had long intrigued me: the whereabouts of the Ark of the Covenant and whether it had ever graced the City of David. After much contemplation, I reached out through prayer, asking the Lord for clarity. To my surprise, His response was unequivocal—He told me that no one would ever discover the Ark of His covenant.

This revelation left me puzzled. Having immersed myself in numerous studies that emphasized the Ark's importance in rebuilding the third temple—a critical element for the fulfillment of prophetic teachings—I grappled with a troubling question: Did this mean that the third temple would never exist?

Before I could fully process my thoughts, the Lord spoke to me again, reiterating the profound statement: "They will never find the Ark of the Covenant." Each word resonated deeply, stirring both wonder and apprehension about what this could mean for the future and the unfolding of divine plans.

In a moment that felt like an eternity, I asked Him, "Why?" His response resonated deeply: "I have hidden it in you." The weight of those words sent shockwaves through my soul. Bewildered, I thought to myself, "What is wrong with me? Have I truly lost my mind?" Standing there, enveloped in a haze of confusion, I felt compelled to repent, pleading for His forgiveness, convinced I had somehow misunderstood His profound message.

I stumbled into my bedroom, my heart racing, and collapsed onto the bed, grappling with disbelief. Indeed, I must have misheard. The idea that I was carrying the Ark of the Covenant seemed utterly absurd. I am just a woman, not of Jewish descent, and I certainly don't fit the criteria that such a sacred responsibility would demand. How could this possibly be true?

His voice was familiar; it had echoed in my heart throughout my life. Yet, I had never perceived myself as someone extraordinary. Deep within, I knew the anointing of the Lord was with me, but for years, I had naively believed that everyone experienced His presence as I did and whispered to all as intimately as He did to me. Learning that millions had never indeed known Him was a harsh revelation.

What did the Ark of the Covenant symbolize? It was the embodiment of God's power on earth. Had God deemed me worthy enough to house that divine essence within me?

Over the centuries, countless souls have lived without encountering Adonai's Holy Presence since Moses' time. Yet, here I stood, blessed beyond comprehension to walk in a personal relationship with God.

I remained oblivious to the miraculous nature of my experiences. My days were filled with a love that transcended understanding and a respect that wrapped around my very being. Every moment, my thoughts lingered on Him, bathed in reverence.

With a heavy heart, I found the courage to question Adonai again. "But, Lord," I implored, "the people will never accept this. How could they possibly conceive of building the third temple in Your honor without the precious Ark of the Covenant?"

His response was humbling and profound: "I entrusted you with my anointing." The realization struck me like lightning—He had transformed the Ark into another chosen vessel that bore the weight of His presence: me.

Overcome with humility, I said to the Lord, "I'm unworthy of this task. What if I fail you as others have failed?" A trembling resolve enveloped me as I continued, "Please, be by my side. I never want to bring you shame or lead your people astray."

At that moment, a deep longing stirred within me. Was there more I needed to grasp to fulfill this divine destiny?

I felt an undeniable sense of divine anointing enveloping me, tangible evidence of miracles, signs, and wonders I had witnessed throughout my life. Those remarkable stories, rich with spiritual significance, are recounted in the other six volumes of this series. Yet, despite this profound awareness, my heart was set on standing in the very places where sacred history was made—specifically, in Jerusalem, where profound events were said to have unfolded.

Another place that called to me with an urgency I couldn't ignore was the Western Wall, a site steeped in spiritual significance. I yearned to feel the presence of Adonai there.

I am blessed with the privilege of entering His presence daily. When I do, a physical manifestation of holiness envelops me and those around me, reminiscent of the divine atmosphere surrounding Moses at the Tent of Meetings in the wilderness.

A few years prior, I had approached my Uncle, who had delved into our family genealogy, with a burning question: Did we have any Jewish ancestors? His answer was unexpectedly intriguing. "Yes, why do you ask?" he replied, curiosity flickering in his eyes. As I elaborated on my interest, he revealed that our family name was once different, tied to a lineage that had served God in the original temple. Moreover, I discovered that my mother's ancestry traced back to German Jews. However, his revelation left me craving more than familial connections; I wanted concrete proof to substantiate this newfound heritage.

My pursuit of knowledge led me to immerse myself in the history and origins of various topics, guiding me through the aisles of numerous bookstores. One day, while on a quest for enlightenment in a quaint bookstore in Dallas, Texas, I encountered a Jewish man at the checkout counter wearing a yamaka, his head covering signifying a deep-rooted faith. Intrigued, I struck up a conversation, inquiring about the process of conversion to Judaism.

To my surprise, he identified himself as a Rabbi, a title that filled me with both respect and curiosity. I asked him to elucidate the rules and laws surrounding conversion, expressing my complexities regarding my Jewish ancestry. "If both of your parents are Jewish," he probed gently.

"Yes," I confirmed, "my mother's family originated from Germany." At that moment, in the warmth of that cozy bookstore, I was truly educated on the facts of my lineage, and the intricate tapestry of my heritage began to unfold before me.

In the United States, lineage typically revolves around the father's side; however, in Judaism, one's Jewish identity is established through the mother. During a significant conversation, I learned this truth from a knowledgeable source who assured me that I didn't need to undergo a formal conversion; I was automatically considered Jewish because my mother was.

I vividly recall the pivotal moment when Adonai's anointing deepened. A transformative decision marked it: I chose to stop observing Sunday as the Sabbath and distanced myself from celebrating Pagan holidays such as Christmas, New Year's Eve, Valentine's Day, Easter, Halloween, and even Thanksgiving. My research unveiled the stark reality that these holidays were often festive, harmless, and initially rooted in pagan rituals dedicated to other deities. This understanding prompted me to remove them entirely from my life.

I can still picture the day I stood before my congregation, a wave of conviction sweeping over me as I declared, "Things were changing." My quest for truth led me to delve deeper into the origins of various cultural practices in America. As I examined the tapestry of holidays and their histories, I became increasingly aware of how these celebrations had been intertwined with beliefs I no longer wanted to uphold.

In the late '90s, I embarked on a mission to write several books that tackled a profound concern: how Satan has ensnared Christian churches, leading them away from the authentic, transformative power of God. Driven by an insatiable curiosity, I sought answers to why we seemed to lack the divine movement described in the Bible. My journey of discovery took me through extensive research at universities and public libraries, all under the attentive guidance of Adonai. Through my investigations, I uncovered the struggles faced by those yearning to believe in God and seeking validation for their faith.

The culmination of my research brought me to James L. Kilgore, one of the District leaders of the United Pentecostal Church International. When he saw the mound of materials I had meticulously assembled in numerous Xerox boxes, he was impressed and encouraged me to write a book.

Embarking on this journey was nothing I had ever experienced; it felt monumental in scope and significance. Nevertheless, fueled by a profound conviction that these truths had been divinely revealed to me, I summoned my courage and dove headfirst into the writing process of my inaugural book, "Be Ye Holy."

The book achieved remarkable success, captivating readers and selling over 100,000 copies in its first year, all through enthusiastic word of mouth and without the benefit of a formal advertising campaign or a flashy book cover.

As I basked in the accolades of my first work, I was approached with opportunities to write a second book.

In the subsequent year following the release of "Be Ye Holy," I noticed a striking cultural phenomenon: a genuine fascination with communication with angels. This emerging trend deeply troubled me, prompting me to ponder why so many people gravitated toward angels instead of seeking a direct connection with God. I felt a deep-seated reluctance to delve into this subject, especially with the potential implications it might have on my understanding of the origins of Christmas.

Determined to explore this intriguing topic, I researched to uncover the truth behind Christmas, hoping to demonstrate that it was neither inherently wrong nor rooted in pagan traditions.

My love for God was an undeniable force in my life, and I recognized that many Christians often followed popular beliefs without questioning their validity. This time, however, my research would adopt a different approach; I was intent on proving that Christmas was a celebration worth cherishing. After all, it held a special place in my heart, second only to Easter. At that moment, I still wholeheartedly believed that Jesus was God and that I was profoundly honoring His death, burial, and resurrection through Christmas.

That's when I began writing my book, "What's Up With Them Angels?"

I had become increasingly aware that churches had adopted an overwhelming reverence for angelic beings, a trend that filled me with unease. This curiosity ignited a fervent quest within me to unearth the origins of these beliefs.

As I delved into my research, I found myself unearthing the rich tapestry of Christmas traditions and exploring other Christian holidays celebrated during this season. Christmas had always held a special place in my heart; I delighted in adorning my home with festive decorations. However, I made a significant shift—trading the traditional Christmas tree for a carefully arranged nativity scene. Yet, my love for the holiday remained steadfast, even as I grappled with overwhelming evidence that challenged my understanding. Eventually, I reached a point where I could no longer participate in the holiday celebrations as I had known them.

Time blurred as I moved from Christmas to Easter, perhaps only a few months later. During this period, I felt a profound stirring within me as God urged me to confront the presence of pagan idols and rituals that had infiltrated the church. Being attuned to the nudges of His Spirit, I could not ignore what I was uncovering in libraries and bookstores.

My unexpected exploration into the origins of these holidays left me questioning the very fabric of the Christian faith. What had transpired within the churches? Why did it seem like the Spirit of God was absent? Amidst the fiery preaching about miracles, I observed a disheartening lack of tangible evidence. In many places, there was a palpable spiritual disconnect from Adonai that I could not overlook.

This unsettling awareness gnawed at me, and I quickly realized I was not alone in acknowledging this pervasive issue. My intent was not to be critical but to seek out the truth behind this alarming trend. After extensive research, I finally understood why Christian teachings often contradicted the miracles preached.

I knew I had to alter my course urgently, especially before another church service concluded. How could I continue to be like many others, inadvertently misleading my congregation with deep-rooted traditions? I vividly remember the day I stood before my congregation, bracing myself to deliver a message that could threaten my standing as their leader. I was uncertain if they would remain after I revealed the truth. All I knew was that if faced with a choice, my loyalty would lie with God, and I was prepared to rebuild from the ground up if necessary. The propagation of false doctrine had to end, and it had to happen now!

As I descended the worn, wooden stairs, a wave of apprehension washed over me. I took my place behind the pulpit, a spot that had been both a source of comfort and a reminder of my authority. My heart raced as I looked over the congregation, their curious faces awaiting my words.

"Sincerely, I said, 'First, I want to ask for your forgiveness.' The weight of my admission hung in the air. 'I have taught you to adhere to the traditions of Christianity, unknowingly leading you toward a devil's hell.'

I paused, letting the impact of my confession sink in. 'I wouldn't blame you for walking out of this building; that's what I would do in your position.'

Their expressions shifted, a blend of uncertainty and intrigue, and I could feel the tension building in the room."

Then, with unwavering clarity, I declared: "From this day forward, we will no longer keep Sunday as our Sabbath or observe Easter." As I surrendered my hands, the air shimmered with electric energy, proclaiming boldly, "Instead, we will observe the true Sabbath, from Friday sundown until Saturday sundown."

At that moment, an extraordinary shift occurred; it felt as though the very foundations of the building trembled. The Holy presence of God enveloped the congregation, a tangible warmth that caused both astonishment and reverence.

In that sacred stillness, I looked upward, my heart swelling with recognition as I whispered to God, "So that's what we were missing." It was like a veil had been lifted, revealing a profound truth. Everything in my spiritual journey transformed that day, igniting a hunger to seek understanding that has guided me for over 24 years.

The first Passover we observed together was on Wednesday, April 16th, 2003, a date etched into my memory. Then, the profound peace of the Sabbath fell upon us on April 19th, 2003. Through the pages of this series of books, I share the intimate details of my journey to know the Creator of the Universe. I call Him Adonai, while others may refer to Him simply as God or HaShem; one thing remains certain—He will never be called Jesus Christ.

In a forthcoming book, I will delve deeper into this truth, offering clarity and further revelations as they unfold. I adjusted my course with each new understanding—often unaware of its grander purpose until 2023.

Reflecting on the tapestry of my journey, I find myself enveloped in a profound sense of gratitude that words often fail to capture. The moment I encountered the true Creator of the Universe was transformative, humbling, and awe-inspiring.

My most profound hope and desire is for you to experience the same intimate familiarity with Him that I have been blessed to know. I want you to understand His divine purpose for humanity. I have been richly blessed to experience His presence, and I want you to know that Adonai is real.

Throughout history, Adonai has always harbored a divine plan for humanity.

Unfortunately, some spiritual leaders lost their way, prioritizing their agendas over the divine guidance He offers. In response, He raised a woman willing to serve Him wholeheartedly, without reservation.

Understand this: the anointing of Adonai is not bestowed upon those who merely beg or plead for divine recognition. It is a sacred choice made by God, who selects those He can trust to carry out His purpose and fulfill His grand vision.

I never sought this role; my humble prayer was for Him to walk beside me, guiding me to become my best in His service. The fact that Adonai chose me, however, was entirely by His design. Initially, I grappled with the question of why He would select a woman of non-Jewish descent for such a sacred task. It was only within the last five years that I discovered my Jewish lineage; for most of my life, I grew up within a Christian family, far removed from an understanding of Jewish traditions until 2023.

Consider this: an elderly widow in her 70s was selected to bring His Spirit into the world. I approach this holy calling with a sense of responsibility and reverence that weighs heavily on my heart. As you read these words, you can understand why I felt compelled to journey to the City of David—to fulfill a calling much more significant than myself.

I find myself in the ancient city of Jerusalem, grappling with an unshakeable question: why has God led me to this hallowed ground? Is there a message that the Almighty, Adonai, wishes to unveil to me amidst the vibrant tapestry of this land?

My understanding of Judaism has been limited until now; I have never taken the time to dive into its teachings and haven't felt a pull to visit. However, my curiosity about the roots of Christianity and its deep connection to the Jewish faith is undeniable.

As my pilgrimage to Israel draws close, with only 18 days remaining, I must pause, reflect, and seek divine guidance. I decided to stay put in my modest apartment, immersing myself in prayer, asking for clarity and direction on what steps to take next.

Looking back, I need to piece together the memories of the places we've journeyed to.

One of the earliest sites we visited was the revered Church of the Holy Sepulcher. My senses were overwhelmed by the sheer number of visitors, a relentless flow of pilgrims from all corners of the globe, each one drawn to the location believed to be the site of Jesus' burial. The air buzzed with excitement, filled with the murmurs of countless tours carrying the weight of history.

Seated on the steps outside the church, I observed the crowds of individuals entering with reverence. Tour guides, charismatic and knowledgeable, narrated their stories in a symphony of languages—Spanish, Russian, Mandarin—creating a rich tapestry of shared faith. It struck me as extraordinary that people would dedicate their savings to stand in this crowded sanctuary, seeking a connection to Jesus, the one they believe to be the Savior of humanity.

As I watched, it was impossible not to notice the palpable sincerity etched into their faces. Their eagerness was contagious, and I moved as I listened to their stories—tales of transformation and profound encounters with Jesus. Their heartfelt narratives echoed in my ears, reminding me of my journey over my 50 years as a Christian, filled with trials and revelations.

Yet, amidst this passion, I was overcome with astonishment and sorrow as I witnessed some individuals engage in poignant yet troubling actions—kneeling at the tomb, leaving behind personal items such as photographs and clothing, and performing rituals with various objects that seemed more aligned with superstition than faith.

Some pressed their lips to a stone, an act of devotion that seemed reckless in light of health concerns, especially given the impending global crisis that would soon sweep through the world.

It broke my heart to witness such desperation and adoration bestowed upon a tomb that, as history might suggest, was unlikely to be the actual resting place of Jesus.

Ironically, we would later discover a different site called the Garden Tomb, an equally commercialized spot that claimed the same significance. The irony was not lost on me: the intertwining of faith with tourism creates a web of beliefs that can often obscure the truth.

Wandering along the storied Via Dolorosa, the path Jesus is said to have walked on his way to the crucifixion, I was reminded of its established history that dates back to the 18th century. Now marked by 14 Stations of the Cross, this route meanders through the old city and is a cherished pilgrimage for countless Christian travelers.

Further, along our exploration of the Old City, we stumbled upon a sign that pointed towards the Pool of Bethesda—a site not initially on my itinerary but one that immediately piqued my curiosity. As I approached the expansive area, I saw a deep, stark void where the pool once lay. The sight was jarring—a dry and empty basin, void of the healing waters that had once drawn so many hopefuls.

Our group of young explorers, energized and eager, asked if they could traverse the desolate terrain. I nodded, encouraging them to investigate the remnants of history beneath their feet. I felt no trepidation, as no signs advised against it.

Standing at the edge of the site, I pondered the permanence of Adonai's miracles. If the account of the angel stirring the waters for healing was valid, I wondered why such miraculous events weren't still occurring today. Wouldn't that serve as a profound testament to skeptics? Wouldn't people still congregate around that pool, yearning for a chance to be the first to enter the troubled waters centuries later?

As I took in the sights and sounds around me, I realized I was searching for something beyond the sites deemed sacred by Christians or those commodified by the forces of tourism. My journey was about discovering the layers of faith intertwined within this ancient land and the more profound truths waiting to be revealed.

CHAPTER EIGHT
Idolatry Destroyed

In the previous chapter, "Prayer Tower," I mentioned that pagan worship occurred in Jerusalem. I want to provide evidence for this statement now.

In writing this series, you will read about the two ways God is referred to in Judaism.

Adonai and Hashem are both Hebrew terms used to refer to God in Judaism, but they have distinct usages and levels of reverence:

Adonai (אֲדֹנָי): Meaning: "My Lord" or "My Master" is primarily used in prayer and liturgical settings. It is considered a sacred name and is pronounced with great respect. **Context:** It directly addresses God, expressing reverence and submission.

Hashem (השם): "The Name" is used in everyday conversation and writing to refer to God without explicitly saying the unpronounceable name. **Context:** It is a respectful and indirect way of referring to God, avoiding the direct use of the sacred name.

Key Differences: Reverence: Adonai is considered more sacred and is reserved for formal religious contexts, while Hashem is a more general term used in everyday speech. **Directness:** Adonai directly addresses God, while Hashem is an indirect reference. **Pronunciation:** Adonai is pronounced, while the unpronounceable name (YHWH) is often replaced with "Adonai" during reading. Hashem, on the other hand, is always pronounced.

By understanding the distinction between Adonai and Hashem, we can appreciate the nuanced ways Jews express their reverence for God in different contexts.

"God" often refers to Adonai, especially within specific religious contexts. The interpretation of God can differ widely across various religions and cultures. Below are some common interpretations:

1. **Creator and Supreme Being**: In numerous religious traditions, God is seen as the ultimate creator of the universe and everything it encompasses. This entity is typically characterized as all-powerful, all-knowing, and inherently good.

2. **Source of Morality and Guidance**: Many believe God is the foundation for moral laws and ethical principles. This perspective holds that God provides essential guidance and support to individuals throughout their lives.

3. **Central Figure of Worship**: God is often regarded as the primary figure of worship and devotion in various religions. Followers engage in prayer and rituals to honor and establish a connection with the divine.

These diverse interpretations reflect the rich tapestry of beliefs surrounding the concept of God across different cultures and faiths.

The Lord took me on a journey and revealed the truth about Israel's idolatry. Israel professed to love God while selling items representing and honoring other gods.

I witnessed the celebrations and practices associated with their observance of these "Holy Days." I was left puzzled as I reflected on the current state of society. How can a nation claim to honor one God while acting in contradiction to that claim?

These questions burned within my soul, and I felt compelled to seek answers. Thousands of people had gathered in Jerusalem to celebrate Yom Kippur, the holiest day of the year in Judaism. It occurs annually on the 10th of Tishrei, corresponding to a date in late September or early October.

For traditional Jewish individuals, Yom Kippur primarily focuses on atonement and repentance.

According to Merriam-Webster, repentance means turning away from sin and dedicating oneself to amending one's life. Sin is an offense against religious or moral law that separates an individual from Adonai. Seeking forgiveness and committing not to repeat the offense—whether to God or another person—brings about reconciliation.

According to Wikipedia, Yom Kippur's main observances consist of total fasting and asceticism, extended prayer services (usually at synagogue), and confessions about sin. Many Jewish denominations, such as Reconstructionist Judaism (vs. Reform, Conservative, Orthodox, etc.), focus less on sins and more on one's goals and accomplishments and setting yearly intentions.

Somewhere, the true meaning of repentance has been lost.

Alongside the related holiday of Rosh Hashanah, Yom Kippur is one of the two components of the High Holy Days of Judaism. It is also the last of the Ten Days of Repentance.

The greatest sin for humanity is to observe any other deity by participating in holidays that acknowledge other deities. In the United States, the violation of the First and Second

Commandments are ever present in the celebrations.

Below is a list of some of these holidays most commonly observed by the Christian faith.

As you review this list, remember that it is only an overview. You, the reader, can look these up on your own. Start with the terms' history and origin, then name the holiday you want to research.

The History of New Year's Celebrations: New Year's celebrations have a long and varied history, dating back to ancient civilizations. The ancient Romans, for example, celebrated the new year on January 1st to honor the god Janus, the God of beginnings and endings. The Romans believed that Janus had two faces, one looking forward and one looking backward, and they associated the new year with new beginnings and a fresh start.

Valentine's Day: The ancient Romans may also be responsible for the name of our modern-day love. Emperor Claudius II executed two men, Valentine, on February 14th of different years in the third century. The Catholic Church honored their martyrdom with the celebration of St. Valentine's Day. Though no one has pinpointed the exact origin of the holiday, one place to start is ancient Rome.

The evolution from a Christian feast day into a widely celebrated holiday is still being determined. One theory is that Valentine's Day was meant to replace the pagan holiday of Lupercalia. Indeed, the Catholic Church often tried to erase pagan traditions by scheduling Christian holidays at the same time, but there isn't much evidence of the two being connected on purpose.

From February 13th to 15th, the Romans celebrated the feast of Lupercalia. The men sacrificed a goat and a dog, then whipped women with the hides of the animals they had just slain.

The Roman romantics "were drunk. They were naked," Noel Lenski, now a religious studies professor at Yale University, told NPR in 2011. Young women would line up for the men to hit them, Lenski said. They believed this would make them fertile.

The brutal fete included a matchmaking lottery in which young men drew the names of women from a jar. The couple would then be married for the festival's duration—or longer if the match was right.

Paganism becomes apparent through the symbolism used during this holiday.

Cupid: If Valentine's Day has a mascot, it's the winged, arrow-wielding baby known as Cupid. Next to the heart, he's the most common holiday symbol. His path from powerful Greek God to lovable cherub was not always obvious.

Cupid was the Roman name for the Greek God Eros, the God of erotic love. Suppose you need clarification about why a tiny baby was chosen. In that case, the original Eros appeared more often as a mischievous young adult who went around making people fall in love with one another. He was also one of the most influential figures in Greek mythology, whose power could be hazardous. Yet by the time the Romans adopted Eros as Cupid, he had aged down and became a more light-hearted figure, always being punished by his mother, Aphrodite, for causing trouble. Classics professor Richard Martin has theorized that this is because the adult Eros was frightening. So new stories — starting around the fourth century BCE — would "constrain" him by having him under his mother's control. Whatever the reason for the popularity of Young Cupid, his image lived on through the Roman Empire.

The idea of Cupid continued to shape over the centuries. As Christianity became dominant in Europe, Roman gods were mainly discarded, but cherubic Cupid continued appearing in art as a symbol of love, though a less lustful love. His popularity took off again in the art of the Renaissance, which used him, among many other symbols from antiquity, as an allegorical symbols in paintings. Cupid was a fanciful way of representing longing.

When 19th-century Valentine's Day card makers sought ideas to decorate their cards, Renaissance Cupids were an obvious choice. Not only was he a well-known symbol of love, but his appearance as a naked flying baby was both cute and inoffensive.

Roses: In Greek mythology, Aphrodite was the mother of Eros and the creator of the rose. There are a few different stories explaining the rose's birth in mythology. One is that the thorn of a white flower scratched Aphrodite, and her blood turned red. Another is that when her mortal lover Adonis died, she wept, and from her tears grew a rose. Beyond this one story, roses have been considered the crown jewel of flowers worldwide.

To find the origins of sending roses on Valentine's Day, we return to 18th—and 19th-century England. During that time, the idea of "flower languages" caught on, meaning people would convey various messages using flowers.

Different flowers meant different things, with forget-me-nots symbolizing remembrance or white lilies meaning "innocence." Perhaps unsurprisingly, there were a few other choices regarding saying "I love you." Red carnations, tulips, and roses were all given on Valentine's Day in the Victorian era, but roses won out in the long run. Today, they're the most famous Valentine's flower by far.

In the article Easter From Equinox to East, BY THE ARCHAEOLOGIST EDITOR GROUP, the topic of Uncovering the

Origins of Easter: From Pagan Traditions to Christian Beliefs, written on August 24th, 2023

Easter is a Christian holiday commemorating Jesus Christ's resurrection from the dead. It is one of the most important Christian holidays, celebrated by billions of people around the globe. In addition to its religious significance, Easter has become a significant subject of archaeological research as scholars seek to understand its origins and evolution.

The origins of Easter can be traced back to ancient pagan celebrations of the vernal equinox, which were observed in numerous cultures around the globe. As symbols of new life and rebirth, these celebrations frequently included feasting, dancing, and the exchange of eggs in Europe. With the spread of Christianity, these pagan traditions were incorporated into the new religion, and Easter took on a new significance to celebrate Jesus Christ's resurrection.

Archaeologists have discovered evidence of ancient Easter celebrations in multiple locations around the globe. In Greece, excavations at the ancient city of Mycenae have uncovered evidence of a festival held in honor of the goddess Demeter, which may have been a precursor to the Christian holiday of Easter.

Archaeologists in Italy have discovered catacombs decorated with images of the resurrection, which shed light on early Christian beliefs and practices.

The Tomb of Jesus, located in Jerusalem's Church of the Holy Sepulchre, is one of the most well-known Easter-related archaeological finds. According to Christian tradition, Jesus was buried and resurrected at this location. Archaeologists have conducted extensive research on the tomb and have uncovered evidence of multiple burial chambers and site modifications over the centuries. Although the tomb's authenticity has been contested, its significance as a Christian pilgrimage site has not diminished.

Archaeologists have also examined Easter-related material culture, including the traditional Easter egg. Eggs are symbols of new life and rebirth, dating back to ancient pagan rituals; Christians later adopted the practice as a symbol of resurrection. Eggs have been discovered in numerous archaeological contexts, such as ancient Roman tombs and medieval castle ruins, and their use as Easter symbols has persisted.

Easter has deep roots in Christian and pagan traditions, and its significance has made it an essential topic of archaeological study. From ancient pagan celebrations to early Christian catacombs and the Tomb of Jesus, archaeologists have unearthed an abundance of evidence regarding the origins and evolution of this significant holiday. As we continue to investigate the past, we gain new insights into the meaning and significance of Easter and its enduring place in the human experience.

This article alone states that Easter originated in Paganism. Why would a nation that honors God allow these lies?

The answer is for commercialism to make money from sincere people who want to value their faith in Jesus Christ.

If the Jewish people believe in one God, then allowing the teachings of the Christians believing that Jesus Christ is God is a violation of the two commandments. Why aren't they teaching the Christians the facts instead of spreading a lie and propaganda?

What is propaganda? Dissemination of information—facts, arguments, rumors, half-truths, or lies—to influence public opinion. It is often conveyed through mass media.

Propaganda is the more or less systematic effort to manipulate other people's beliefs, attitudes, or actions using symbols (words, gestures, banners, monuments, music, clothing, insignia, hairstyles, designs on coins and postage stamps, and so forth). Deliberateness and a heavy emphasis on manipulation distinguish propaganda from casual conversation or the free and easy exchange of ideas. Propagandists have a specified goal or set of goals. To achieve these, they deliberately select facts, arguments, and displays of symbols and present them in ways they think will have the most effect. To maximize impact, they may omit or distort pertinent facts or lie, and they may try to divert the attention of the reactors (the people they are trying to sway) from everything but their propaganda.

Jerusalem needs tourists for financial gain. This agenda has never been about truth.

What is the First Commandment?

God began the 10 Commandments this way: "I am the LORD your God, who brought you out of the land of Egypt, out of the house of bondage. *<u>You shall have no other gods before Me" (Exodus 20:2-3).</u>*

What is the Second Commandment?

<u>Exodus 20:1-6 NKJV: And God spoke all these words, saying: "I am the LORD your God, who brought you out of the land of Egypt, out of the house of bondage. "You shall have no other gods before Me. "You shall not make for yourself a carved image--any likeness [of anything] that is in heaven above, or that is in the earth beneath, or that is in the water under the earth; you shall not bow down to</u>

them nor serve them. For I, the LORD your God, am a jealous God, visiting the iniquity of the fathers upon the children to the third and fourth [generations] of those who hate Me, but showing mercy to thousands, to those who love Me and keep My commandments.

The Second Commandment does not just say, "Do not worship idols." It says, "Do not worship God through an idol."

Where the First Commandment tells us to worship the right God, the Second Commandment tells us to worship the right God the right way.

The Bible has two good examples of how people broke the 2nd Commandment.

1. The Golden Calf - In Exodus 32, when the people of God saw that Moses was taking so long to come down from the mountain, they gathered around Aaron and said, "For they said to me, 'Make us gods that shall go before us; as for this Moses, the man who brought us out of the land of Egypt, we do not know what has become of him.' (verse 23, New King James Version)."

The people made the golden calf because it symbolized God's strength and power. They danced around the calf (see Exodus 32:19), bowed down to it, and sacrificed it (Exodus 32:8).

Because of their disobedience, 3,000 of them were killed (Exodus 32:28), and the people were struck with a plague (Exodus 32:35).

God does not tolerate idols, and He does not tolerate worshipping Him through an idol.

2. King Jehu - When Jehu became King of Israel (2 Kings 9-10), he demolished the sacred stone of the God Baal and tore down the temple of Baal. He essentially eliminated Baal worship throughout the nation of Israel, even killing off the Prophets of Baal (see 2 Kings 10:28-29).

Jehu obeyed the First Commandment by not having any other gods. So far, so good. However, 2 Kings 10:28-29 tells us Jehu broke the 2nd Commandment:

2 Kings 10:28-29 NKJV: <u>*Thus, Jehu wiped out Baal from Israel. But Jehu did not turn aside from the sins of Jeroboam, the son of Nebat, which he made Israel sin - that is, the golden calves in Bethel and Dan.*</u>

The golden calves were made in Bethel and Dan to worship God, but this was inappropriate and ultimately broke the Second Commandment. When we worship God through something, we limit our understanding of God and make an idol that does not represent the totality of God. Jehu should have eliminated the golden calves.

2 Kings 10:18-28 NKJV: <u>*Then Jehu gathered all the people together, and said to them, "Ahab served Baal a little, Jehu will serve him much. "Now therefore, call to me all the prophets of Baal, all his servants, and all his priests. Let no one be missing, for I have a great sacrifice for Baal. Whoever is missing shall not live." But Jehu acted deceptively, intending to destroy the worshipers of Baal. And Jehu said, "Proclaim a solemn assembly for Baal." So they proclaimed it. Then Jehu sent throughout all Israel; and all the worshipers of Baal came, so that there was not a man left who did not come. So they came into the temple of Baal, and the temple of Baal was full from one end to the other. And he said to the one in charge of the wardrobe, "Bring out vestments for all the worshipers of Baal." So he brought out vestments for them. Then Jehu and Jehonadab the son of Rechab went into the temple of Baal, and said to the worshipers of Baal, "Search and see that no servants of the LORD are here with you, but only the worshipers of Baal."So they*</u>

went in to offer sacrifices and burnt offerings. Now Jehu had appointed for himself eighty men on the outside, and had said, "If any of the men whom I have brought into your hands escapes, whoever lets him escape, it shall be his life for the life of the other." Now it happened, as soon as he had made an end of offering the burnt offering, that Jehu said to the guard and to the captains, "Go in and kill them; let no one come out!" And they killed them with the edge of the sword; then the guards and the officers threw them out, and went into the inner room of the temple of Baal. And they brought the sacred pillars out of the temple of Baal and burned them. Then they broke down the sacred pillar of Baal, and tore down the temple of Baal and made it a refuse dump to this day. Thus Jehu destroyed Baal from Israel.

2 Kings 10:29-31 NKJV: **However Jehu did not turn away from the sins of Jeroboam the son of Nebat, who had made Israel sin, that is, from the golden calves that were at Bethel and Dan. And the LORD said to Jehu, "Because you have done well in doing what is right in My sight, and have done to the house of Ahab all that was in My heart, your sons shall sit on the throne of Israel to the fourth generation." But Jehu took no heed to walk in the law of the LORD God of Israel with all his heart; for he did not depart from the sins of Jeroboam, who had made Israel sin.**

Allowing the recognition of pagan deities in a land that belongs to Adonai is a compromise. Adonai will not bless the nation or the people.

Halloween: Halloween and witchcraft are intertwined through a complex cultural exchange and appropriation history. Here's a breakdown of the connection:

Pre-Christian Origins: Samhain: Halloween's roots trace back to the Celtic festival of Samhain, celebrated around November 1st. The Celts believed this was when the veil between the worlds of the living and the dead was thinnest, allowing spirits to roam freely.

Witches and Magic: In Celtic and other pre-Christian cultures, specific individuals, often women, were seen as having special powers or connections to the spirit world. These figures were sometimes associated with healing, divination, and other forms of magic and were often feared and revered.

Christian Influence: All Hallows' Eve: When Christianity spread, the Church incorporated pagan traditions into its calendar. Samhain became All Hallows' Eve, the night before All Saints' Day.

Witches as Villains: The Church often portrayed those practicing traditional beliefs as witches, associating them with evil and the devil. Persecution resulted from the fear of witchcraft, especially during the Middle Ages.

Modern Halloween: Witches as Symbols: Witches have emerged as a prevalent symbol and costume choice during Halloween, often portrayed lightheartedly or whimsically. This evolution in representation reflects changing cultural attitudes toward witchcraft, indicating a shift from fear and superstition to a sense of fascination and intrigue. As a result, witches are now embraced as part of the celebratory aspects of Halloween, highlighting society's evolving perspectives on this once-dreaded figure.

Magic and Mystery: Halloween retains supernatural and unknown elements, aligning with the historical connection to witchcraft and the occult.

In Summary, while Halloween and witchcraft share historical connections, the modern understanding of witchcraft is vastly different from the historical persecution. Today, witchcraft is often associated with spirituality, nature, and personal empowerment. On the other hand, Halloween is a secular holiday focused on fun, costumes, and community. However, the historical link between the two continues to influence cultural perceptions and Halloween traditions.

Several scriptures state that witchcraft and other forms of dark arts are against God.

2 Chronicles 33:6 NKJV: <u>***Also he caused his sons to pass through the fire in the Valley of the Son of Hinnom; he practiced soothsaying, used witchcraft and sorcery, and consulted mediums and spiritists. He did much evil in the sight of the LORD, to provoke Him to anger.***</u>

The Jewish holiday most similar to Halloween is Purim. Here's why:Costumes:

Both holidays involve people dressing up in costumes. On Purim, costumes often represent characters from the Megillah (the Book of Esther), which tells the holiday story. Celebration: Purim is a festive occasion with joy, laughter, and revelry. It's a time for feasting, drinking, and having fun.

Treats: Purim involves the exchange of treats called mishloach manot. These are baskets of food and gifts shared with friends and family.

However, there are some key differences:

Meaning: Purim commemorates a historical event in which the Jewish people were saved from destruction. Halloween has roots in Celtic traditions and focuses on themes of death and the supernatural.

Giving Back: Purim emphasizes acts of kindness and charity, such as donating to people experiencing poverty (matanot la'evyonim). Halloween is primarily about trick-or-treating and costumes.

While Purim and Halloween share some similarities, they are distinct holidays with their unique traditions and significance.

Although Purim is referred to in the Old Testament, the traditions have been adapted throughout history.

Any holiday or holy day that involves alcohol and or drugs is associated with a pagan god related to drinking.

One of the most prominent pagan gods associated with drinking is Dionysus (also known as Bacchus) in Greek mythology. He is the God of wine, fertility, festivity, and ritual madness.

<u>Dionysus is often depicted with a thyrsus, a staff topped with a pine cone, and a kantharos, a drinking vessel.</u>

Other deities associated with drinking include Aegir, the Norse God of the sea and ale; **Bacchus, the** Roman counterpart of Dionysus; **Ash, the** Egyptian God of wine and oases; and **Acan, the** Mayan God of alcohol.

These deities are often celebrated in festivals and rituals involving the consumption of alcoholic beverages, reflecting the cultural significance of drinking in many ancient societies. Several Jewish holidays involve drinking, often as part of the religious rituals or cultural traditions associated with the holiday. Here are a few of the most prominent:

Purim: This holiday celebrates the miraculous salvation of the Jewish people from the evil Haman. It is customary to drink wine or other alcoholic beverages until one "cannot distinguish between 'Cursed be Haman' and 'Blessed be Mordechai.'"

Passover (Pesach): During the Passover Seder, four cups of wine are traditionally drunk, symbolizing God's four expressions of redemption in the Torah.

Shabbat: The Jewish Sabbath is marked by the recitation of Kiddush, a blessing over wine, and Havdalah, a ceremony that marks the end of Shabbat, which also involves wine.

Tu B'Shvat: This holiday, also known as the "Jewish New Year of the Trees," is often celebrated with wine, as it is considered a fruit.

There is no reason that a person who loves and honors God should drink alcohol or use drugs, regardless of the occasion. When you do, you honor a pagan god who is all about partying.

The purpose of the dietary laws was for health reasons. However, this is contradictory when it comes to smoking and drinking alcoholic beverages, including beer, and drugs. Indulging in these habits destroys the body both physically and mentally.

When participating in the revelry or party life, a person goes into an altered state of consciousness. Demonic spirits control their behavior. They are causing violence and abuse of other individuals.

The reasons given for eating kosher are provided here.

<u>Eating kosher, which follows the dietary laws outlined in the Torah, serves several purposes for those who observe it, including:</u>

Religious Observance: For many Jews, keeping kosher is a commandment from God, fulfilling a spiritual obligation that expresses their faith and commitment. **Cultural Identity:** Following kosher laws helps maintain Jewish cultural and ethnic identity, especially in diverse societies. It fosters a sense of community among those who observe these practices.

Health Considerations: Some believe that kosher laws contribute to healthier eating habits, as they emphasize certain foods and cooking methods. **Ethical Treatment of Animals:** The rules of kashrut include guidelines for the humane treatment of animals, appealing to moral concerns about food production. **Mindfulness in Eating:** Keeping kosher encourages awareness and mindfulness about food choices and their origins, promoting thoughtful consumption. Historical Continuity: Keeping kosher connects individuals to their heritage and the historical practices of their ancestors, fostering a sense of continuity.

Eating kosher is multifaceted, intertwining spirituality, identity, ethics, and health.

When eating dairy and cheese, let's review this lie. Rabbis go to a farm where the cattle are all grazing on the same land with no special diet.

How does the Rabbi know if the cattle are pure? There are no unique markings. As the cattle are moved into the barn for milking, the Rabbi selects a percentage of milk to be marked kosher. The farmer must pay an extra fee to have the milk blessed.

The Rabbi says a blessing; magically, the cow is supposed to be pure.

Tradition has demanded that Kosher be observed for health reasons. Why don't spiritual leaders teach people not to participate in activities that cause an individual's body to become diseased?

The food processed with chemicals for preservation should be where the focus is, so that foods can bring about optimal health.

More on the topic of Kosher later.

The origins of Christmas are indeed intertwined with pagan traditions. Here's a breakdown of the critical connections:

Pagan Festivals: Saturnalia: This Roman festival, celebrated from December 17th to 25th, honored the God Saturn. It involved feasting, gift-giving, and general merrymaking, mirroring some of the festive aspects of modern Christmas. **Yule:** A Germanic winter solstice festival, Yule celebrated the rebirth of the sun and the promise of spring. It involved decorating evergreen trees, feasting, and the exchange of gifts.

Pagan Symbols and Customs: Evergreen Trees: The evergreen tree, symbolizing eternal life, was central to Roman and Germanic winter solstice celebrations. Decorating trees with ornaments and lights is a direct continuation of this pagan tradition. **Mistletoe:** This plant was sacred to the Druids and associated with fertility and peace. The custom of kissing under the mistletoe is a remnant of this pagan belief. **Holly:** Another plant sacred to the Druids, holly was associated with the winter solstice and used to ward off evil spirits. It's still commonly used as a Christmas decoration. **Yule Log:** This is a large log burned during the Yule festival, symbolizing the return of the sun and the promise of warmth and light.

Christianization: In the 4th century, the Church sought to Christianize the pagan winter solstice celebrations. They chose December 25th as the date for Christmas, aligning it with the Roman festival of Saturnalia. We allowed them to incorporate popular pagan customs into Christian celebrations, making the conversion process smoother.

In Summary, while Christmas is a Christian holiday celebrating the birth of Jesus Christ, many of its traditions have their roots in pagan winter solstice festivals. The incorporation of these pagan elements into Christmas celebrations reflects the Church's strategy of adapting to existing cultural practices to facilitate the spread of Christianity.

Only a few of the holidays or holy days are mentioned in this text.

If Jesus were God, why would he allow these activities? If the Christian faith is the example that humanity is supposed to live by, then why does the religion violate numerous commandments?

Why would a believer want to break the commandments when Jesus taught the people to obey them? Isn't that a hypocritical statement? He teaches one thing, and his followers do the opposite.

I was a Christian, and I do know why we were taught this, and I never could understand how Jesus was supposed to become God. He never was and never has been God.

The God that I serve loves humanity and would never send a human sacrifice for our sins. He destroyed nations because of human sacrifice, and what makes you think that he was okay with Jesus being a human sacrifice for sin?

Adonai provides a simple guideline for repentance. If we are sincerely sorry for actions that have offended Him or any individual, then all we need to do is talk to Him, ask His forgiveness, and resolve in our hearts never to do that again.

When a person truly repents, they are remorseful and turn away from the actions that caused hurt or pain to others.

How could anyone ask the holy, righteous creator of the universe to forgive them for their past transgressions while standing in violation of the most critical of commandments?

The scriptures do not mention acknowledging or worshipping other gods and idols, yet thousands stood before a stone wall, pleading with HaShem to forgive them of their actions that may have offended him during the past year.

While forgiveness through repentance was being sought from HaShem, their actions were contradictory. The stone wall, known as the Western Wall, is a place that many go to daily to pray, believing that the wall has power and that the glory of God is in that place. This idea is far from true. Where did all of this come from?

Two definite offenses occur during pilgrimages to these sacred places: one is erecting idols. It became holy in a place where innocent blood was shed during conflicts. The area where the Western Wall is located is surrounded by idols. Violation of the first two commandments negates repentance.

In the dream, I asked the professors why they say one thing yet practice another. At first, I was ignored, and the leaders turned to walk away. I shouted louder. Can you hear me, and then give me an answer?

Why do you only honor HaShem with your lips, and your heart is far from Him? The silence was deafening. I walked over and looked at the gentleman next to the podium. Can you answer me?

He angrily said, "Woman, what are you talking about?" My response was to look at the people. Why haven't you told them their actions were in vain? Enraged, he asked how people do this. I explained that they practice witchcraft and magic and participate in that which is unclean, and the leaders ignore the facts.

In anger, he turned to walk away. I screamed Don't walk away; answer my question. That's when I pointed out that witchcraft was all around us. Were the people so blind that they couldn't see the obvious?

The people were on automatic pilot, moving, obeying, and fearful of questioning. They were walking zombies.

Desperately, without thinking, I stepped into the zone, and before I knew it, the atmosphere changed. There, standing with me, was a large body of celestial beings. I couldn't see them at first, but then my spiritual eyes opened, and a host was fighting with me for the people.

Suddenly, where I was standing, a force rose to silence me, but I couldn't be silenced. With greater power and strength, I knew I would fight for those who were sincere.

I said No more will this country honor other gods. I was not prepared for what happened next.

Those who knew what they had done turned to attack me, and when they did, an angelic force rose up and immediately destroyed them.

No one could raise their hand or voice against me, for all that did were destroyed immediately.

Miraculously, the atmosphere changed as the war raged on, and the heavenly army took control of the city.

CHAPTER NINE
Western Wall

The Dung Gate is the closest gate to the Western Wall. It leads directly to the Western Wall Plaza.

There is a sign posted at the Western Wall's security entrance. The first time I saw it, I thought it was unique. It is not directly in front of the visitor but off to the right-hand side, and it is not a large sign. I didn't see any people stopping to read it, but I thought how exciting and insightful the hearts of those who wrote it were. The sign read.

Dear visitors, You are approaching the holy site of the Western Wall, where the Divine Presence always rests. Please ensure you are appropriately and modestly dressed so as not to harm this holy place or the feelings of the worshippers. Sincerely, Rabbi of the Western Wall and holy sites.

Curious about the Western Wall and its spiritual importance to the Jewish people, I wanted to go and embrace the atmosphere. I respect the people and their beliefs, so I researched as much as possible before going to the sacred place.

I had read some about the Jewish faith when I learned that my ancestors were Jewish. The Rabbi in Dallas told me that I was naturally Jewish because of my mother, but still, I moved cautiously; I had been deceived by the Christian faith and offended Adonai. Determined never to let that happen again, I would research every ritual of a religious group before embracing another faith. I would like to know why various rituals were taught.

Oliver Wendell Holmes, Sr., once said that some people are so heavenly-minded that they are no earthly good. This quote expresses that just because a person may appear intelligent and talented, it doesn't make them accurate.

Before dedicating your life to a cause, ask yourself these questions: Who, What, When, Where, Why, and How. Refrain from obeying anyone who can't explain why they believe a specific dogma. Know why the belief or ritual was instituted.

For Christians, there is a difference between worldly wisdom and God's wisdom. In Isaiah 55, God reminds us that our thoughts are not even close to his. If a spiritual leader can't explain the reasons behind the rituals and they can't be founded on history or biblical facts, beware.

Respectfully, I wanted to understand the significance of this monument. Going to the Western Wall was a challenge for me since I am in a wheelchair. The paths to that location inside the old city were challenging and sometimes impossible. The area wasn't conducive to people with disabilities or older adults. Fortunately, I had my senior staff members with me, and they pushed the wheelchair to get me to our destination.

Although I had seen numerous pictures and videos of people praying at the Western Wall, the power is in the editor's hands to convey their agenda. The photos and videos didn't depict the full magnitude or significance surrounding the purpose behind people going there to pray verses in their homes or at the synagogue.

When entering the area where the Western Wall is located, security checks bags since there have been incidents of violence in the area. Once we passed security, I told the Staff to slow down and let me see where I wanted to park my wheelchair. My attention was drawn to the side where the men were located.

I told my Staff that I wanted to park my wheelchair on the left-hand side in the area close to the water fountain. I wanted to see the purpose of the water fountain. I watched as men came up to wash their hands; they used a two-handle cup. There was also an area to fill your drinking water jug. As I watched, I noticed only some people washed their hands before going into the area to pray.

Inside the area, there were three sections. They are not of equal size. It was apparent that each area served a specific purpose. In the front, there were two areas. That area was for prayer.

On the left-hand side is the designated area for men to pray, and on the right is the designated area for women. I could understand that because some Christian Churches have separate prayer rooms for men and women.

There was a fence that separated prayer from visiting. Again, I understood the reason for that. That is where people would meet and mingle. There was more visiting going on than praying. Young people may go to the wall for a few minutes and spend the rest of the evening talking with others. The way the girls were dressed, they had the young men's attention. The third area was the most active.

It became apparent that only some were there for prayer. Those who did pray stayed at the wall only briefly, maybe less than 10 minutes.

Jewish people often recite prayers from a prayer book called a siddur, which contains the prayers' text, instructions, and commentaries.

However, it's important to note that prayer is not just about reciting words from a book. For many Jews, prayer is a personal and meaningful experience that involves connecting with God on a deeper level. They may use the siddur as a guide and bring their thoughts, feelings, and intentions to their prayers.

Jewish prayer occurs three times a day: in the morning (Shacharit), in the afternoon (Mincha), and in the evening (Ma'ariv).

I was fascinated by how the people were praying. The men and women rocked back and forth. The swaying motion is called Shuckling (also written as shokeling), from the Yiddish word meaning "to shake." Shuckling is the ritual swaying of worshippers during Jewish prayer, usually forward and back but also from side to side.

This practice can be traced back to at least the 8th Century and possibly as far back as Talmudic times. Rabbi Akiva said that when he prayed by himself, he would start in one corner and end up in another because of all his kneeling and bowing; Maharil (14th Century) noted this link. Yehuda Halevi mentioned the practice in the 12th Century.

Shuckling, or swaying during prayer, is a traditional Jewish custom not limited to gender. Both men and women may engage in this practice, although it is more commonly associated with men in many communities. Shuckling is often seen as a way to enhance concentration and devotion during prayer.

The practice has deep roots in Jewish tradition. As you've noted, it can be traced back to ancient times, including references in the Talmud and writings from various Jewish scholars throughout the centuries. Rabbi Akiva's intense devotion during prayer is a well-known example that illustrates the significance of physical movement in enhancing spiritual engagement.

In contemporary practice, women's acceptance and participation in shuckling can vary depending on the community and its customs. In some more traditional or Orthodox communities, women may not shuckle as frequently as men, while in more liberal or egalitarian communities, women may shuckle freely during prayer. The practice is a personal expression of spirituality that anyone can embrace, regardless of gender.

I had to see why this was one of the most sacred places in Judaism. I thought about what each individual goes through to get there.

There are several ways to enter the old city. One is the Dung Gate, the closest gate to the Western Wall, leading directly to the Western Wall Plaza.

The first entrance we used was the Jaffa Gate. It's located on the western side of the Old City walls and is the most popular tourist entrance.

Getting there requires walking or riding the light rail to the property's exterior.

The first thing you see when entering the city is all the various merchants selling idols representing the occult or other deities. Most people need help understanding the occult meaning behind these trinkets or souvenirs.

Although numerous souvenirs represent other gods and the occult, I want to point out two of the most common: the Hamsa and the Nazar.

The Hamsa, also known as the Hand of Fatima or the Hand of Miriam, is a palm-shaped amulet with a rich history and diverse meanings across various cultures and religions. It is primarily recognized as a symbol of protection against the evil eye and negative energies.

Key Meanings: •**Protection:** The open hand is believed to ward off evil influences and bring good fortune. •**Power and Strength:** The outstretched fingers represent the five pillars of Islam or the five books of the Torah, symbolizing divine power and strength. •**Blessings:** The Hamsa is often associated with blessings, health, and happiness. •**Good Luck:** It is a potent charm for attracting good luck and positive energy. •**Connection to Divine:** Some believe it represents the hand of God or a significant religious figure, providing spiritual protection.

Cultural Variations: •**Islam:** In Islamic culture, it's known as the Hand of Fatima, named after the daughter of the Prophet Muhammad. It is believed to protect against the evil eye and bring blessings. •**Judaism:** The Hand of Miriam is named after Moses and Aaron's sister. It is often used as a protective amulet and a symbol of divine protection. •**Other Cultures:** Hamsa's origins can be traced back to ancient Mesopotamia. It has been adopted by various cultures throughout history, each adding its interpretations and symbolism.

Standard Features: •**Eye in the Palm:** The eye, often blue or green, is a powerful symbol against the evil eye. •**Fish:** Some hamsas include fish, symbolizing abundance and prosperity. •**Inscriptions:** The Hamsa is often adorned with religious verses, prayers, or blessings for added protection.

The Hamsa's versatility and powerful symbolism have made it a popular choice for jewelry, home decor, and other items. It continues to be a cherished symbol of protection, good fortune, and spiritual connection for many people worldwide.

The Hamsa is the most common symbol used in Israel to ward off the evil eye. It is a hand-shaped amulet with an eye in the center, often decorated with other protective symbols like the Star of David or a fish.

The Hamsa is believed to protect against envy, jealousy, and other negative energies. It is a famous symbol in Jewish and Muslim cultures in Israel and can be found in jewelry, home decor, and other objects.

The symbolism of the eye varies across different cultures and contexts. Here are some common interpretations:

Protection and Watchfulness: •Eye of Providence: Often depicted as an eye within a triangle, it symbolizes divine watchfulness and protection. •Evil Eye: In many cultures, the eye is believed to ward off evil and protect against negative energy. Amulets and talismans featuring eyes are commonly used for this purpose. •Horus Eye: In ancient Egyptian mythology, the Eye of Horus represents healing, protection, and royal power.

Knowledge and Insight: •All-Seeing Eye: This symbol suggests omniscience and the ability to perceive everything. •Third Eye: In some spiritual traditions, the third eye is associated with intuition, psychic abilities, and enlightenment.

Power and Authority: •Royal Symbolism: In many cultures, the eye has been used to symbolize royal power and authority. •Military Symbolism: The eye can represent vigilance, surveillance, and the ability to see threats.

It's important to note that the specific meaning of an eye symbol can vary depending on the cultural context and the particular design.

Nazar and Hamsa are symbols used to ward off the evil eye, a belief that envious or malicious gazes can cause harm. While they share this common purpose, they have distinct characteristics and cultural associations:

Nazar: •Appearance: Typically, a blue bead with concentric white and blue circles resembling an eye. •Origin: The belief in the evil eye is widespread across various cultures, including the Middle East, North Africa, and Europe. •Symbolism: The eye-like design mimics the evil eye, deflecting its harmful gaze. The blue color is often associated with protection and warding off evil.

Hamsa: •Appearance: A hand-shaped amulet, often with an eye in the palm. It can be found in various styles, materials, and colors. •Origin: The Hamsa is a symbol with roots in ancient Middle Eastern cultures, and it has been adopted and adapted by different religions and communities. •Symbolism: The hand is seen as a protective gesture, shielding the bearer from harm. The eye in the palm often represents the evil eye, while the five fingers can symbolize the five pillars of Islam or the five books of the Torah.

Similarities: •Purpose: Nazar and Hamsa protect against the evil eye and negative energy. •Cultural Significance: They are deeply rooted in Middle Eastern and North African cultures, and their use extends to other regions they influence.

Differences: •Appearance: Nazar is a simple, eye-shaped bead, while Hamsa is a more elaborate hand-shaped amulet. •Symbolism: Nazar's symbolism primarily focuses on warding off the evil eye, while Hamsa has broader protective and spiritual connotations.

It's worth noting that Nazar and Hamsa are often used together, as their combined power is believed to provide even more robust protection.

What are Amulets and Talismans? •Amulets are objects believed to have protective powers, often worn on the body. •Talismans are objects believed to have magical powers used to attract good fortune or influence events.

Historical and Cultural Context: •Ancient Civilizations: Amulets and talismans have been used throughout history by various cultures, including ancient Egypt, Mesopotamia, and Rome. They were often associated with religious beliefs and used for protection, healing, and good luck. •Occult Practices: Amulets and talismans are often created with specific intentions and imbued with magical energy. They may incorporate symbols, sigils, or sacred geometry associated with various occult traditions.

It is important to note that all amulets and talismans are connected to evil, magic, and witchcraft. Remove them from your life.

The proprietors are also known as business owners. They know the hidden meanings behind these items.

The people are ignorant of these symbols and would not buy them if they knew the truth.

The scripture that says, "My people are ignorant," ***Hosea 4:6 New King James Version:*** <u>***"My people are destroyed for lack of knowledge; because you have rejected knowledge, I reject you from being a priest to me. And since you have forgotten the law of your God, I also will forget your children."***</u>

This verse is part of a more significant passage in which the Prophet Hosea condemns the Israelites for idolatry and moral corruption. He accuses them of rejecting God's law and knowledge and warns them that they will be punished for their ignorance.

Israel is supposed to be an example to the world of God's power, righteousness, and love. This nation, along with the city of Jerusalem, belongs to Adonai.

If we are to worship God only and honor him in our lives, why are we allowing other representations of other deities to be represented in the nation?

Has the 10 Commandments been compromised? The first is to have no other gods. The second is not to have idols that represent other gods.

Has a compromise been made to gain a financial profit?

Millions come to Jerusalem to connect to God and leave with shattered hopes and great disappointment. People purchase these items and need to learn what they are doing. By possessing them, you invite demons into your life.

We are to teach and instruct the people about these dangers and practices. If sincere individuals know the true meaning behind these items, they will remove them from their lives.

Keeping them will bring excellent heartache because Adonai will not hear your prayers and will not enter where these things are.

Deuteronomy 7:26 New King James Version: <u>**"Nor shall you bring an abomination into your house, lest you be doomed to destruction like it. You shall utterly detest it and utterly abhor it, for it is an accursed thing.**</u>

This verse is part of a more significant passage in which Moses warns the Israelites not to adopt the pagan practices of the Canaanites, whom they were about to conquer. He warns them against bringing idols or other objects associated with false gods into their homes.

How have we guarded the truth? God abandons the people because they disobey His commandments. His anger is then turned against us. These trinkets are not worth God's wrath.

Before reaching the wall, you must go through the areas where these abominations are sold.

Other items of clothing I noticed were significant in the life of the Jews and represented their faith.

One item of clothing has substantial meaning, and that is the kippah. A kippah (plural: kippot), yarmulke, yamaka, bullcap, or koppel is a brimless cap, usually made of cloth, traditionally worn by Jewish males to fulfill the customary requirement that the head be covered. It is the most common head-covering worn by men in Orthodox Jewish communities during prayers and by most Orthodox Jewish men at other times. Some non-Orthodox Jewish individuals wear them most of the time. In contrast, most wear them only during prayer, while attending a synagogue, or at other ceremonies, and others wear them rarely or never. Kippah – Wikipedia

When entering the prayer area, men are given a Kippah regardless of whether they are Jewish. Wearing the skull cap is one of many places this is enforced; when visiting other sites, don't be alarmed or offended if the men in your group are asked to put one on.

One of the other items worn is called a tallit. Tallit - Wikipedia

A tallit is a traditional fringed garment worn as a prayer shawl by religious Jews. This garment features special twined and knotted fringes, known as tzitzit, attached to its four corners. The fabric portion of the tallit is referred to as the beged (meaning "garment") and is typically made from wool or cotton. In some cases, silk is used for a tallit gadol, a larger Jewish prayer shawl worn over outer clothing during morning prayers (Shacharit) and all prayers on Yom Kippur. The term "tallit" commonly refers to the tallit gadol in this context.

In Hebrew, "beged" means garment, with the plural form being "begadim," which denotes clothes. Unlike the English word "clothes," which is derived from "cloth," the root of "beged" carries a different connotation. The term "boged" translates to "traitor," referring to someone who has broken faith. This meaning is echoed in the biblical verse from Isaiah (24:16), which laments, "Woe is me, bogdim bagadu - the faithless have acted faithlessly."

There are different traditions regarding the age at which a tallit gadol is used, even within Orthodox Judaism. In some Sephardi communities, boys wear a tallit even before their bar mitzvah. In some communities, it is first worn for a bar mitzvah (though the tallit katan is worn from pre-school age). In many Ashkenazi circles, a tallit gadol is worn only from marriage. In some communities, it may be customarily presented to a groom before marriage as a wedding present or as a dowry.

As the men pass through the opening leading to the inner gate of the Western Wall, they come in prepared to pray with their customary garments on. They never turn their backs on the wall. When they leave, they walk backward, a sign of respect for what represents God's holy presence.

Prayer is ritualized. Many carry a prayer book; once inside, most stand swaying back and forth. A set of scriptures or passages from the Torah is read three times daily at specific hours. As I observed what was happening, I wondered why, if they had prayed the same prayers since childhood, they had to read the passages out of a book.

Wouldn't they have them memorized when a few years passed?

Chairs were provided for those who couldn't stand for physical reasons, and lecterns were around the area.

In the Christian Faith, very few men practice their faith. To see the Jewish men practice theirs was fascinating.

With great anticipation, I silently prayed and felt nothing. I knew the actual presence of God and what an incredible experience that is, but I was waiting to see if the same thing was at the Western Wall.

I waited with great anticipation. Was Adonai there? Would I experience His presence like I have for over twenty years? No, it wasn't anything, and my heart broke. Why wasn't Adonai there? Why wasn't He there if this was His people, country, and city?

After waiting, Adonai spoke to me and said, "I am not here. For the people have sinned against me and honored other gods." Then I realized that the people had no idea what had gone wrong.

While I thought about these things, my heart was broken. How would they ever know the authentic Holy Presence of God?

Sitting in my wheelchair, a lady approached me and said, "I don't mean to stare, but there is something very different about you."

Are you from here? I told her no. I was from the United States. She asked what state I lived in, and my response was Texas. She was from New York. She asked what brought me to Israel, and I told her I was here to celebrate 50 years of serving God.

She inquired about my religious background, specifically if I identified as Jewish. This question prompted me to share a significant part of my life journey. I recounted how, in the past few years, I became aware of my Jewish heritage through the diligent research of my uncle. He delved into our family lineage and discovered that we have Jewish roots. To my surprise, I learned that I belong to the tribe of Levi, a lineage that holds substantial historical and spiritual significance within the Jewish community. This revelation deepened my understanding of my ancestry and sparked a profound interest in exploring my newfound identity.

Just minutes after I shared this information with the woman, her husband approached us. I'll never forget his words when she introduced me to him and mentioned where I lived in the United States. She also brought up my recent discovery of Jewish heritage and the tribe I belong to.

At that moment, he took my hand and said, "Holy woman of God, can you tell me when the Messiah will come?"

After a brief moment of hesitation, I provided a timeframe and told the couple it would be within three to four years.

I realized I couldn't give a specific date, which will become clear as you read this book.

They would have been surprised to know who they were standing next to.

I asked them how often they visit Jerusalem, and they said they come every year to wait for the Messiah.

At this juncture, it is vital to provide a more in-depth exploration of the characteristics of the Messiah.

In the Christian faith, the Messiah is identified as Jesus Christ, believed to embody divine qualities and fulfill numerous prophecies outlined in the scriptures. Christians hold that Jesus is not just a historical figure but the Son of God, sent to offer salvation and redemption to humanity through His teachings, sacrificial death, and resurrection.

Central to Christian eschatology is the belief in Christ's second coming, when He is expected to return to Earth. This event is often associated with the rapture concept, in which believers will be taken up to meet Him, signifying an ultimate deliverance from earthly trials and tribulations. This anticipation of His return fosters hope and faith among Christians, who look forward to His reign and the establishment of God's kingdom in its full glory.

The concept of the Messiah encompasses a profound understanding of a divinely anointed individual chosen by God for a significant purpose. This figure is characterized not only by their anointing but also by their ability to transform the spiritual and emotional atmosphere. When the Messiah engages in teaching, worship, or prayer, a palpable shift occurs, making the presence of Adonai felt by all, whether they are physically present in the vicinity or participating from afar through online platforms.

Throughout history, the Messiah has been recognized as an instrument of God, performing miraculous acts that confirm their divine mission. These miracles are not random or self-serving; they are profound demonstrations of God's power working through the Messiah. When the Messiah prays, transformative changes occur in individuals' lives. Those who are bound by spiritual oppression often find freedom, while many who suffer from debilitating illnesses like cancer experience healing.

Remarkably, there are accounts of the physically impaired regaining their ability and even instances where the dead are brought back to life, showcasing the extraordinary influence the Messiah wields through divine intercession.

It is important to note that the Messiah does not presume to dictate terms to God or sway divine will according to personal desire. Instead, the Messiah exemplifies perfect obedience and attunement to the divine will, striving to fulfill God's plans with utmost humility and devotion. This alignment with God's purpose sets the Messiah apart as a beacon of hope and a source of radical change in the lives of many.

Not every individual will experience the miracles I stated in this paragraph, but God's physical, holy presence is the greatest miracle of all. Now you can understand why my heart was broken to know that the people desperately needed God, and He wasn't at the wall. One of the interesting points of this trip was seeing many graves. It is reported that over 200,000 graves are located on the Mount of Olives, and more graves are outside the Golden Gates. I found this article today and wanted to share it with you.

The world's largest Jewish cemetery is on the side of the Mount of Olives, which slopes down into the valley that separates it from Jerusalem. Why be buried here?

The Scriptures teach that when the Messiah descends, His feet will stand on the Mount of Olives east of Jerusalem, and He will judge the nations (Zachariah 14:4). Scattered along that hillside today, thousands of Jewish graves testify to the hope that those buried there will receive a more benevolent resurrection when Messiah comes.

On the other side of the Kidron Valley, sloping up towards the Temple Mount, a prominent Muslim cemetery blocks the eastern gate, or Golden Gate, which is even bricked closed. One tradition suggests that the Messiah will enter Jerusalem through this gate after He appears. Therefore, the graves represent an attempt to "defile" anyone who would ascend the hill to enter the gate.

I noticed something else while watching the people go into prayer: pieces of paper were inserted in the wall's cracks. These were special requests for God's mercy and intervention.

The Temple Mount in Jerusalem has been the site of significant historical and religious events, though it is not primarily known for significant battles like other locations.

However, it has been involved in various conflicts throughout history, especially during periods of Conquest and religious upheaval.

Here are some notable events and disputes associated with the Temple Mount:

•Jewish-Roman Wars (66-135 CE): Roman forces under General Titus destroyed the Second Temple in 70 CE during the First Jewish-Roman War. This pivotal moment in Jewish history began a significant shift in religious practice and the Jewish diaspora.

•Muslim Conquest (636 CE): The early Muslim military campaigns resulted in the Conquest of Jerusalem, and the Temple Mount became an important Islamic holy site following the construction of the Al-Aqsa Mosque and the Dome of the Rock.

•Crusades (1099-1291): During the First Crusade, the Crusaders captured Jerusalem in 1099 and established control over the Temple Mount, converting Muslim holy sites into Christian ones. The site changed hands multiple times during subsequent Crusades.

•Mameluke and Ottoman Periods: The Temple Mount continued to be a significant religious site, but direct military engagements were less frequent. •However, the area was involved in broader conflicts over control of Jerusalem. •Arab-Israeli Conflict (20th Century): The Temple Mount has been a focal point in the ongoing Israeli-Palestinian Conflict, with tensions surrounding access and control of the site. Clashes have occurred, particularly during periods of heightened tensions.

While the Temple Mount has not been the site of many traditional battles, it has been a crucial point in the religious and political conflicts that have shaped Jerusalem's history.

There have been instances of violence and casualties at the Temple Mount.

Some of the most notable incidents include:

•1990 Temple Mount Killings: Also known as the Al-Aqsa Massacre, this event resulted in the deaths of 17 Palestinians and injuries to many more. •2017 Temple Mount Shooting: Two Israeli police officers were killed by Arab Israeli assailants. •Other incidents: There have been numerous other instances of clashes, stabbings, and shootings at the Temple Mount, leading to casualties on both sides.

It's important to note that the Temple Mount is a highly sensitive and contested religious site, and tensions often run high. These incidents highlight the ongoing Conflict and the region's complex political and spiritual dynamics.

The Temple Mount holds immense religious significance for Jews, Muslims, and Christians due to its historical and spiritual associations:

For Jews: •Holiest Site: It's considered the holiest site in Judaism, as it was the location of the First and Second Temples, where Jewish people worshipped God. •Biblical Significance: The Temple Mount is associated with numerous significant biblical events, including the binding of Isaac and Jacob's dreams. •Messianic Hope: Jews believe the Third Temple will be built on the Temple Mount when the Messiah comes.

For Muslims: •Third Holiest Site: The third holiest site in Islam is Haram al-Sharif (Noble Sanctuary). •Muhammad's Night Journey: According to Islamic tradition, Prophet Muhammad ascended to heaven from Jerusalem. •Shared Heritage: Muslims also revere the site as a place where Abraham almost sacrificed his son Ishmael.

For Christians: •Biblical Context: The Temple Mount is mentioned in the New Testament, and Jesus visited the Temple during his ministry. • Shared History: Christians recognize the historical and religious significance of the site for Jews and Muslims.

Both Judaism and Islam have strong prohibitions against killing. The Torah, the central text of Judaism, contains the commandment "Thou shalt not kill" (Exodus 20:13).

Similarly, the Quran, the central religious text of Islam, prohibits killing without justification (Quran 5:32).

However, both religions recognize circumstances where killing may be justified, such as in self-defense or just war.

With the area inside the Old City considered sacred to all monotheistic religions, why is there great hostility if all serve the same God?

Chapter Ten
Ark of the Covenant

We planned on going to the City of David, and I wanted Kris and Jason to go with us. I asked Kris, and he said they would, so we made the plans. We found out which taxi would take me since I had a wheelchair, and some would take the bus.

Witnessing Kris and Jason's bond as they interacted was a beautiful sight. Their laughter echoed softly through the ancient corridors, a contrast to the stillness of the surroundings. Feeling a mix of anticipation and nostalgia about what lay ahead, I decided to leave the wheelchair at security and took a confident step toward the mouth of Hezekiah's Tunnel.

As I approached the entrance, I glanced back to catch Kris and Jason immersing themselves in exploring the Tunnel's historical wonders. The flicker of their camera flashes illuminated the damp stone walls as they snapped photos, capturing the essence of this unique experience. I chose to hang back in the shadows, wanting to give them the space to enjoy this moment together without interruption.

Kris and Jason had overcome so many challenges to be here, and I understood that this could be a rare opportunity for them to connect on a deeper level. The extent of their friendship was evident in how they exchanged smiles and shared excitement over every little discovery. I felt a sense of gratitude for witnessing this particular time they had carved out for each other amidst their busy lives.

As we passed through the Tunnel, we came to a section where a spring flowed.

Questions burned in my mind: Was there a spiritual presence in the Tunnel?

During my visit to the Western Wall, I was struck by the deep history and rich spirituality that envelop this revered site. Standing before the ancient stones, I couldn't help but reflect on the countless prayers and hopes offered there over the centuries. For many, the Western Wall is not just a wall; it is a sacred place, a remnant of the Second Temple, where the divine presence of Adonai was once palpably felt. Pilgrims and visitors from around the world come to touch the worn stones, insert notes of prayer into the crevices, and connect with a profound sense of heritage.

Amidst the powerful atmosphere, I confronted a personal realization.

Despite the collective faith and devotion around me, I knew that the Presence of Adonai, which many seek in that place, was not felt there.

However, it's intriguing to consider that this location, while significant, may be different from the original site where the Ark of the Covenant rested in its early days. Historically, the Ark, which held immense importance for the Israelites, was housed in a different location altogether, highlighting the complex layers of faith and tradition that envelop these ancient grounds.

I had reached the end of my journey. As I stood gazing at the steady stream of water, I talked with the Lord and expressed how hard it was to realize that I was not like anyone else.

I told the group to go on. I was going to stay at the bridge for a little while. That's when some of the group, including my grandson, decided to follow the water through the Tunnel.

Jason wanted his dad to wade into the water with him, but Kris didn't. He was afraid of water and couldn't swim, so he saw that the current was very swift.

Those who chose to walk through the Tunnel had yet to learn how far it went. At times, the water was deep; at one point, Julian put Jason on his back and continued walking. It took them about an hour to navigate to the end, and we waited for them. Kris waited for Jason as they met us at the Tunnel's exit.

In a profound revelation, I was told that the Ark of the Covenant was within me, a notion that surpassed my understanding. I embarked on a comprehensive research journey to validate this claim, dedicating time to reading extensively and watching numerous historical videos. My pursuit of knowledge was fueled by an intense desire to uncover the truth.

I explored various suggested locations for the Ark's resting place throughout my research. According to biblical accounts, King David significantly relocated the Ark of the Covenant to the City of David, recognized today as Jerusalem. Once there, it was housed in a tent that David had prepared specifically for it. The Ark remained in this location until the completion of Solomon's Temple, where it was ultimately placed in the Holy of Holies.

These verses indicate that the Ark was brought to Jerusalem, the City of David.

2 Samuel 6:9-19 New King James Version: *David was afraid of the LORD that day, and he said, "How can the ark of the LORD come to me?" So David would not move the Ark of the LORD with him into the City of David, but David took it aside into the house of Obed-Edom the Gittite. The Ark of the LORD remained in the house* *of Obed-Edom the Gittite three months. And the LORD blessed Obed-Edom and all his household. Now it was told King David, saying, "The LORD has blessed the house of Obed-Edom and all that belongs to him, because of the ark of God." So David went and brought up the Ark of God from the house of Obed-Edom to the City of David with gladness. And so it was, when those bearing the Ark of the LORD had gone six paces, that he sacrificed oxen and fatted sheep. Then David danced before the LORD with all his might; and David was wearing a linen ephod. So David and all the house of Israel brought up the Ark of the LORD with shouting and with the sound of the trumpet. Now as the Ark of the LORD came into the City of David, Michal, Saul's daughter, looked through a window and saw King David leaping and whirling before the LORD; and she despised him in her heart. So they brought the Ark of the LORD, and set it in its place in the midst of the tabernacle that David had erected for it. Then David offered burnt offerings and peace offerings before the LORD. And when David had finished offering burnt offerings and peace offerings, he blessed the people in the name of the LORD of hosts. Then he distributed among all the people, among the whole multitude of Israel, both the women and the men, to everyone a loaf of bread, a piece of meat, and a cake of raisins. So all the people departed, every*one to his house.

The Ark of the Covenant is a sacred chest mentioned in the Bible that contains the original tablets of the Ten Commandments. It served as a central religious artifact for the Israelites and is regarded as one of the most significant objects in Jewish and Christian traditions.

According to biblical accounts, the Ark was constructed from acacia wood and overlaid with gold. It featured a decorative lid known as the mercy seat. The Israelites carried the Ark during their wanderings in the wilderness, and it was eventually placed in the Holy of Holies within Solomon's Temple in Jerusalem.

The Ark is surrounded by mystery, and its ultimate fate remains unknown.

It is a topic of much speculation and holds significant religious importance, continuing to fascinate people today.

The Ten Commandments are moral and religious principles central to Judaism and Christianity. They are considered a divine revelation from God to Moses, as recorded in the Book of Exodus in the Hebrew Bible and the Old Testament.

The Ten Commandments are divided into two parts:

Part 1. The first four commandments relate to our relationship with God: •1. You shall have no other gods before Me. •2. You shall not make idols. •3. You shall not take the name of the Lord your God in vain. •4. Remember the Sabbath day to keep it holy.

Part 2. The last six commandments relate to our relationship with others: •5. Honor your father and your mother. •6. You shall not murder. •7. You shall not commit adultery. •8. You shall not steal. •9. You shall not bear false witness against your neighbor. •10. You shall not covet.

The Ten Commandments are considered to be a fundamental guide for moral living.

They have had a profound influence on Western culture and law, and they continue to be a source of inspiration and guidance for many people today.

When Adonai revealed that the people would search in vain for this invaluable artifact, I realized how many individuals had dedicated years to uncovering this remarkable representation of Adonai's Spirit. Countless explorers, scholars, and seekers of truth have embarked on arduous journeys, driven by their passion and zeal, only to be met with obstacles and mysteries that have kept the artifact hidden. Each attempt, laden with hope and determination, has only deepened the enigma surrounding this sacred treasure, a testament to the powerful legacy and divine essence of Adonai that it embodies.

Although I knew the facts, I had to go to the City of David to see for myself.

According to what I had read, the Ark of the Covenant had to be by a fresh body of water for sacrifices to be made.

I wanted to go to the Gihon Spring inside Hezekiah's Tunnel, which I knew was once the only source of pure spring water.

The Gihon Spring holds immense historical and religious significance, making it a crucial landmark in Jerusalem. Here's why it's important:

Historical Significance: •Reliable Water Source: It was a primary water source for ancient Jerusalem, enabling the city's growth and development. •Strategic Importance: Control over the Gihon Spring was vital for military defense, as it ensured access to water during sieges. •Archaeological Discoveries: The area around the Spring has yielded numerous artifacts and structures, providing valuable insights into the city's ancient history.

Religious Significance: •Biblical References: The Bible mentions the Gihon Spring as the site where King David was anointed king of Israel. •Pilgrimage Site: It's a popular destination for religious pilgrims, particularly Jews and Christians, who trace biblical events to the holy site. •Mystical Significance: Some believe the Spring's waters have healing properties, adding to its spiritual importance.

Modern-Day Importance: •Tourist Attraction: The Gihon Spring and its surrounding archaeological sites are significant attractions in Jerusalem, drawing visitors worldwide. •Water Source: While no longer the city's primary water source, the Spring still flows and symbolizes Jerusalem's enduring history.

The Gihon Spring is a testament to Jerusalem's rich past, strategic importance, and spiritual significance.

The story about this Tunnel was fascinating. In 701 BCE, the king oversaw its construction. This Tunnel is a single tunnel deep within the earth. It was said to have started at two opposing tunnels and tapping sounds; the connection happened in the Middle.

Hezekiah's Tunnel, also known as the Siloam Tunnel, is a remarkable feat of ancient engineering located in the City of David in Jerusalem. Constructed during King Hezekiah's reign in the 8th century BCE, it served as a vital water source for the city during the Assyrian Empire's siege.

The Tunnel was carved through solid rock, stretching approximately 533 meters (1,752 feet) from Gihon Spring to the Pool of Siloam. The engineering marvel lies in the remarkable precision with which two teams of workers, starting from opposite ends, met in the Middle, creating a gentle gradient for the water to flow.

However, it's important to note that this event is described in the Hebrew Bible and is considered a matter of faith by many. There is no archaeological evidence to confirm the existence of the Ark of the Covenant or its presence in Jerusalem.

I wanted to stand in the possible location of this momentous event. Being close to the area was essential, so I asked Adonai to show me where it once stood.

I can't explain the significance other than wanting to validate that when Adonai told me he placed the covenant inside me, I never wanted to be elevated to a place of adoration. I love God, and comprehending everything was hard.

I never considered myself unique or super spiritual. When I worshipped or sang to the Lord, I worshipped him with all my heart. When I prayed for people, I felt a great deal of empathy.

Empathy is the ability to understand and share another person's feelings. It involves putting yourself in someone else's shoes and trying to see the world from their perspective. Includes understanding their emotions, thoughts, and experiences.

Empathy is an essential social skill that helps us to build solid relationships and connect with others on a deeper level.

Because I had experienced so much trauma and drama, I could relate to almost everyone that I came in contact with. I understood their pain and heartache.

This empathy brought about a great deal of compassion for all that I came in contact with.

Compassion is a powerful emotion involving empathy for another person's suffering and a desire to help alleviate their pain. A complex interplay of cognitive and emotional processes drives us to connect with others on a deeper level and take action to make a positive difference in their lives.

Many times, when someone shared what they were going through, I felt their physical and emotional pain. By listening to them, I would connect with God and enter His presence to plead their cause. I was not responsible for the results; I knew they needed Adonai.

When Adonai healed cancers, and the lame walked again, diseases were eradicated, blind eyes opened, emotional and mental health was reestablished, lives and families were restored, and even the dead came back to life. I never took credit for the miraculous. It was and has always been Adonai, the master of the universe and creator of humanity.

His love made the difference.

Everyone is different; God has always brought the result, not me. There have been many times in this journey when I was amazed, just like the next person, and I never viewed the results of my being powerful. At first, I questioned why, but later, I learned that God controls and judges an individual by the heart. He knows the future, and the greatest act of faith is trusting Him regardless of the end game. No one can manipulate God.

It can also help us to resolve conflicts and make more compassionate decisions.

In this series, I have shared my dramatic journey with you. You will ask why God didn't change the people around me and events. My response now and always will be that God never forces anyone to serve Him. We are all given free will, and no matter what we do, we must trust Adonai's wisdom. I see only a tiny picture of the events when He sees the hidden.

At this juncture in my spiritual journey, I had yet to receive all the insights and revelations that Adonai would eventually impart. I remember feeling a mixture of anticipation and curiosity, knowing that greater understanding was on the horizon.

These profound truths and lessons would unfold in 2023, reshaping my perspective and deepening my connection with the divine. The waiting period was both a challenge and an opportunity for growth as I navigated through uncertainties with faith and hope in what was yet to come.

Always remember that when God is actively shaping your life and guiding your path, an equally persistent force will be at play—Satan, lurking in the shadows, crafting intricate distractions designed to pull your focus away from your divine purpose. You can often discern who might be unwittingly serving as instruments of this negativity; those closest to you may unknowingly become conduits for these disruptive influences. Satan's most effective tools are often found among the people you interact with daily.

All went well with the team. As the day ended, we headed back to the apartment. Things were more settled. Marie was gone, yet she kept calling Kris. With each phone call, she tormented him more. I could tell when she called that Kris expressed how she had returned to her boyfriend and sent pictures.

He said this trip would save and reunite his family, but that would never happen.

I told him we were over 7,000 miles from Texas, and there wasn't anything he could do right now but make the best of the trip and spend time with Jason.

CHAPTER ELEVEN
Singing in the Streets

Things always seem to work out in your mind, but application is another thing. In the States, the youth group practiced singing, even going to a retirement center to sing for older people.

They were super excited. They took the songs that I had approved and added hand jesters and choreographic movement.

When I was younger, the Pastor of the church I attended in Albuquerque, New Mexico, molested me for over a year, and I was held captive through fear and intimidation.

I left that state and moved to Houston, where the church elders in the organization blamed me for the incident, even though there was a 23-year difference in our ages. I was told I could not participate in activities in the churches I attended. The restriction lasted about six years.

It had always been a dream of mine to be able to sing and travel with a church choir.

However, I wasn't allowed to participate because of the horror I had experienced in my late teens.

I never wanted anyone to be deprived of the opportunity to participate in activities at the church I now Pastor, so the young people had my support.

I would provide everything they needed, but I didn't plan on singing with them. Of course, I would sing and worship on the sidelines, but I never wanted to be the focus of attention. I am a perfect introvert and must force myself to be in public. I am a very private person, and I work best behind the scenes.

They had worked hard, and I was excited for them. It was the first time they had formed a worship team. Anyone who wanted to be in the group would sing karaoke-style along with pre-recorded songs.

No one had to be professional. Just sing and worship Adonai with your heart.

When traveling to a foreign country, you need to be familiar with the laws and customs of the host country to avoid offending anyone.

For the first few weeks we were in Israel, I was so busy fighting hell that I couldn't seem to get direction on where we needed to go or how to approach singing in the streets of Jerusalem.

With less than ten days to go before the trip was over, I was at a complete loss about how to approach going onto the streets of Jerusalem and worshipping God. To some who have experience singing in open squares, this might have seemed like an insignificant task, but to me, I was his anointed servant and had to use wisdom in everything I did. I rely entirely on the Lord's direction before attempting anything I do for Him.

After all the chaos I had dealt with, it would have been easier to pack things up and head back to Texas. Yet I couldn't do that. God brought me to Israel for a reason, and I had to find out why. I couldn't bail out and forget the mission.

I had to stop and look at the bigger picture, shake myself off, and examine the purpose behind the mission. I knew I was the only one with God's power, and the world needed what God had given me. I must keep focused.

I gathered the team around me and told them we were going out that evening to find the best place. Everyone didn't need to understand the technical side of things. I have always been a person of my word, and if I tell someone I will do something, I will. I might not know when or how, but I will always keep my word.

The most critical trait of serving Adonai is integrity.

Integrity is the quality of being honest and having strong moral principles. It's about doing the right thing, even when no one is watching. It involves being truthful and fair and having a solid sense of what is right and wrong.

Here are some critical aspects of integrity: •Honesty: Being truthful and sincere in your words and actions. •Fairness: Treating everyone with respect and equality. •Responsibility: Taking ownership of your actions and their consequences. •Courage: Standing up for your beliefs, even when difficult. •Consistency: Acting following your values and principles.

Integrity is essential in all areas of life, from personal relationships to professional endeavors. It builds trust, strengthens relationships, and helps to create a more just and equitable society.

Here are some ways to cultivate integrity: •Reflect on your values: What do you believe? What is important to you? •Practice honesty: Be truthful in your words and actions. •Be fair: Treat others with respect and equality. •Take responsibility: Own up to your mistakes and learn from them. •Be courageous: Stand up for what you believe in. •Be consistent: Live your values every day.

By practicing integrity, you can become more trustworthy and respected and help create a more positive and ethical environment for everyone.

I have lived by this for 50 years, and it is not something that most people live by. How the world sees me, including my family, is vitally important. I honor Adonai in everything I do.

I have been a videographer for over 25 years and have been self-taught through experience. Anything that I do for the Lord must be my best.

When we started, I had no idea where we would go. It would have to be wheelchair accessible. I want to insert here that I am not permanently disabled; I had an accident and could not afford treatment. It wouldn't be until 2022, when my Medicare went into effect, that I would be led to the best physician to perform surgery.

Going out the apartment's door was the first act of faith, and believing God would lead me was absolute.

As I was being pushed, I prayed and listened for the Lord's directions. Then, I told everyone to stop; I felt like I had found the place to set things up.

We didn't have an extensive sound system because our luggage was limited, so I found some tiny Bluetooth speakers called Ultimate Ears UE Boom 3 and bought those so I could daisy-chain them to cover a larger area.

We would also use Julian's Surface laptop to play the music.

It didn't take long, and I found what I thought would be a perfect location. It was between two buildings, with a walkway down the middle for entering and exiting. This configuration would allow the music to bounce off the buildings and create a natural amplifier.

Everyone was naturally nervous since no one had ever sung in public. We had no idea how things would turn out since we had yet to test the equipment. It took a little while to set up, and then I told them, "Let's go ahead and start."

We had a few issues when the music started, but we came there on a mission so that we would continue. The first song started playing, and the team looked at each other and gave a hand signal to begin. They were singing with extraordinary enthusiasm, and the team looked at each other, and people started responding.

At first, there were the curious, and within minutes, other onlookers came. By the end of the first song, the crowd had quickly grown. The response was terrific.

I watched and paid close attention to the technical side of things, staying in the background. When the team finished all the songs designated for the evening, it was time to return to the apartment.

I noticed that the chorus had vanished, and when I looked out the window, I saw them outside practicing. They took this mission seriously and wanted to be well-prepared for their next performance.

We planned to go out again, this time to explore Zion Square. This location has more activity, which would provide the team with greater exposure.

Although it was chilly outside in late November, foot traffic was frequent on the main street. At first, the idea of moving to the new area seemed great; however, there was one significant detail I should have considered: the noise from the light rail train.

The train comes at varied times with no set schedule. When the singing began, it was right before the train came by. Everything was moving on the list of songs, but then the train drowned out the music.

Our small speakers were no match for the mighty train or the street noise.

To make matters worse, I looked at the adults with us. I wanted everyone to support the team, but that was asking for it to snow in Africa.

Every time we prepared to sing, Rachael, Kim, and Toni sat on the sidelines, appearing not to be with the group. Their expressions were a total embarrassment.

It never shocks me how Satan will use those who are carnal and have attitudes to hinder or stop the sincere. There is one thing that I have learned over the years: never pay attention to expressions. That's one of the devil's tools to promote doubt.

I told the team we needed to return to where we started; we had better acoustics there.

More determined than ever, no one would stop our meager endeavor. In selecting the songs for the team, I wanted people to hear songs of encouragement and a message that lifted their spirits if they were going through a hard patch in life. Most importantly, I wanted songs that expressed our love for God.

It is essential to tell the reader what was going on while we were reaching out to those God wanted to reach. The battle zone never stopped. Imagine the mental stress that was happening while I was attempting to lead this group.

Once again, Kris was troubling me. I didn't know where he was, and neither did Jason.

Jason would ask me, "Grandma, have you heard from Dad?" Then Jason would say, "I want him to come listen and watch us." I told him no, son, and I had tried calling him several times, but it went straight to voicemail.

Kris was not the only one disgruntled. Rachael, Kim, and Toni had their share of issues.

They were never happy with the apartment's small size and having to share a roll-out sofa. Keep in mind that none of them paid for the accommodations. At one point, I told them, "If you have the money to get another place, do so, so no one is telling you to stay in this apartment."

The battle with Kris continued from when we left Dallas on November 11th until we returned on December 6th. Because of my position as a Pastor, I refused to cause confusion and disrupt everyone's trip. Things erupted when everyone left the apartment, and I refused to fight with him. Instead, I tried to defuse any issue by reasoning with him and listening to why he was so angry.

It got to the point where I was not too fond of his phone ringing. It was like a ticking time bomb. I told him to block Marie's calls and only handle his business calls, but he refused. You might wonder why I didn't put him on a plane and send him back to Texas.

If you have ever had a relationship where you loved someone with all of your heart and wanted your marriage to work, you did everything possible to resolve the issues.

I knew Kris loved Marie and would do anything to have her back. He could never give up on her, and I couldn't give up on him. He was my son, and I knew what he had been through. It was never in my heart to abandon him, and I didn't. I was there for him from his infancy to the end.

I could see the pain, and at times when she hadn't called, she upset him with her wildness. He was the most intelligent, loving, supportive, hilarious man I've ever met. His employees loved him, and so did the family. He was brilliant and successful in building a business from the ground up. He helped everyone in need and encouraged those around him. His mental stability was essential to me and vital to Jason.

He was the most fantastic dad who ever walked on the earth. He loved Jason and had taken care of him since infancy. He called him my love. Jason loved him but had learned to escape his parents' issues. He had lived with me for almost five years, and I spent much time listening, talking, and praying with my grandson. I became the mother he never had. Kris wouldn't tell me what was happening in his marriage, but it was apparent. I, like Kris, wanted to believe that the trip to Israel might help her realize how critical the family was.

The trip didn't go as planned, and few knew what happened when the rages occurred.

Only my three close assistants knew what was happening. The main reason they knew was that their bedroom was next to ours. Plus, when the battles occurred, everyone was gone, and I was alone in the apartment. I didn't go out much due to having to use the wheelchair, and it was a significant inconvenience, so I would tell everyone to go out and enjoy being with their friends and families.

I spent time praying and seeking direction from God as to our purpose here.

Kris was restless, going in and out of the apartment at all hours of the day and night.

Coming in, he would wake me and my grandson up. He wanted us to make more room on a full-size bed, which was nearly impossible when considering three grown adults in the bed. Sleeping was impossible. I would be sleeping at the foot of the bed in a small ball, which was no easy task for a woman 65 years old.

Regardless of how I tried to help my son, I needed something to work on. We were scheduled to sing the next night, and I couldn't push through wanting to reschedule. I regrouped, prayed for strength, and asked God to help me accomplish what I came here for. The mental stress was not anything new to me; I had lived through unbelievable tragedies with very few breaks in life.

Sometimes, Kris would disappear for long periods, and being concerned about his well-being, I would call his cell phone. One day, he was gone for almost 24 hours, and when he came back, I asked him where he had been. He said, "I fell asleep on the train." They woke me up when I got to the border, and I didn't know what they were saying. Finally, I realized where I was and headed back to Jerusalem.

After this, I realized how shattered he was. He had to be suffering from sleep deprivation. It kept me on edge, concerned about his whereabouts, what was going on, and if he was lost in the everyday things when you were going to a foreign country.

The next evening, we planned to worship the Lord on the streets. My grandson knew that his dad had been causing me massive issues, and he wanted his dad to come and listen to them sing and dance. But Kris wouldn't commit, and later, we would find out he was standing in the background.

On our way to the location, my grandson was pushing me in the wheelchair and then spoke the words that, to this day, echo through my mind. He said Grandma, I know Dad has upset you, but please ignore him and do your thing. If you don't, then the world will never know God.

What was my grandson talking about? My oldest son eventually termed what I do as stepping into the zone. When I go into the zone, my mind blocks out everything, and my focus is on God. With all my heart, I pray and sing, expressing my love to Him. That is when God's

Holy Presence comes down upon all the people. The experience is miraculous.

All set and ready to go, the young people started singing and dancing. The crowd gathered and watched. Everyone who came stayed. Then the words of this song, Waymaker, got my attention. The Lyricist Sinach wrote the music. The song starts with You are here, moving in our midst, I worship You, I worship You, You are here, working in this place, I worship You, I worship You. I started focusing on the words, and they sang when the chorus came. You are a Way maker, miracle worker, Promise keeper, and light in the darkness. My God, that is who You are.

Immediately, I entered the zone. I lifted my hands and focused on the Lord, singing to Him. I forgot everything around me. Adonai had come into the area.

The atmosphere shifted. Everyone sensed the Holy Presence of God was there. I was so focused that I hadn't noticed the crowd repositioning around me. When I opened my eyes, I was unprepared for what I saw: cell phones pointed at me, live-streaming the event. That's when I heard my grandson's words again echoing in my mind. I stepped back into the zone and continued worshipping God. Throughout this experience, the crowd continued to grow, and people approached me as soon as the song ended.

People worldwide wanted to shake my hand, hug me, or touch me, but because of the language barrier, I didn't know what most people said; with their eyes filled with tears, it was easy to see that God had touched them. Some people tried to give me money. At first, I declined, but they insisted. I felt extremely humbled. I knew that I had not done anything special, but Adonai had.

It was amazing to see the people's response, and then hearing the team's reaction was beyond words. Everyone's excitement was apparent, and they were full of energy, so they decided to get something to eat. This evening was the highlight of the trip.

The following day, the team was ready to do the same thing as the night before. I knew in my heart that it would be different. We went out to set up and couldn't get any equipment to work. Julian is excellent at audio and knows what he is doing, so he doesn't need my direction.

While waiting for the equipment to return online, the Lord told me I was to stay still.

There was someone whom I was to meet.

Finally, Julian got the Bluetooth to connect, and the young people started singing and dancing. For the first few songs, everything was going to run smoothly. That night, I had just started to go into the zone when the music suddenly quit.

Julian immediately tried to reconnect, but nothing worked. At that point, I remembered what the Lord had said: I was to meet someone here. The team started coming to me individually, asking if we were done. I told them to be still and wait. Within minutes, a lady came up to me. Her name was Sister Gayle. When she walked up, she said she could feel the spirit of God out on the other street. She said I had to find out where it was coming from. Then, she invited me to take the group to the prayer tower the next night.

I told my staff to close things down, and I knew what we were to do next. I wanted to find out where we were invited to go the next day.

We went for a walk to find the location she had told us about, and when we got there, we took the elevator to one of the top floors. When we knocked on the door, they opened it, and we met the most amazing people staying there.

God was leading me to see why He brought me to Israel. The next day, we went to the Prayer Tower.

CHAPTER TWELVE
Prayer Tower

Gayle explained that the purpose of the prayer tower was to provide Christians with a location to come and pray when they were in the country. She showed us the facility and the view from the window, where she explained the places of interest, pointing out the government buildings and the old city.

During our conversation, we were told about the Israel Prayer Tower and how it was founded by Dr. Paul Dhinakaran, the co-founder and chairman of Jesus Calls Ministry. I took this information from their website.

Jesus Calls ministry is dedicated to praying for the broken-hearted. It was started following God's vision and mandate given to the late Bro. D.G.S. Dhinakaran to serve the people through love and compassion. Jesus Calls has opened over 75 Prayer Towers in India and 10 Prayer Towers worldwide, dedicated to praying for all who seek God and are in need.

I found the following statements on the Prayer Tower website. Their vision: We desire the Israel Prayer Tower to provide a House of Prayer for the local body of believers in Israel and the Nations to seek the Lord and experience His presence through prayer and worship.

Strategically located on the 20th floor in downtown Jerusalem, the spectacular panoramic view of the Mount of Olives, the Old City, the Temple Mount, and the modern city of Jerusalem captivates visitors and inspires them to pray for the peace of Jerusalem (Psalm 122), the governments of the world, global revival, and the second coming of Yeshua (See below to read Dr. Paul's Israel Prophecy).

Gayle then shared how the group from India is connected with the man who owned the building. She said that others from other countries pray during the day. After investigating what this group was about, I felt confident enough to take everyone to the prayer tower the next day to sing and dance.

With everything set into motion, it was time for us to try to get some rest. By this point in the trip, Kris was becoming more settled and started to enjoy Jerusalem, even stating that he loved the city and would someday like to live there. Kris and Jason were spending more time together, and there seemed to be a break in the emotional storm.

The day was here, and the young people would sing for those in the prayer tower. It was time to pack the equipment and make the journey.

When we arrived, we started greeting everyone who came up to us and were met with extreme kindness. After setting things up, it was time to sing and worship God.

At first, I wouldn't sing; I would sit in the front row on the right-hand side. As the team finished setting up, I was asked to come and help sing. The team needed a choir leader, and they knew the concert would be a struggle if I didn't step into the zone.

Once again, as the melodies of worship filled the air, I felt an overwhelming sense of divine connection. I was stepping into a sacred space where the Presence of God enveloped the room like a warm embrace.

With my heart focused on the music and the words flowing from my lips, I consciously disregarded the myriad of responses from the congregation around me. I wanted to fully immerse myself in this moment, free from distractions that could distract me from the profound worship experience.

Stacey, my steadfast protector, stood vigil nearby. With her keen eyes scanning the crowd, she always ensured my safety during these special services. Her fierce loyalty comforted me; I knew she was there, carefully observing the assembled congregation to ensure that no one with ill intentions could approach me. Meanwhile, other members of my Senior Staff were strategically positioned throughout the room, engaging warmly with the attendees, offering support, and creating an atmosphere of connection and fellowship.

Once the service concluded, I was surrounded by a wave of eager faces. People flocked to me, hoping for a moment—a photograph, a handshake, an opportunity to share a brief connection. Families held up their phones, vying for my attention so I could pray for their loved ones. As they displayed images on their screens, I felt honored to meet their cherished ones, even if just through the glow of a device. Each face represented a story, a struggle, a hope, and I was grateful for the privilege of being woven into their lives, even in such a small way.

Throughout it all, I was reminded of the transcendent power of the Spirit of God, which often goes beyond mere words and cultural differences. His love is boundless, reaching out to embrace everyone, irrespective of language or background. In moments of prayer and connection, I witnessed how God responds authentically and warmly, reminding us that His hand is always extended toward those in need.

We returned the next day, and to my surprise, the crowd had grown. From the response of those who came the day before, I knew they had been telling people about the service.

The room buzzed with excitement and high expectations. Every person in attendance was fully engaged in the event unfolding before them.

The next time we gathered at the tower to sing, the group from India quickly approached us.

The conversation soon turned to me, as they were excited about the Lord's presence during the previous night's service.

During that meeting, the group expressed their desire for me to meet Dr. Paul. However, Sister Gayle informed them it wasn't possible because he was overwhelmed with work and wouldn't be in Israel for several weeks. I couldn't understand why meeting him was so important to them, as it had been years since I had been impressed by someone's status.

My Senior Staff noted that several women were discussing me, urging one another to pay close attention. They mentioned that when I speak in an unknown tongue, it's as if heaven itself responds. They made it clear that I was someone to watch closely. If I had known this sooner, I wouldn't have held back my worship and prayer. I don't seek to draw attention to myself, but my impact on others is undeniable.

We had been at the prayer tower at least three times when a young woman and her mother came into the service. As I looked over the congregation, the Lord spoke to me that she was demon-possessed and to pray for her. At first, I waited to respond. I was used to dealing with people possessed by evil spirits. So, knowing her status was not terrifying to me.

I wanted to approach this with wisdom so that attention wouldn't be drawn to her, which would embarrass her. It wasn't long before the young woman's mother told one of my Staff members that she wanted me to pray for her daughter.

With discretion, one of my staff members told me the two ladies wanted me to pray for them. I responded quietly, walked over, and knelt. When I began to speak to them, I realized they were from another country, which didn't hinder me. I knew they could see the Spirit of the Lord on me and felt the compassion and love.

It's important to note here that when I pray for an individual who is demonically possessed, I never put my hands on them. The laying on of hands on the individual transfers spirits.

Instead of making an announcement telling the congregation what I will do, I have my Staff tell everyone to pray. Unfortunately, this never stops the onlookers and the curious. Not wanting to embarrass anyone, I speak to the evil spirits and tell them it's time for them to leave. I focus my attention on the Lord, and He delivers the individual. I am not the miracle worker; I am the conduit or vessel God uses.

The atmosphere immediately changed when I started praying, and God's Power swept the room. It wasn't like there was this announcement that God was there. No one had to say anything.

In the spirit world, when there has been a spiritual deliverance, I see the demons leave the room.

Let me explain. It is not like a visual effect; the natural eye can't see this, but once again, the atmosphere changes.

When God freed this young woman, you could see the physical transformation on her face. The peace of God came over her. When I stopped praying, she grabbed and hugged me and her mother.

People have heard about miracles and are now seeing them; this always draws attention. The people at the prayer tower called Dr. Paul and told him he had to come to Israel and meet me.

We would go to the prayer tower one more time before preparing to return to the United States.

Kris arrived at the tower but was not present when the events began. He quietly joined a congregation and watched Jason multiple times in the various areas where they sang. Jason knew his dad loved him, and they shared a strong bond. Kris often followed wherever Jason went, and they would spend time together afterward.

You might wonder why I didn't pray for my son's deliverance. First, I wouldn't know he was in the service until close to the end. Also, I refuse to single out an individual or call them out in front of a group. It's one thing if someone comes up for prayer, but it's another if you call someone out before the congregation; that approach can create resistance, humiliation, and embarrassment, turning the situation into a battle zone.

As the prophetess of Adonai, I can only act according to God's instructions.

On the last day, we were at the prayer tower; I had no idea Dr. Paul had flown to Israel to investigate the reports he had received about how God was moving there among the people.

For at least 30 years, I had a standing policy that I was never to be left alone with any individual. I never wanted to be falsely accused of any abuse or immoral act. For years, I would only counsel people with at least two staff members present. I wouldn't be a part of a scandal or false accusations.

Individuals put safeguards in place if you or another person is called to visit.

I remember one time during a church service, the Lord was moving powerfully, and one young lady came up to hug me and whispered in my ear Can you feel my nipples? I am excited and want you.

I quickly pushed her away, and from that day on, I put distance between myself and everyone I interacted with. That's when I started implementing safeguards. I always kept my office door open, and if a Staff member wasn't available, I rescheduled appointments. I refused ever to be put in a position where anyone could accuse me of inappropriate conduct.

There was one time that I could recall my Staff abandoning me, and this was one of them. The plan was to make sure no one cornered me to speak privately. At the end of the service, one of Dr. Paul's staff members approached me and asked me to go with them to the office. I was then told that Dr. Paul wanted to meet me. I looked at Stacey and told her I had been asked to go with them. Somehow, the communication line had dropped. I was headed to an office located through several doors and secluded. Three men were in the office. By a process of elimination, I figured out which was Dr. Paul, who shook my hand when I walked into the office and told me he had heard fantastic reports about me. I immediately said to him that God was touching people's lives. He talked with me about his plan for the worldwide prayer towers and how he came to do this work. I found his story very interesting.

When it came to my turn to tell about my vision, the power of the Lord entered the room, and it caught everyone off guard. From that point on, their attitudes went from superior to realizing that I was the anointed of God. We talked for a while longer.

Little did I know that once Julian realized I was gone, he was determined to find me, and no man could stand in his way. Julian was faced with opposition, but that didn't stop him. He said he would listen outside the door to ensure I was ok.

Once Julian heard my voice, he sat beside the door and listened to what was happening behind closed doors. At some point, Dr. Paul asked me if there was a way I could pray for him. I replied absolutely and prayed. I found Dr. Paul gracious and sincere.

When I came out of the office, several people from India asked me if Dr. Paul prayed for me, and I responded no; instead, he asked me to pray for him.

Dr. Paul expressed interest in collaborating with me in the future, and I informed him that I couldn't commit right now and would need to consider it.

He had a location in Dallas, Texas, and invited me to visit the facility. I accepted the invitation, and when we returned to Texas, Stacey, Julian, and I set out to find the location.

Upon our arrival in Dallas, no one was expecting us. I was given a tour of the facility, where the guide explained their mission. I found their goals admirable; however, I realized I needed to avoid getting involved in their efforts. That was the last time I interacted with the group.

I must admit that when I discovered that Dr. Paul had a large group of people who followed him and felt honored that he wanted to work with me, I knew in my heart that it would never transpire.

At first, I thought it would be great to be involved with a significant ministry. Then the reality hit me: There was no way I could do that. We taught two different messages. By this time, I no longer believed Jesus was God and had made those declarations.

I couldn't see any common ground. If I were involved with another ministry, the people would assume I agreed with the group leader. I couldn't allow confusion or send out mixed messages.

Adonai was taking me on a different path. At the time, I had no idea what was happening. By the end of this book, the reader will see that the mission Adonai had me on was unlike anyone else's.

Each day, God spoke to me and led me to follow Him. I had no idea where this journey was taking me, but I knew I loved Adonai and would serve Him.

It was time to pack up, leave Israel, and return to Dallas, with no plan of ever returning. I had come to see what was called the Promised Land and was not impressed. Looking at old sites didn't thrill me.

I had everything I ever wanted in the Lord. Over the years that I have served Him, I have never focused on being someone tremendous or famous; I have focused on being my best for Him as His servant.

I was looking forward to returning to Dallas. Uncertain about what to do next, I would wait at my house for the next direction. I loved my church family and would continue to teach and instruct regardless of the crowd.

When the Lord directed me to start this work, I told him I would do the best I could, even for the sake of one.

Reflecting on the trip to Israel, I can see how God blessed those we encountered, even amid the battle.

I thought of the millions coming into Jerusalem looking to connect with Adonai. I recalled those who were disappointed in their spiritual experiences in Israel.

Had Satan blinded the eyes of Israel, causing them to violate the 1st and 2nd Commandments?

Through years of research, I could recognize all the pagan idols in Jerusalem and knew that Adonai would not bless the nation because of violating His commandments.

It troubled me that people would never see the beauty of His Glorious Presence. My heart was heavy knowing that Adonai walked with me, and only through His love, mercy, and kindness could I ever know His depth of love.

Chapter Thirteen
Return to Dallas

The next time I plan a mission trip for a group, the first requirement will be to leave your attitudes and demons behind.

This trip was supposed to be momentous, and I will never forget my 50th anniversary.

What is crazy is that I am writing this book when I celebrate 55 years of serving Adonai.

It was time to head back to Texas, first stop Ben Gurion International Airport in Tel Aviv.

Since there were 15 people with over 40 pieces of luggage, we were still determining the best way to get to the airport.

Only three people could comfortably ride inside each taxi, and the trunk was so small that the only thing that would fit inside was my wheelchair and maybe a couple of backpacks. Getting everyone to the airport would take at least four or five taxis.

One of the massive issues with this group has been the need for more communication.

I had brought audio-video equipment to live stream the singing on the street, which required me to carry extra suitcases. When we left Dallas, I divided the equipment suitcases among those traveling so that each person could be responsible for helping transport the gear to Israel.

When everyone headed to their respective taxis, they forgot they had helped me get the extra suitcases with the mission equipment to Israel.

They took only their items when they left the apartment and forgot about the gear.

The one vital characteristic when organizing a group adventure is communication. This group would make excellent spies; if captured, they would never give away secrets since they don't communicate.

I am notorious for having meetings to inform everyone about the action plan and provide step-by-step details. The only problem is that people need to take notes and focus.

No one worked as a team following the action plan, so it would have appeared that a meeting of the minds had occurred.

It didn't come as a shock that the exit plan would be forgotten. I had already expressed how important it was for everyone to stay together and communicate. The way things happened, it didn't come as a shock that my instructions were ignored entirely.

This group's action reminded me of a fox entering the chicken coop. Everyone was running everywhere and getting nowhere.

When Kris, Jason, and I left the apartment and headed to the elevator, Kris pushed my wheelchair. We had yet to learn that we would be looking at the bulk of luggage when we entered the lobby.

That's when Kris asked me where everyone was. I told him I didn't know what was happening, so let me find out.

Everyone except the five of us had left for the airport.

Kris was furious. He said, "How did they think I was going to push you in the wheelchair and take the luggage?" I told him we must do our best to get to the taxi. I then looked at our circumstances and started giving him instructions on how to get our luggage to the street without making multiple trips since we were pressed for time.

He said, "Mom, this doesn't seem right. No one should ever be treated this way." I told him it wasn't my top priority. We focused on figuring out how to get the suitcases to the taxi.

During this period, I decided to organize our load. I told Kris to give me the suitcases. I extended the handles all the way and turned them back-to-back. Fortunately, all the suitcases had wheels. Kris put two backpacks on each shoulder, and we started walking.

Jason grabbed the remaining suitcases, several backpacks, and other items, and the three of us headed toward the street. Julian, Stacey, and the rest of their luggage and gear were waiting for us.

The sidewalks all over the city had loose bricks that desperately needed repair, making pushing any wheelchair or walking device challenging. On top of all of that, we would have to go uphill. With all the tourists coming into the city, the infrastructure needed resurfacing so people wouldn't fall.

I can't do anything about this right now, so I have to focus on making it to the airport.

Traveling always involves massive stress, especially when you are in a foreign country and have yet to learn the procedure for leaving.

We made it to the taxi, and the reality of everyone leaving me set in. That was the day when selfish behavior hit me hard. I had given my emotional and financial all, trying to accommodate everyone and neglecting myself.

One would have thought that my well-being would have been a concern.

Instead, all I saw was that the action was selfish.

I am incredibly blessed to have Julian and Stacey at my side, and they never let me down. As Kris, Jason, and I struggled with the suitcases we could handle, the dynamic duo forged ahead and secured us a larger transport taxi to the airport.

Once we were at the airport, we had to find out where everyone was. Since no one had listened in the meeting, it was time for a scavenger hunt.

For those who have never heard of a scavenger hunt, it is a game in which participants search for a list of items within a specific time frame.

We only had a short time to get through customs. Senior Staff members carried most of the passports, especially those of the youth choir.

When we arrived at Ben Gurion International Airport in Tel Aviv, Kris went to talk to Jeremiah. Jeremiah not only worked for Kris but was also Kris's godson. Kris wanted to know why he left his godmother without ensuring everything was handled and that I was okay.

One look at Jeremiah, and you can tell he didn't like being called out. Then Kris told Jeremiah, "Forget it; there is no excuse." Kris turned and walked away. Immediately, I knew the trip back to the States would again be filled with attitudes.

I knew Kris had been on the phone with Marie all morning, and the flight back to Dallas could be just as explosive as the flight to Israel. Kris was on edge, dealing with the fact that he would face Marie for what had happened, and he wanted to get back as fast as possible.

I was shocked. The flight appeared peaceful, with no outbursts, until we landed in New York.

While gathering our belongings from the overhead bins, everything went smoothly. We were headed to baggage claim to collect our luggage and prepare to go through Homeland Security immigration and customs.

There was another exchange of words and looks. I couldn't tell you what that was about. I told Jeremiah and Kris to grow up and stop acting immature.

Jeremiah couldn't let things die. He smarted off at Kris pushing into him while we waited for the elevator. Jeremiah sneakily did that so no one, but the two guys and I, paid attention.

Kris called him out and said, "Stop it, man." One look at Kris's face told the story: Two exhausted individuals are on edge, marking their territory like dogs. The action was getting ready to ignite.

Then Jeremiah said, "Come on, let's handle this right here and now." He stepped up to Kris face-to-face and glared at him. It was then that Julian stepped in to talk to Jeremiah.

At the same time, Julian was talking to Jeremiah, the elevator door opened. I rushed Kris into the elevator, getting up in his face and telling him enough of this insanity. I wasn't putting up with it one more day.

"I have reached my limit. If you want to get arrested here, I am going home."

Then I said Grow up and act like a man. All Kris said was Mom, he disrespected you, and I can't be silent about that. I told him he had no choice if we were to catch the flight home. I told him we were family and didn't settle differences in a public airport terminal.

We still have hours to wait in New York before heading back to Texas, and my final instructions to Jeremiah and Kris were that I had better not see either of you in the same area.

Imagine how Jason felt when his Dad was ready to fistfight with his close friend, who was like his cousin.

After a few hours, things started calming down, but I still insisted they stay separated.

When we arrived in Dallas, it was only hours before Jeremiah apologized to Kris and me, saying he was acting stupid and was sorry. The family dispute was settled.

Once on the airplane, I had plenty of time to reflect on the trip's events.

I know that whenever God is ready to act, Satan often reveals his influence over those who are spiritually weak.

Looking back on our time in Israel, three people consistently caused conflict: Marie, Kris, and Rachael. Satan notably used them to create drama.

The reader has been following the drama between Kris and Marie, but you might wonder how Rachael fits into the story.

Rachael was in her 70s and was very self-absorbed. She was the most outspoken member of our group and constantly tried to take control. The issue was that no one ever listened to her. I often questioned whether Rachael's behavior stemmed from prejudice or jealousy. Her treatment of our diverse group, which included individuals from various ethnic backgrounds, raised concerns.

Kim and Toni never caused any problems. They were accommodating. There was a day I walked into the kitchen and noticed Rachael, Kim, and Toni preparing to leave. I asked them where they were headed. I was told about the Dead Sea. Then I informed them that the group would be singing that night and was unsure when someone would be at the apartment, but to go and enjoy themselves.

Kim and Toni said they would stay with the young people; they wanted to be with the team. They followed up, and she could go if she wanted, but they had changed their minds.

Rachael's reaction spoke volumes. She was unhappy with Kim and Toni's desire to support the team.

Remember that Rachael initially told the rest of the group that they needed to stay in Texas if they were going on this trip to sightsee. Here, she was upset about the change of plans.

Rachel decided to stay and go with the young people, yet it was apparent when we went out that she wasn't happy. She stood off and acted as if she weren't with the group. The insane part was that we accidentally caught this on video.

The other time I knew she was angry was when we were in prayer, and she started shaking, trying to lay hands on various team members. The young people took this to their Dad, Julian, and said she had better keep her hands off them. If they wanted prayer, they would go to their Nana.

Important note: I am the Nana of all the young people who went on the trip.

I had watched Rachael during prayer, and what she was doing caught my attention. She was trying to take over and lead this group, and no one appreciated her actions. I asked Julian and Stacey to go and talk to her and explain that the young people had no idea who she was and were uncomfortable with what she was doing.

You may ask, Why didn't I handle that? I have always believed that if you have a problem with an individual, it is the responsibility of the one who is offended to make the first approach, and if nothing is resolved, then I will step in.

When they talked to her, she told them she was over 70 and no one would tell her what to do. I knew that was coming.

I couldn't wait to get home to Dallas. As far as I was concerned, the jet couldn't fly fast enough. I knew the first thing I would do was take a long bath and lie down in my nice, comfortable bed.

When the plane landed in Dallas, I waited for people to clear so I wouldn't feel rushed and forget anything. The three ladies rushed by, and Stacey noticed the one giving us trouble, who walked off, and left my laptop in the overhead bin. Stacey retrieved that, along with other things she left that were mine.

Everyone headed to baggage claim, and while waiting for the luggage, I focused on ensuring I received all of our luggage. Within minutes, Rachael rushed out of the airport, and it was apparent that she was distraught. If you were allowed to go on a trip that wasn't in the first place designated for you, the least you could do is say thank you for allowing me to tag along. Nope, that didn't happen. The last time I saw Rachael was when she rushed by me on the plane after we landed. That would be the last time I ever heard from her.

Looking back, I can say that Satan used every person he could to stop what God did in Israel.

I was finally home in my peaceful surroundings.

Kris and Jason left the airport and headed to their house.

I called JD and told him I was home, and he said, "Great, then I am coming over." He lived only a few blocks from me and wanted to hug me. That was his way of checking on me.

JD told me Kris had been on the phone with him throughout the trip. Then he apologized and said, "Mom, this was supposed to be a celebration, and from what I hear, it was not that at all."

Then I told JD it was good that he and his family didn't go to Israel. He would only have ended up fighting with his brother.

I told JD about the flight to Israel and what had happened with Kris and Marie. I didn't get far in the conversation when JD told me that both of them were on drugs. He said Marie is on the hard stuff plus drinking, and she would be going out of her mind with desperation trying to get more drugs.

I had suspected that Kris was using drugs and drinking, but I didn't have any proof, and when I asked Kris if he was using, he always responded no.

When Kris came to my house, he would stay about 15 minutes and then dash out. Kris allowed Jason to choose to stay with me or go home.

So he bounced between my home and his Dad's. I had a bedroom set up for my grandson, and he would usually stay with me.

My book, titled Trapped in Another Dimension, addresses the issues a person faces when a loved one is addicted to drugs and alcohol.

We had been home for approximately six weeks when Kris came to me begging me to move him to Mexico. I told him we had yet to return from Israel long ago, and I wasn't ready for another out-of-country trip. He said, "Mom, I have to get out of here. The fighting every day is messing me up." I told him I would consider it, but could not guarantee anything.

I didn't know then that Marie was living with a man and still seeing Kris. To make matters worse, Kris had been living with another woman off and on for about just over a year, but she had left before Kris decided to go to Israel with Marie. Her name was Endora, and she was ten times worse than Marie.

One day, Kris rushed into my house in a panic, saying they were trying to kill him. He was out of his mind, rambling, not making sense. I asked Jason what was happening, and he wouldn't tell me. Then Kris showed me the places where he was burned, beaten with a belt on his back, and had cuts on his wrists and arms. Endora was a practicing witch, and she wanted Kris's finances since she didn't work and had two boys living with her. This story is covered in the book Trapped in Another Dimension.

I told him that he couldn't keep taking these women back. He had to get away from all of the physical and emotional abuse.

After finding out what was happening, I reconsidered taking Kris and Jason to Mexico, especially after what I saw. I told him he needed to if he was serious about getting away.

He said he would move his stuff into a storage unit, and they couldn't find him.

Famous last words. Once the decision was made, Kris started putting his things into storage.

I looked online for the best airfare and decided to leave Texas on February 29, 2020.

CHAPTER FOURTEEN
Leap Year-February 29, 2020

The flight to Guadalajara took less than two hours. While waiting for the flight to leave, Kris poured his heart out to me, expressing how he had made massive relationship mistakes. Kris told me, "Mom, when we get to Mexico, I want to help you with the school." Shocked by his offer to help, I told him I would appreciate it.

There were multiple reasons that I had gone to Mexico in the first place.

The news reported on ObamaCare, later known as the Affordable Care Act. I had been listening to and watching the news about how the new healthcare promoted end-of-life conditions for those in their 60s and above who had health issues.

As soon as the bill was released to the public, I downloaded the 1,000-page article. I wanted to see for myself if this was true. Had there been provisions included in the text about how your family would be encouraged to seek medical advice about the quality of life and counsel from medical professionals on how to best end the life of the one suffering from a catastrophic illness?

It became increasingly clear that the medical industry prioritized financial gains over genuine patient care and well-being.

The article I'm sharing delves into the intricacies of the plans laid out for the care of you and your loved ones, especially as we approach end-of-life considerations. For a thorough exploration of this critical topic, you can find the article "ObamaCare Dives Into End-Of-Life Debate" on the Forbes website.

David Whelan wrote ObamaCare Dives Into End-Of-Life Debate.

Former Contributor. I cover health care costs, quality, entrepreneurship, and business. July 24, 2009, 12:15 pm EDT Updated June 19, 2013, 04:54 pm EDT. This article is more than ten years old.

Buried halfway through the current version of "America's Affordable Health Choices Act," the House version of ObamaCare includes a set of proposals regarding end-of-life care.

The bill is still awaiting passage by at least two more congressional committees. (See "Punting On Paying For Health Care.") However, in its current draft form, ObamaCare would authorize Medicare to pay for a consultation between a patient and her doctor or nurse to discuss how much or little medical care is desired in the event of incapacitation.

The end-of-life language originates from a different bill, the Advance Planning and Compassionate Care Act, introduced earlier this year by Senators. Jay Rockefeller, D-W.Va, and Susan Collins, R-Maine. In addition to the consultation, which Medicare will pay for every five years, the bill also says that patients will be informed about the benefits of hospice and palliative care. Hospices are facilities or home-based services for terminally ill patients to receive pain medicine and other comforts before they die.

The proposed legislation says that patients should be instructed on how to write an advanced health care directive. It defines standard categories of care that can be included in such a document, such as nutrition, hydration, antibiotics, and resuscitation in the event of a lack of pulse. It would also create a tracking system to see if doctors promote and follow advanced care directives. Sen. Rockefeller's office released a statement Friday saying the measure has bipartisan support and the backing of groups like the AARP.

Why the focus on end-of-life care? Sen. Rockefeller announced at the time of the original bill's introduction that he wanted to encourage the use of hospices and help families make the right decisions as death approaches.

Yet, end-of-life care is also a vital issue regarding slowing the growth of health care costs. About a quarter of all spending by Medicare, more than $100 billion, takes place during a patient's final year of life. President Obama has referred multiple times to the fact that his grandmother received an expensive hip replacement. At the same time, she was terminally ill with cancer, holding it up as an example of spending that sometimes takes place near the end of life. He's wondered whether the country can afford those bills, even though he said he would have paid out of pocket for his grandmother's hip.

Historically speaking, in the early 1980s, hospices and living wills, a type of advanced directive, became more commonplace in response to concerns about the cost of end-of-life care. The last Bush administration deliberately increased Medicare reimbursement rates for hospices to promote their use as an alternative to more expensive hospital stays. Hospices have become a big business. Chemed Corporation has earned over $800 million (revenue) for the hospice chain Vitas. The Cincinnati company also puzzlingly owns Roto-Rooter plumbing franchises. It has one public competitor, Dallas' Odyssey, and many regional for-profit and nonprofit hospices.

Hospices, not surprisingly, support efforts in ObamaCare to promote their services. "It's a good provision," says Jon Keyserling, general counsel for the National Hospice and Palliative Care

Organization in Alexandria, Va. "I've seen an inference that government doctors will be steering patients to choose less care, and that's not the intent," he says, referring to some of the controversy that's emerged around this part of the bill.

Opponents of ObamaCare argue that this five-page section of a 1,000-page bill is an attempt to pressure senior citizens into opting out of expensive lifesaving therapy.

It brings to mind Boomsday, a 2007 satirical novel by ForbesLife editor at large Christopher Buckley, in which the government solves its fiscal problems by offering tax breaks to those who kill themselves before retirement age.

The idea that ObamaCare is promoting physician-assisted suicide for older adults or encouraging them to forgo medical care late in life has made its way into partisan rhetoric among the bill's opponents. "The bill would require every senior to have a mandatory counseling session with a government bureaucrat every five years on ways to 'die with dignity '; starvation, dehydration, stuff like that," Republican strategist Lawrence Lindsey wrote in a memo.

In a post entitled "The Democratic Culture of Death is Terrifying," one blogger wrote, "First they came for our light bulbs, then they came for our SUVs. Now, they are coming for our senior citizens." Other commentators have made a connection between the bill and the Terry Schiavo episode, in which a woman on life support in Florida starved to death after a feeding tube was removed when her husband prevailed in a prolonged legal battle.

The bill says nothing about death with dignity or any other code words for euthanasia. It also does not make these counseling sessions mandatory--it just says that Medicare will start reimbursing for them.

Still, some activist groups not necessarily opposed to ObamaCare are concerned about the end-of-life proposals in the bill. Marilyn Golden of the Disability Rights Education and Defense Fund in Berkeley, Calif., has been active in opposing physician-assisted suicide at the state level. Many disabled people worry that legalizing suicide would lead to euthanasia.

Golden points out that many doctors, when counseling patients, push for do-not-resuscitate orders or have them sign boilerplate documents that can lead to the premature denial of lifesaving medical care. "I don't want to say we're opposed to the language in the bill," she says. "But there are legitimate concerns about how advance directives are administered."

"There is reason to be concerned," says Diane Coleman of Not Dead Yet, a group in Rochester, N.Y., that opposes physician-assisted suicide and what it calls medical killing. "The disability community," she says, "often experiences pressure to sign treatment-withholding orders."

She cites a case of a woman who works in her building who developed quadriplegia 11 years ago. Her physicians encouraged her family to remove life support while she was on a ventilator for five months, even though she was improving and eventually recovered to the point where she could live independently with a wheelchair.

Those concerned about unwittingly getting the plug pulled are advised to make it very clear to all their medical providers that they do not have a "DNR" and that if they stop breathing or their heart stops, they want to be revived.

"Society does devalue older and disabled people," Coleman says. "And the medical profession is not always very accountable."

David Whelan, I was a staff writer at Forbes for eight years, covering health care. Now, I work in hospital administration, where ObamaCare is tackling the end-of-life debate.

A heavy dread settled in my chest as I carefully read through the details of this bill. It became painfully clear that two individuals I cherished deeply might fall victim to the ominous implications of this legislation, potentially subjected to a grave and unjust fate. I felt a burning resolve within me; I could not stand idly by while this act of murder loomed on the horizon. I was determined to fight against it, to protect those I loved at all costs.

Among those who touched my life deeply was my mother, a vibrant woman whose laughter once filled our home. In 2000, she faced the daunting diagnosis of non-Hodgkin's lymphoma, a battle that would forever alter our family's landscape. Alongside her was my cherished friend Jennette, a remarkable individual whose strength I admired immensely. She had endured a series of debilitating strokes that challenged her spirit and resilience. Jennette wasn't just a friend but an integral part of my church community, where she served on my staff. Her presence was a comforting constant, and her family, with children and grandchildren, filled the pews, creating a warm tapestry of fellowship and love that defined our church. I was honored to serve as their Pastor, guiding them through trials and triumphs.

The economy was in turmoil, a shadow cast over daily life, and during a moment of deep reflection and prayer, I felt a stirring in my heart to journey to Mexico. I needed to explore the possibility of ensuring the continued care for those I held dear. The remarkable women I was thinking of were thriving physically, their spirits shining bright, but their safety weighed heavily on my mind.

In my heartfelt pursuit of God through prayer, I felt a renewed determination to find the right path for my family. As I sought guidance, a profound message resonated: the Lord instructed me to lead my loved ones on a journey to Mexico.

The driving force behind my urge to investigate this opportunity was solid and unwavering. I resolved that I would protect my loved one from harm at all costs. The thought of euthanasia was unthinkable to me; I could never find it in my heart to support such a decision. Instead, my thoughts raced with ideas about how I could provide care and support, striving to create a safer and more nurturing environment for them.

After weighing all my options, I was drawn to the vibrant city of Guadalajara, Mexico. The thought of exploring its rich culture and bustling streets excited me, even though I had no concrete destination. I felt an adventurous spark within me, trusting that the perfect spot would reveal itself once I arrived in the city. The anticipation of wandering through its colorful mercados and bustling plazas filled me with curiosity and wonder.

Before going to Mexico, I met a man in Grand Prairie, Texas, who said if I ever go to Mexico, I need to go to Chapala. That was a few years before we made the trip to Guadalajara.

Guadalajara was so large that I couldn't feel that it was where we were supposed to go. Stacey, Julian, and I took a bus trip to Puerto Vallarta, but we were still looking for a place to move our family members.

Convinced that I had overlooked some vital message from God regarding our journey to Mexico, we began to prepare for a return to Texas. However, just before we set off, a memory sparked in my mind—the suggestion from the man I had spoken to about the picturesque town of Chapala. Intrigued by the idea, I proposed that we take a detour to explore the charm of that enchanting area before leaving.

The following day, the sun had just begun to rise when Stacey, Julian, and I hailed a taxi to Chapala, our hearts guiding us as we sought confirmation from the Lord. As the taxi wound through the picturesque town, I asked the driver, "Could you point us to where most expats reside?" With a friendly smile, he replied, "That would be Ajijic." Without hesitation, I urged him to take us there, eager to explore this vibrant community.

God works in mysterious and unique ways. While driving through the charming town, I suddenly became captivated by an irresistible craving for barbecue when I spotted the inviting sign for Bubba's Barbecue. We had eaten Mexican food for over two weeks, and the aroma of smoky meats seemed to waft through the air, tugging at my appetite. Without hesitating, I eagerly suggested that we pull over and step inside the restaurant to indulge in a delicious bite to eat.

When we went into the restaurant, we met the owner, who was from Texas. I started asking Bubba many questions about the area and what it was like to live there. After our conversation, I knew that was the area that we needed to take our family members to.

The following day, we discovered a charming little spot to call home in the picturesque town of Ajijic. The vibrant colors of the buildings and the warm smiles of the locals welcomed us as we settled in. Within just a few days, we eagerly embarked on the process of completing our paperwork to secure permanent residency in beautiful Mexico.

As time passed, we couldn't help but share the allure of our new life. Gradually, we began to relocate several family members to join us in the enchanting Lake Chapala area, where the tranquil waters and breathtaking mountain views created a serene backdrop for our growing family community.

It was refreshing to know that I had followed Adonai's instructions.

Fifteen years have passed since that pivotal moment, and during this time, I've felt a deep calling to make a difference in the lives of those less fortunate. This inspiration drove me to embark on a transformative journey to establish a school dedicated to providing quality education and opportunities for children who might otherwise be overlooked.

Stacey, Jennette's beloved daughter, and her husband, Julian, stood together as pillars of support during a challenging time for their family. Their deep sense of loyalty and love for Jennette was evident as they rallied around her in her fight for life. In just four months, a dedicated team would be established in Mexico, ready to assist and ensure their cherished family member received the care she desperately needed.

Initially, we had only a small private school there because financial constraints prevented us from fully expanding the mission.

On February 29, 2020, Kris offered to help me prepare the school so we could open its doors to the public. I was shocked and excited. Maybe now, after all these years, we will see the fulfillment of my dream of having an educational facility open to those who wanted an education but couldn't afford it.

When we arrived at the Pueblo, I saw an immediate change in Kris and Jason.

Everything was turning around. The minute we pulled in front of the house, the two took their luggage up and decided to go for a walk.

I felt that I could finally relax and watch my son begin to heal. For about two weeks, everything seemed perfect. Then, one day, Kris asked if he and Jason could move out to the RV about three miles from our house at a resort. This RV used to be my mother's home, which I inherited after she passed away, but I hadn't stayed there. Therefore, I decided not to decline his request.

He asked if he could use my mom's truck. Since I wasn't driving it then, I agreed but mentioned that I needed it daily. I told him he would have to pick me up and take me where I needed to go. He said that wouldn't be a problem and asked if I would be working at the school. He assured me he would work with my schedule, so picking me up would be fine.

CHAPTER FIFTEEN
Endora the Witch

Chapter 15. Endora the Witch

For over 35 years, I have dealt with the occult. I didn't fully understand the operation of the dark world. I had lived a sheltered life and did not interact with society. Since I was raised on the Navajo Reservation, their rituals have been a part of the area where I lived as a child.

When I became a Christian, I was more isolated due to my religion. Primarily, since the Church group I belonged to taught that we didn't fellowship with works of darkness and that people who didn't serve God were considered undesirable.

I always needed clarification on that. How would we lead sinners to God if the world were considered evil?

When I started the Church, I had pastored for over 36 years. I went to the streets of Dallas and Arlington, where I taught people under bridges.

My sons watched when they were younger how I helped those less fortunate.

Since I didn't have extra money to pay for a building or advertisement, I went dumpster diving to collect cans and raise money.

In my zeal, I couldn't have projected the outcome or how my boys would adopt the same idea of helping others.

When I met my first husband, Robbie, he was a Christian. I had been taught that in the Christian faith, we were not to marry someone outside our denomination. The scriptures stated that we were not to be unequally yoked with non-believers.

I was 23 when I married and felt like it was God's will for me to be with him. In one of the earlier books in this series, I talk about my journey in this marriage.

Less than six months later, Robbie's brother Paul started coming around and influencing Robbie to hang out. I knew Paul was a Christian at one point, but I didn't know anything about his background.

Back in that period, we were taught that women were to be submissive and that the man was the head of the household.

The man was to lead the family spiritually and not question his authority. I never asked questions when Paul came around, but over the next nine months, Robbie started smoking weed and eventually became a drug addict and alcoholic.

When I turned to the church leadership for direction, I was rebuked. I never thought that these spiritual leaders didn't know anything about deliverance or demonic possession. Thinking that Pentecostals base their faith on the books of Acts and the New Testament, they would be the best ones to address spirits because we were of the Pentecostal faith, also known as Apostolic.

What I discovered was shocking: Our Pastor didn't know how to advise me, and I would be on this journey alone.

Never realizing that churches are the best places for evil spirits to reside, they can hide among the people and take them captive.

2 Timothy 2:23 NLT: *<u>Again I say, don't get involved in foolish, ignorant arguments that only start fights.</u>*

2 Timothy 2:24 NLT: <u>A servant of the Lord must not quarrel but must be kind to everyone, be able to teach, and be patient with difficult people.</u>

2 Timothy 2:25 NLT:<u> Gently instruct those who oppose the truth. Perhaps God will change those people's hearts, and they will learn the truth.</u>

2 Timothy 2:26 NLT:<u> Then they will come to their senses and escape from the devil's trap. For they have been held captive by him to do whatever he wants.</u>

Reading these scriptures, one would believe that you handled all conflicts with understanding. These scriptures were written to believers who were supposed to follow the same guidelines.

It didn't address those who were addicted to drugs and alcohol—those people who would deliberately cause conflict. Robbie was one of those who would come in the front door after work and start verbally attacking me, and I was at a loss as to how to handle that environment.

I had become a shell of a woman who had lost my identity from all of the abuse. I knew what it was like to be physically, emotionally, and sexually abused by people whom I trusted.

I had two little boys to raise, and I had to be my best and stay strong.

In 1987, we moved from Fort Worth to Arlington, Texas. We had visited Faith Tabernacle; it seemed like the perfect Church. The Pastor had been a missionary to Africa. I thought that since the Pastor and his family had lived in Africa for several years, he was bound to know about demon possession.

Robbie was demon-possessed, and in my heart, I felt that if anyone could help Robbie, it would be the Pastor in Arlington.

I was wrong. Once again, I would have to face the reality that no one could; I would have to seek my answers. It's important to mention that I highly respected the Pastor and his family.

When I left their Church, it wasn't because they did anything wrong. They were extremely kind, and I loved them very much.

So when God spoke to me about going out on the streets of Arlington and then said that he would raise a church that would worship him within a year, leaving the local assembly was one of the most challenging moves I had ever made. I knew the voice of God and decided to go out on the streets and try to be the one to help those whose lives Satan had destroyed.

How could anyone in my situation go out and start a church?

I would follow the Lord's direction every step of the way. I didn't know what I was doing, but I loved and cared for hurting people.

My obstacles would be continuous, for it was during that time frame that women pastors were considered taboo.

Every time I turned around, I was quoted these scriptures. I am going to provide you with two different versions. I never allowed this to hinder me, for the position I was called to was that of a prophetess, and I still serve the Lord in that position today. Numerous Old and New Testament scriptures supported that position.

I address this topic in detail in my series and provide the proper interpretation.

1 Corinthians 14:34 KJV: **_Let your women keep silence in the churches: for it is not permitted unto them to speak; but [they are commanded] to be under obedience, as also saith the law._**

1 Corinthians 14:35 KJV: <u>And if they will learn any thing, let them ask their husbands at home: for it is a shame for women to speak in the Church.</u>

Comparing these two versions, you will understand what was being addressed.

1 Corinthians 14:34 NLT: <u>Women should be silent during the church meetings. It is not proper for them to speak. They should be submissive, just as the law says.</u>

1 Corinthians 14:35 NLT: <u>If they have any questions, they should ask their husbands at home, for it is improper for women to speak in church meetings.</u>

More determined than ever to reach out to those in impossible situations became my focal point. One of the first individuals I became acquainted with was once on America's Ten Most Wanted for Bank Robbery. She had a son several years older than my boys. He had a magnetic personality but was into breaking the law.

His Mom had spent ten years in the Federal prison, so his grandfather and his uncle raised him. Violence seemed to run in the family. His grandfather, one day, walked into a church in another state and shot two people, killing a church deacon. What brought this action was that the boy's grandfather had heard his wife was having an affair; this was only a rumor with no proof, just speculation.

Looking back, I can see my mistakes. The first was not teaching my sons to keep a distance from those up to mischief. How could I? That would mean I would have to exclude their father from our lives.

When I started the Church at 33, I was not experienced enough to deal with all the pitfalls and obstacles. Due to my lack of wisdom and not instructing my sons about the pitfalls of Satan, later, I would be faced with demons through several women attacking my son.

Today, I refuse to allow anyone to walk in the dark trying to figure things out. This series addresses numerous topics.

In this chapter, I will share information on the occult and what to look for in life. I have learned these things over the years, and while sharing my story, I hope you will learn how to handle these issues.

You may ask why I didn't address the demons in my family. When I realized how deep Satan's tentacles had reached into their lives, they were grown men. I looked for the opportunity to address these issues, but there was only one major problem: they were seldom around me.

Initially, I didn't know that Endora was involved in Witchcraft. She was an eclectic witch who drew inspiration and practices from various spiritual and magical traditions rather than strictly adhering to a single path. They pick and choose what resonates with them, creating a unique and personalized practice. This approach allows flexibility, creativity, and a deep connection to the individual's spiritual journey.

Key characteristics of an eclectic witch: •**Diverse influences:** They may incorporate elements from Wicca, Paganism, Shamanism, Hermeticism, or other spiritual traditions. •**Personalization:** They tailor their practices to their own beliefs and goals. •**Flexibility:** They are open to learning and experimenting with new ideas and techniques. •**Inclusivity:** They embrace diversity and accept people of all backgrounds and beliefs. •**Respect for nature:** They often profoundly connect to the natural world and may incorporate nature-based practices into their rituals.

Standard practices of eclectic witches: •**Spellcasting:** Creating spells and rituals to manifest desires and intentions. •**Divination:**

Using tools like tarot cards, runes, or pendulums to gain insight and guidance. •**Herbalism:** Working with herbs for healing and magical purposes. •**Meditation:** Connecting with their inner selves and the divine. •**Honoring deities:** Working with deities from various pantheons or personal spirit guides.

Ultimately, an eclectic witch is curious, open-minded, and committed to their spiritual growth. They are free to explore and experiment, creating a unique and meaningful path that resonates with their soul.

It is straightforward for people who are practicing occultists to hide in churches. Due to ignorance and lack of knowledge, the leadership in a church is clueless about what is happening.

Before continuing, I want to share some vital information about exposing the world of darkness.

With Texas being close to Mexico, Catholicism is vital to the culture. Within Catholicism, Witchcraft is openly practiced. By the outward appearance, the non-suspecting innocent people don't know this.

The Catholic Church has a complex relationship with the occult. While the Church officially condemns occult practices, there are historical and cultural connections that have led to speculation and controversy. Here are some key points to consider:

Official Stance: •The Catholic Church strongly condemns occult practices, considering them incompatible with the Christian faith. •The Catechism of the Catholic Church explicitly warns against practices such as divination, astrology, magic, and spiritualism.

Historical Connections: •Some historical figures associated with the Church, such as certain popes and religious orders, have been accused of engaging in occult practices. •The Church's early history was intertwined with various pagan beliefs and practices, which were gradually assimilated or suppressed over time.

Cultural Influence: •The Church's rich symbolism, rituals, and sacred art have influenced various occult traditions. Some occult groups have adopted or adapted elements of Catholic symbolism and practices. •The Church's authority and power have often made it a target of occult fascination and conspiracy theories.

Modern Interpretations: •Some individuals argue that the Church's teachings and practices contain hidden, occult meanings or esoteric knowledge. •Others suggest that the Church's emphasis on ritual, symbolism, and spiritual experience can be seen as a form of occult practice, albeit one that the Church sanctions.

It's important to note that these are complex and often controversial topics. The relationship between the Catholic Church and the occult is a matter of ongoing debate and interpretation.

The Catholic Church and Santeria have a complex and intertwined history, particularly in Cuba. Santeria, an Afro-Cuban religion, emerged from the blending of West African Yoruba beliefs and Roman Catholicism during the transatlantic slave trade. Enslaved Africans were forced to convert to Catholicism, but they secretly maintained their traditional religious practices. They associated their deities (orishas) with Catholic saints to blend their beliefs with Catholicism and avoid persecution. This syncretism allowed them to practice their religion while outwardly conforming to Catholicism.

As a result, Santeria rituals often incorporate Catholic elements, such as prayers to saints, the use of holy water, and the lighting of candles. For example, the orisha Oshun, associated with love and fertility, is often linked to the Virgin Mary. Similarly, the orisha Chango, associated with thunder and lightning, is often linked to St. Barbara.

While the Catholic Church officially condemns occult practices and does not recognize Santeria as a legitimate religion, the two faiths continue to coexist in Cuba and other parts of the world. Many Santeria practitioners also identify as Catholics, participating in both Catholic and Santeria rituals. This syncretism reflects the resilience of African religious traditions and the ability of people to adapt and blend their beliefs in the face of oppression.

The occult encompasses a wide range of beliefs and practices, so there are many different types of occult groups. Here are some of the most common:

• **Hermetic Orders:** These groups focus on the teachings of Hermes Trismegistus, a legendary figure believed to know alchemy, astrology, and magic. The Hermetic Order of the Golden Dawn is **one of the most famous examples.** • **Theosophical Societies:** These groups believe in the unity of all religions and the existence of a universal spiritual principle. The Theosophical Society, founded by Helena Blavatsky, is a well-known example. • **Wiccan Covens:** Wicca is a modern pagan religion emphasizing nature worship and magic. Wiccans often gather in covens to practice their rituals and spells. • **Satanic Groups:** While often misunderstood, Satanic groups do not worship the Christian devil. Instead, they focus on individualism, self-empowerment, and critical thinking. The Church of Satan is one of the most well-known Satanic organizations. • **Magical Orders:** These groups focus on practicing magic, often through rituals, symbols, and tools. The Ordo Templi Orientis

(O.T.O.) is a well-known magical order. • Spiritualist Groups: These groups believe in the ability to communicate with the spirits of the dead. Spiritualist churches and societies hold séances and other events to facilitate communication with the spirit world. • **New Age Groups:** The New Age movement encompasses many beliefs and practices, including meditation, yoga, and energy healing. Many New Age groups incorporate occult practices into their teachings.

It's important to note that this is not an exhaustive list, and many other types of occult groups exist. The occult is a diverse and ever-evolving field, with new groups and practices emerging all the time.

Wicca is a relatively new, modern pagan, nature-based religion that emerged in England in the 1950s. Wiccans believe in a Goddess and a God, often called the Triple Goddess and the Horned God. They honor the cycles of nature and celebrate the seasons through rituals called Sabbats.

Wicca is a diverse religion with many different traditions and practices. Some standard practices include:

• Spellcasting: Using words, symbols, and energy to bring about desired changes. • **Divination:** Using tools like tarot cards, runes, or astrology to gain insight into the future or the present. • **Herbalism:** Using plants for healing and spiritual purposes. • **Meditation:** Focusing the mind to connect with the divine and oneself.

Wicca is often misunderstood and stereotyped. It is not a religion of black magic or evil. Wiccans believe in a positive, life-affirming path emphasizing harmony with nature and all living things. This description entices people; however, Wicca is still part of Witchcraft and violates the scriptures.

Walt Disney and his Magic Kingdom gradually introduced Witchcraft into the world. His creative cartoons and fairy tales captivated audiences worldwide.

Bewitched is a classic American sitcom aired on ABC from 1964 to 1972. It revolves around the life of Samantha Stephens, a young witch who marries a mortal advertising executive, Darrin Stephens. The show humorously explores the challenges of maintaining an everyday suburban life while possessing magical powers.

Samantha, played by Elizabeth Montgomery, often uses her magic to solve everyday problems or to teach her husband a lesson. However, her meddling mother, Endora, played by Agnes Moorehead, frequently interferes and causes chaos. The show's iconic theme song and the comedic timing of the cast members made it a popular and enduring television series.

Bewitched was known for its clever writing, witty dialogue, and memorable characters. It tackled various social issues of the time, including gender roles, marriage, and family dynamics, often with a humorous twist. The show's popularity led to a spin-off series, Tabitha, which focused on Samantha and Darrin's daughter.

Bewitched remains a beloved classic, remembered for its charming blend of fantasy and comedy. Its enduring popularity is a testament to its timeless appeal and the talent of its cast and crew.

This series promoted problem-solving through magic and Witchcraft.

Harry Potter: The Harry Potter series has had a profound and far-reaching impact on popular culture, influencing literature, film, gaming, and social norms. Here are some of its key influences:

Literature: **•Resurgence of Reading:** The series sparked a renewed interest in reading among young people, with many crediting Harry Potter for their love of books. **•Complex Characters:** Rowling's characters are multi-dimensional and relatable, inspiring a new generation of writers to create more nuanced and engaging protagonists. **•Magical World-Building:** The creation of the Wizarding World, with its intricate rules and lore, has influenced countless fantasy authors.

Film: **•Pioneering Special Effects:** The Harry Potter films pushed the boundaries of visual effects, creating stunning and immersive magical worlds. **•Box Office Success:** The films have broken records and remain among the highest-grossing movie franchises ever. **•Cultural Phenomenon:** The films have generated massive fan followings and sparked global cultural events like midnight book releases and movie premieres.

Gaming: **•Interactive Magic:** The Harry Potter video games have allowed fans to experience the magic firsthand, exploring Hogwarts and casting spells. **•Immersive Experiences:** The series has inspired the creation of immersive theme park attractions where visitors can enter the Wizarding World.

Social Impact: **•Tolerance and Acceptance:** The series promotes tolerance, acceptance, and standing up to injustice. **•Literacy and Education:** The books have been used in classrooms to encourage reading and critical thinking. **•Philanthropy:** J.K. Rowling's success has allowed her to support various charitable causes related to children's welfare.

The Harry Potter series has left an indelible mark on popular culture, inspiring readers, filmmakers, and gamers alike. Its enduring legacy continues to shape how we think about storytelling, magic, and the power of imagination.

It's a fictional creation by J.K. Rowling, drawing inspiration from various sources like folklore, fairy tales, and mythology. Real-world practices like Wicca and other forms of Witchcraft are present in every book, promoting a connection to the occult.

Churches remained silent and never taught against Witchcraft. They promoted this series, desensitizing the world to the truth about the powers of darkness.

J.K. Rowling is a renowned British author, best known for her iconic Harry Potter series. Born Joanne Rowling on July 31st, 1965, she later adopted the pen name J.K. Rowling to appeal to a broader audience, particularly young boys.

The Harry Potter series spans seven books and has captivated readers worldwide. It has sold over 600 million copies and has been translated into 84 languages. It has also spawned a massive global media franchise, including films, video games, and theme park attractions.

Rowling's success with Harry Potter has made her one of the most successful authors ever.

Santería: Santería, also known as Regla de Ocha, Regla Lucumí, or Lucumí, is an Afro-Caribbean religion that developed in Cuba during the late 19th century. It is a syncretic religion that blends elements of the traditional Yoruba religion of West Africa, Roman Catholicism, and Spiritism.

Critical aspects of Santería: • **Orisha:** Santería is a polytheistic religion that centers around worshiping deities called orisha. These orishas are associated with various natural forces and human qualities.

- **Syncretism:** Santería practitioners often equate the orisha with Catholic saints, allowing them to practice their faith discreetly during the colonial period. • **Divination:** Divination, mainly through cowrie shells (Ifa), is a central practice in Santería. It is used to communicate with the orisha and seek guidance. • **Rituals and Ceremonies**: Santería involves various rituals and ceremonies, including offerings, sacrifices, and feasts. Animal sacrifices, often of chickens or goats, are performed to honor the orisha. • **Spirit Possession:** Practitioners may experience possession by the orisha, allowing the deity to communicate directly with the devotee.

Santería has spread beyond Cuba to other parts of the Caribbean, the United States, and the world. It is a vibrant and complex religion that continues to evolve and adapt to new cultural contexts.

Spiritism: Spiritism is a belief system that originated in 19th-century France. It was founded by the educator Hippolyte Léon Denizard Rivail, who wrote under Allan Kardec. Spiritism posits the existence of spirits who can communicate with the living through mediums.

Fundamental beliefs of Spiritism: • **Spirit World:** Spiritists believe in a spirit world that exists alongside the physical world. • **Reincarnation:** They believe in reincarnation, where souls progress through multiple lifetimes to achieve spiritual growth. • **Communication with Spirits:** Spiritists use mediums to communicate with the spirits of the deceased. • **Moral and Spiritual Development:** Spiritists emphasize the importance of moral and spiritual development. • **God and Jesus:** Spiritists believe in a supreme being, often called God or the Supreme Intelligence, and recognize Jesus as a great spiritual teacher.

Practices of Spiritism: • **Mediumship:** Mediums are individuals who are believed to be able to communicate with spirits. • **Séances:** Séances are gatherings where participants attempt to communicate with spirits through mediums. • **Spiritual Healing:** Spiritists believe that spirits can provide healing and guidance. • **Charity and Social Work:** Spiritists often engage in charitable and social work.

Spiritism has gained significant popularity in Brazil and other parts of Latin America, influencing various cultural and religious practices. It is a diverse and evolving belief system with different interpretations and practices worldwide.

While neo-paganism and the occult share some commonalities, they are distinct concepts with different focuses and practices. Deception is the critical element of these groups that I will teach you about.

Who is Satan, and what terms describe this evil entity?

Satan, or the Devil, has been given numerous names throughout history and across different cultures. Here are some of the most common names associated with him:

• Satan: This is the most common name, derived from the Hebrew word meaning "adversary" or "accuser." • **Lucifer:** This name, meaning "light-bearer," is often associated with Satan, particularly in the Christian tradition, as a fallen angel. • **Devil:** This is a more general term for an evil spirit or demon. • **Beelzebub:** This name, "lord of the flies," is often used interchangeably with Satan. • **Mephistopheles:** This name, popularized by Goethe's "Faust," is a demon often associated with temptation and evil. • **Prince of Darkness:** This title refers to Satan's role as the ruler of hell and the forces of evil. • **Father of Lies:** This title emphasizes Satan's role as a deceiver and liar. • **Tempter:** This title highlights Satan's role in tempting people to sin.

It's important to note that these names often carry different connotations and significance in various religious and cultural contexts. Some of these names may also be used in a more symbolic or metaphorical sense rather than referring to a literal entity.

Neo-Paganism: • Focus on nature and deities: Neo-pagans often draw inspiration from pre-Christian religions and worship nature and deities associated with natural elements and cycles. • Emphasis on community and ritual: Many neo-pagans participate in community rituals and celebrations that connect them to the natural world and their chosen deities. • Diverse beliefs and practices: Neo-paganism encompasses many beliefs and practices, including Wicca, Druidry, Heathenry, and other traditions. • Ethical and spiritual framework: Neo-pagans often emphasize ethical principles such as harmony with nature, respect for all beings, and personal responsibility.

Occult: • Focus on hidden knowledge and esoteric practices: The occult encompasses various practices and beliefs related to secret knowledge, mysticism, and the supernatural. • Emphasis on individual exploration and spiritual development: Occultists often engage in solitary practices and seek personal spiritual growth by studying esoteric subjects and performing rituals. • Diverse practices and beliefs: The occult includes many techniques, such as magic, divination, astrology, alchemy, and spiritualism. • Diverse ethical frameworks: Occultists may adhere to various ethical frameworks, some of which may be aligned with neo-paganism. In contrast, others may be more individualistic or based on specific occult traditions.

Key Differences: • **Focus:** Neo-paganism is primarily focused on nature-based spirituality and the worship of deities, while the occult is more focused on hidden knowledge, esoteric practices, and personal spiritual development. • **Community:** Neo-pagans often emphasize community and shared rituals, while occultists may practice more solitary or individualistic paths. • **Ethics:** While both neo-pagans and occultists may adhere to ethical principles, the specific ethical frameworks may differ.

It's important to note that there is an overlap between neo-paganism and the occult, and some individuals may identify with both. However, they are distinct concepts with different primary focuses and practices.

Neo-Paganism celebrates a cycle of eight sabbats, or holidays, marking the turning points of the solar year. These sabbats are divided into two groups: the Greater Sabbats, which occur at the cross-quarter points, and the Lesser Sabbats, which occur at the solstices and equinoxes.

Greater Sabbats: • **Imbolc:** Celebrated on February 1st or 2nd, Imbolc marks the beginning of spring and the return of life to the land. It is associated with the goddess Brigid and is often celebrated with bonfires and the blessing of seeds. • **Beltane:** Celebrated on May 1st, Beltane marks the height of spring and the beginning of summer. It is associated with fertility and is often celebrated with bonfires, maypoles, and rituals to ensure a bountiful harvest. • **Lughnasadh:** Celebrated on August 1st, Lughnasadh marks the year's first harvest. It is associated with the God Lugh and is often celebrated with feasting, music, and offering first fruits. • **Samhain:** Celebrated on October 31st, Samhain marks the end of the harvest season and the beginning of winter. It is associated with the dead and is often celebrated with bonfires, divination, and ancestor veneration.

Lesser Sabbats: • **Ostara:** Celebrated on the spring equinox, Ostara marks the equal balance of day and night. It is associated with the goddess Eostre and is often celebrated with egg decorating and seed planting. • **Litha:** Celebrated on the summer solstice, Litha marks the longest day of the year. It is associated with the sun god and is often celebrated with bonfires, outdoor rituals, and the gathering of herbs. • **Mabon:** Celebrated on the autumn equinox, Mabon marks the equal balance of day and night. It is associated with the harvest and is often celebrated with Thanksgiving rituals and gatherings of nuts and fruits. • **Yule:** Celebrated on the winter solstice, Yule marks the year's longest night. It is associated with the sun's rebirth and is often celebrated with the burning of the Yule log, gift-giving, and the decorating of evergreen trees.

In addition to these eight major holidays, many Neo-Pagans celebrate festivals and observances throughout the year, such as the solstices, equinoxes, and the full and new moons.

If you compare Neo-Paganism and the occult, while sharing some commonalities, they have distinct approaches to holidays and celebrations.

Neo-Paganism: • **Focus on the Wheel of the Year:** Neo-Pagans primarily celebrate the eight sabbats, marking the turning points of the solar year. These holidays are tied to natural cycles and agricultural traditions. • **Community-oriented:** Many Neo-Pagan holidays involve communal rituals, gatherings, and celebrations. • **Emphasis on nature and deities:** Neo-Pagan holidays often honor specific deities associated with the seasons and natural elements.

Occult: • **Diverse and individualized:** Occult practices vary widely, and no standardized holidays exist. • **Focus on personal spiritual development:** Occult practitioners may celebrate personal milestones, astrological events, or specific magical correspondences. • **Less emphasis on communal celebration:** Occult practices often involve solitary rituals and studies.

Similarities: • **Some shared holidays:** Both Neo-Pagans and some occultists may celebrate certain holidays like Samhain (Halloween) and Yule (Winter Solstice). • **Interest in the supernatural:** Both traditions often involve practices related to the mystical, magical, and spiritual realms.

Key Differences: • **Focus:** Neo-Paganism is more nature-based and community-oriented, while the occult is more individualized and focused on personal spiritual development. • **Holidays:** Neo-Pagans have a structured calendar of eight sabbats, while occult holidays are more flexible and varied.

In essence, while Neo-Paganism and the occult may share some common ground, their approaches to holidays and celebrations differ significantly. Neo-Paganism often involves communal rituals and celebrations tied to the natural world, while the occult is more individualized and focused on personal spiritual practices.

The occult encompasses a diverse range of practices and beliefs, leading to the formation of various groups and organizations. Here are some of the different types of occult groups:

Historical and Traditional Groups: • **Hermetic Orders:** These groups, such as the Hermetic Order of the Golden Dawn, focus on esoteric knowledge, ceremonial magic, and spiritual development. • **Theosophical Societies:** These groups, like the Theosophical Society, explore spiritualism, mysticism, and the interconnectedness of all things. • **Rosicrucian Orders:** These groups, such as the Societas Rosicruciana in Anglia, study alchemy, astrology, and the occult sciences.

Modern and Contemporary Groups: • **Wiccan Covens:** These groups practice Wicca, a nature-based religion emphasizing harmony with the Earth and its deities. • **Pagan Groups:** These groups, such as Druids and Heathens, focus on ancient pagan traditions and the worship of nature spirits. • **Magical Orders:** These groups, like the Ordo Templi Orientis (O.T.O.), practice ceremonial magic, sexual mysticism, and the pursuit of individual enlightenment. • **Spiritualist Groups:** These groups, such as Spiritualist churches, focus on communication with spirits and the afterlife. • **New Age Groups:** These groups, often loosely organized, explore various spiritual practices, including meditation, yoga, and energy healing.

Other Notable Groups: • **Secret Societies:** These groups, often shrouded in mystery, may practice occult rituals and esoteric knowledge. Examples include the Freemasons and the Illuminati. • **Satanic Groups:** These groups, such as the Church of Satan, practice Satanism, a philosophy that emphasizes individualism, self-indulgence, and rejection of traditional morality.

It's important to note that the occult is a vast and diverse field, and these are just a few examples of the many types of occult groups that exist. Each group's beliefs and practices can vary widely, and many individuals may participate in multiple groups or practice independently.

The Bible strongly condemns magic, Witchcraft, and any practices that involve seeking power from sources other than God. Here are some key points:

•Magic and Witchcraft are Abominations: Deuteronomy 18:10-12 clearly states that practices like divination, sorcery, Witchcraft, and consulting the dead are detestable to the Lord.

•Forbidden Practices: Exodus 22:18 prohibits tolerating a sorceress, emphasizing the seriousness of such practices.

•False Gods and Idolatry: Magic and Witchcraft are often associated with the worship of false gods and idols, which the Bible strongly condemns.

•Spiritual Warfare: The Bible presents a spiritual battle between God and Satan. Satan uses practices like magic and Witchcraft to deceive and harm people, drawing them away from God.

It's important to note that the Bible condemns these practices not simply because of superstition or cultural prejudice. It reflects a deep understanding of the spiritual realm and the dangers of seeking power outside God's authority.

Deuteronomy 18:9 NLT: "When you enter the land the LORD your God is giving you, be very careful not to imitate the detestable customs of the nations living there.

Deuteronomy 18:10 NLT: For example, never sacrifice your son or daughter as a burnt offering. And do not let your people practice fortune-telling, or use sorcery, or interpret omens, or engage in Witchcraft,

Deuteronomy 18:11 NLT: or cast spells, or function as mediums or psychics, or call forth the spirits of the dead.

Deuteronomy 18:12 NLT: <u>Anyone who does these things is detestable to the LORD. It is because the other nations have done these detestable things that the LORD your God will drive them out ahead of you.</u>

Deuteronomy 18:13 NLT: <u>But you must be blameless before the LORD your God.</u>

Deuteronomy 18:14 NLT: <u>The nations you are about to displace consult sorcerers and fortune-tellers, but the LORD your God forbids you to do such things."</u>

Exodus 22:18 NLT: <u>"You must not allow a sorceress to live.</u>

Exodus 22:19 NLT: <u>"Anyone who has sexual relations with an animal must certainly be put to death.</u>

Exodus 22:20 NLT: <u>"Anyone who sacrifices to any god other than the LORD must be destroyed.</u>

After reading all this information, finding out what an individual believes before engaging in friendship is essential. Open conversations prevent you from being trapped in a friendship or relationship you will regret someday. Finding out what the individual believes could also save your natural and spiritual life in the long run.

While waiting for our flight to Guadalajara, Kris told me about his life and many regrets.

He said he wanted to start fresh without all of the drama. I told him to do that; he was going to have to block people out of his life who brought him heartache, pain, and especially the ones who abused him, including not answering their phone calls. I told him I would have stepped in and ended all the chaos if I had known all this was happening with the two women. Then I told Kris that Jason didn't need to be in that environment, and neither did he. I said, Son, Jason, seeing these women taking advantage of you, using and abusing you, was not suitable for your family.

He said, "I know you would have stepped in, but Mom, I felt I had gotten myself into the mess. I am a grown man, and it's not your place to babysit me." I told him I loved him with all my heart and couldn't be silent now that I knew what was happening.

When Jason was younger, his parents brought him to visit me in Mexico. It was then that Kris fell in love with the tranquil area. We had lived in the Dallas-Fort Worth area for over 30 years. The area is so large that it is called the Metroplex. Traffic and road rage are a way of life; it's a nightmare, and daily, you deal with the hustle and bustle, along with attitudes. That alone can be challenging.

The flight to Guadalajara is less than two hours long, and I live an hour from there. It was early enough for us to unpack and relax. We weren't in the house for 30 minutes when Kris and Jason wanted to go for a walk. I told them to be careful; it was late and almost time for the switch.

Now is a great time to tell you what the switch is. In Mexico, you learn when it is time to go inside your home. Generally, the streets empty around 9 p.m., when most law-abiding citizens go inside. Then, somewhere around 10 p.m., the atmosphere of the pueblo changes and becomes very chaotic, full of havoc and activity with the cartel.

The area where we lived in Mexico was beautiful. During the rainy season, usually during the hurricane season from June to March or April, the mountains and the surrounding area were like a paradise—lush green landscapes, beautiful flowers, and extraordinary temperatures.

We arrived in Mexico during the cooler months, so Kris and Jason loved to go on walks and did that frequently. The pueblo was small enough to walk anywhere, and we only needed transportation if we went outside the area.

It was a great relief to see Kris and Jason happy. He was still on the phone in the USA, and his business was based in the Dallas metroplex. Due to the type of business he had, he received calls all through the day. I didn't question who was calling; I just watched his attitude to see if it was the two women. If they had called, it would have caused Kris stress.

If Kris hadn't broken ties with Marie or Endora, it wouldn't have been until the last two years that I found out the depth of the threesome. Both women knew Kris made a lot of money and used him for all the money they could get their hands on. Neither of them worked, and after a few weeks without Kris's money, I expected them to get desperate.

When Kris asked if he and Jason could move into the RV, everything seemed to be running smoothly. I never expected what would happen a few days after the guys moved to the RV.

The RV is in a gated community that offers several amenities, which helps strengthen their relationship. They enjoyed walking and visiting the recreational park by the lake, which was only three miles from the house. This proximity meant they could quickly drop by whenever they needed anything.

My Mom owned the RV, a Grand Junction model with three slides that made the interior feel very spacious. She purchased it new, and it became her home.

She lived there for about eight years. After her passing, I found it difficult to move in, so I allowed other staff members to stay there while I continued living in the house in town, which was closer to the school.

When Kris asked to move to the RV, I told him he wouldn't have transportation. Then, he asked to use my truck until he found a vehicle. I told him I needed transportation to get around and to go to school. He said, "Mom, I will pick you up daily and take you wherever you need to go."

After all he had been through, I was concerned about his mental stability. Then, staying at the RV might be a great idea. The RV park was lovely, and many English-speaking people lived there, so that would give him company. I told him it was okay, but he had better handle everything.

The guys had been at the RV for about a week when I received a call late at night. The voice I heard sounded familiar, and I thought, surely not. I asked who this was, and she answered Endora. She then started in on Kris, screaming, "He is running from the police." I said, "What are you talking about? Where are you?" She said, in a smug voice, "In your RV."

Now my blood is boiling. That was the first time that I knew Endora was in town.

Now I was stuck. Kris had my truck, and I had no idea where to go to start looking for him. At this point, I was walking the floor, furious that he allowed this witch to come to where we were.

Within 15 minutes, Kris and Jason were pounding on the front door, sweating and panicking. Once they settled down, I asked them what was going on and why Endora was there.

Kris told me that she had stabbed him in the arm. I asked him what she was doing at my RV. Nothing he was going to say would change my attitude, so I told him I wanted her out of my RV in the morning. She had better get a bus and get out of town.

She had lied when she called me and said the police were after Kris. She then said that the neighbors had reported a stabbing. I was trying to understand what all of this insanity was about. I asked her where Kris and Jason were; she said they were running from the police.

There were some significant facts left out of her report. First, it was Endora who had stabbed Kris in the arm. Kris and Jason took off running on foot, fearing further attacks from her.

On their way to my house, they had to go in front of the Green Cross, an emergency clinic similar to the Red Cross. Kris checked in to see if he needed stitches. The clinic treated his deep wound, gave him some medication, and then they came to my house.

The police weren't looking for Kris to arrest him; they were looking for him to see if he wanted to press charges.

I talked to Kris and Jason, and they filled in the details of what had happened. It took a while for everyone to settle down; it was getting late, and we all needed sleep.

I prayed with them, and Kris said Mom, Jason, and I will sleep in Jason's room and deal with this tomorrow. I told him she had better be on her way back to Texas in the morning.

Kris has always had a soft heart for the underdog. This woman once had five children. The state took three of them, and recently, the father of one came and picked up his son, so now she only had one son left. I found out all of this information over time, and Endora verified it.

The next day, Endora and her son were at the bus station. When Kris saw them, he jumped out of the truck. Jason jumped out and said, "Dad, get back in the truck, don't mess with her anymore." Jason knew there would be more trouble, but couldn't persuade his Dad to listen. So Jason jumped in the truck and said, "Grandma, that's messed up. A witch stabs you, and you try to talk to her."

She didn't leave town that day; instead, she found another place to stay, and I am sure Kris paid for it. Jason would stay with me most of the time, and then stay with his Dad to look after him and ensure his safety.

I repeatedly tried to convince Kris that Endora took immense pride in her identity as a witch and her dedication to the craft. With an air of confidence, she would often brag about how she had used her powers on him, but he remained skeptical, dismissing my concerns as mere exaggeration.

That all changed one fateful day when Kris unexpectedly walked into our dimly lit living room. To his horror, he found Endora sitting lotus-style on the floor, surrounded by an elaborate circle of candles and symbols, engaged in some ritual alongside a mysterious witch doctor. They were deep in concentration, their voices rising and falling in an eerie chant as they called forth evil spirits from the shadows.

In a panic, Kris bolted from the house, his heart racing, unable to comprehend the scene he had just witnessed. Meanwhile, Endora, unfazed and perhaps even amused by his reaction, was away traveling abroad, seemingly disconnected from the chaos she had left behind, adding to the mystery of her character.

During her time in Mexico, she quickly connected with the cartel, making sure she had drug connections to keep her supplied with her drugs of choice.

Santería is one of the prominent occult practices in Mexico, deeply rooted in a blend of African traditions and Catholic beliefs. During her time in Mexico, Endora sought the guidance of a witch doctor — a figure known for their ability to summon and communicate with spirits. This witch doctor performed rituals that evoked demons within the very walls of the house where Kris and Jason resided, creating an atmosphere thick with unease and supernatural tension. In a state of urgency and fear, Kris and Jason raced back to the house, desperate for an intervention to dispel the dark forces at play. Concerned for their safety, I insisted they stay at my home, providing them a refuge from the haunting events around them.

Daily, I was dealing with Satan's attacks on my family. I was at a loss for how to deal with all that was happening.

I recalled the day Endora finally caught a bus and returned to Texas. I asked Phillipe, who worked with Kris when the events happened. His notes show that Endora left the RV on March 16th, 2020. So we hadn't been in Mexico for 16 days when this mess started again.

There are at least five ways a person can become immediately possessed by demons: drugs, alcohol, sex outside of marriage, meditation, altered states of consciousness, and activities that bring immediate demonic possession. Addictions are another word for possession.

Addiction is a complex condition characterized by compulsive engagement in a rewarding activity or substance despite harmful consequences. It often involves changes in the brain's reward system, leading to cravings and difficulty controlling the behavior.

The pervasive presence of media in our lives continuously shapes and influences our society. Programming manifests in many forms, from catchy melodies on the radio to visually striking music videos and stories told through various film and television platforms. Each song, video, and broadcast carries messages and narratives that subtly influence our thoughts, beliefs, and behaviors. This constant stream of media entertains and acts as a powerful tool for programming societal norms and values, weaving itself into the fabric of our everyday experience.

Chapter Sixteen
Arrested Mexican Jail

Endora departed from the RV on March 16, 2020, but her journey has yet to lead her out of Mexico. Instead, she found a new place to settle within the vibrant Pueblo area, where she stayed for at least six weeks after leaving the RV. I turned to Kris for answers about her whereabouts one day, but he remained tight-lipped. It wasn't until a family member visited the park across from my house that I learned Endora was still nearby; they spotted her young son playing innocently on the swings. The revelation hit me hard—she lived a few blocks from my home.

As time passed, I lost track of when she finally decided to return to Texas, but it felt like an eternity. Each day without her departure felt like a heavyweight, and I wished she would leave sooner rather than later.

Each night, I was transformed into a whirlwind of anxiety. As the sun dipped below the horizon, an unsettling sense of dread settled over me, knowing that if anything were to go awry, it would inevitably happen during those late hours when reaching out to anyone for help would be futile. I kept my cellphone ringer at maximum volume, a lifeline to the outside world amid the silence. I learned to sleep with one ear open, attuned to even the faintest rustle or creak that might disrupt the stillness. Every sound became amplified, each whisper of the wind through the trees or faint thump of the night echoing through my thoughts as I lay in restless vigilance.

For more than 35 years, my life has been a journey full of unpredictability. As a Pastor, I dedicated myself wholeheartedly to the service of others, making it a priority to be accessible to anyone who sought my guidance or support. Whether it was a church member grappling with personal challenges or a family member needing comfort, I never turned away a call for help. My door was always open, and I wanted everyone to feel they could rely on me in times of need, knowing that I would listen, console, and provide encouragement.

The clock had just struck eleven, and the night was thick with silence when my cell phone shattered the stillness, its shrill ring slicing through the darkness. I answered it immediately, but the voice on the other end was anything but calm. Kris's frantic screams echoed in my ear, each one laced with raw terror.

"Mom, they're going to kill me! They're going to kill me!" His words tumbled out in a panicked rush, drowning me in an overwhelming fear.

My heart pounded as I struggled to grasp the urgency of my son's panicked plea. "Kris, please! You need to calm down!" I implored, my voice trembling with desperation as I fought to break through the chaos of his hysteria. "Who is after you? Where are you?" Dark possibilities raced through my mind, each one more sinister than the last, as I listened helplessly to his cries, each scream sending a chill down my spine.

His voice pierced through the darkness, raw and frantic, each syllable dripping with a volatile mix of terror and urgency. I strained my ears, trying to locate him amidst the chaos surrounding us. The only hint was his proximity to the convenience store, a modest neon sign flickering in the distance. An oppressive weight of dread hung in the air, thick and suffocating, while confusion clouded my mind like a storm, leaving me disoriented in the shadowy night.

Without a breath to lose, I burst into Stacey's room, my pulse racing as if it were trying to escape my chest. "Come on! We have to go!" I urged, gripping her arm tightly, each word heavy with the urgency of our plight, knowing that time was slipping away like sand through fingers.

As his desperate cries bounced somberly off the dimly lit street, I caught fragments of his panic-stricken shout—something about being "down the block." The vague direction gnawed at me with unease, but instinctively, an unyielding drive surged within me, propelling us forward. With my phone glued to my ear, the cool night air rushed through the truck's open window, a refreshing contrast to the heat of my pounding heart. The stillness of the night wrapped around us, amplifying every muffled noise and starting a race against the unknown as I searched the shadows for any hint that might lead us closer to the source of his voice, eager to unearth the mystery lurking in the enveloping darkness.

I had always been attuned to the subtlest sounds, my acute hearing like a finely tuned instrument, able to catch whispers where others heard only silence. As Stacey skillfully maneuvered the truck through the winding streets, her attention was split between the road and focusing on locating Kris's cries. Every turn seemed to steer us towards a sliver of hope.

Gradually, the faint echoes of his voice began to weave through the city's ambient noise like a ghostly thread pulling at the edges of my consciousness. Initially barely discernible, the sound started to sharpen, becoming a desperate beacon guiding us home. We exchanged fleeting glances, an unspoken understanding passing between us—we had to delve deeper into the shadows and follow that distant call to discover its source.

After what felt like an eternity of searching, we finally located the source of the chilling screams that had echoed through the night. An unsettling sight greeted us as we turned down the narrow street: at least four or five large trucks loomed in the dim light, engines rumbling ominously.

Surrounding them was a menacing group of ten or more men, all clad in the dark uniforms of the Federales, the federal security forces known for their unwavering resolve. They had encircled Kris, their expressions a mix of determination and aggression, creating an atmosphere thick with tension and uncertainty. The scene was chaotic yet intensely focused, and we could feel the weight of the moment pressing down on us as we took in the unfolding drama.

I rushed up to the Federales. When I got to where Kris was, he was on the ground behind a fence with an officer's foot on his head. I screamed Get your foot off of his head. NOW!!

The officers stood frozen for a moment, their expressions a mix of confusion and authority as I let out another cry, this time in Spanish, desperation lacing my voice. My heart raced as I demanded to speak with the Officer in charge, a figure who soon approached and greeted me in English. He met my frantic gaze as I declared, "I am his mother," leaving him baffled and searching for clarity amidst the chaos.

"What is happening here?" I demanded, my voice firm despite the turmoil swirling inside me. It seemed incomprehensible that Kris had somehow found himself behind the sturdy front gate of an unoccupied house, which felt like a strange, disturbing prison. It wasn't until later that I learned the truth about the unfolding events. In his panic, Kris had sprinted to the unadorned front door of the desolate home, oblivious to its emptiness. He had knocked frantically and called out for help, only to have the officers rush in behind him, swiftly closing the gate as they arrived. The scene played in my mind like a harrowing film; each detail etched as I wrestled with the uncertainty and fear of the moment.

A brief insight into the background is essential to grasp the situation's intensity. In Mexico, law enforcement is heavily tainted by corruption, often falling under the sway of the Cartel. The Federales, an elite police force, morph into even more formidable enforcers for these criminal organizations, serving as the muscle behind their evil operations.

Unfortunately, in this challenging environment, it is common for individuals who dare to challenge the Cartel to call upon the Federales for help. However, this can be a fatal mistake; should they decide that a person must be silenced, that individual may vanish without a trace, erased from existence.

This grim reality creates an atmosphere rife with fear and suspicion. Adding to the desperation of the situation, local police officers, struggling with meager city salaries, often resort to fabricating charges to extort money from unsuspecting citizens. In such an environment, it's not surprising that hiring a cop to carry out illicit activities has become a common practice, a troubling testament to how deeply corruption has embedded itself in the very fabric of society.

Confusion and concern surged as I absorbed the chaotic scene around me. My mind raced, desperately seeking to understand the reasons behind Kris's alarming detention. My eyes scanned the fray, searching for any sign of my grandson, Jason, but he was nowhere to be found.

As anxiety tightened its grip on my chest, I turned to Kris, my voice tinged with urgency as I asked about Jason's whereabouts. Instead of a verbal response, he cast a silent gaze toward a looming sight in the distance—a large, foreboding fenced area, its heavy gate closed. The stark, metal structure seemed to exude an air of danger, intensifying my apprehension as I realized it might hold the answers I dreaded to uncover.

Desperate for clarity, I pressed the Officer in charge with a growing sense of urgency, my voice shaking as I demanded to know why my son was apprehensive. My eyes drifted to Kris, who stood a few feet away, absorbed in a call; his brow furrowed as he likely received instructions from someone unseen. The officers' indifference was palpable; it felt like I was invisible, a ghost pleading for recognition. Each question I posed seemed to dissolve into the air, met with stern faces that didn't waver.

After an eternity, a curt response emerged, flat and lacking empathy: they were taking him to jail, and the next steps were entirely uncertain. My heart plummeted at the thought of my son confined behind bars, trapped in a web of circumstances I could barely grasp. The weight of helplessness settled heavily in my chest, mixing with dread as I envisioned him enduring the cold reality of a cell isolated from the world he knew.

As we lingered in anticipation, listening intently for the sound of keys jingling that would signal the unlocking of the heavy metal gate and Kris's release from his confinement, an inexplicable urge tugged at me to venture toward the nearby construction storage site. This place was a fortress of heavy-duty trucks and towering construction equipment, a stark contrast to the urgency of our situation.

I stepped cautiously into the dimly lit yard, the atmosphere thick with tension as a vigilant officer accompanied me, his eyes scanning the gloom for any flicker of movement that might signal trouble. The chilly air wrapped around us, heightening my senses as my gaze roamed across the rows of colossal vehicles, each looming like a sentinel in the encroaching twilight, their metal surfaces dull and scratched from years of neglect. My curiosity was piqued, and I was drawn to the scattered pieces of abandoned equipment in the far corner—a chaotic array of rusting tools and forgotten machinery that seemed to whisper stories of past endeavors. I methodically combed through the shadows, inspecting every inch of the cramped space, but despite my diligent search among the eerie silhouettes and the scent of decay, I found no trace of Jason.

Suddenly, Kris's urgent voice sliced through the silence, filled with raw desperation. "Mom, please find Jason; I immediately promised Kris I would find him." His broad, pleading eyes were brimming with fear, and I nodded solemnly, vowing to scour for Jason once we resolved this situation. I leaned closer and whispered into Kris's ear, trying to offer a glimmer of hope: "He's probably at our house."

A chilling wave swept over me as the Officer and I approached where Kris had been anxiously waiting. His face was pale and drawn, and his voice quivered with raw emotion as he recounted the harrowing events.

"They were kicking him with their boots," he said, each word laced with pain, "until they saw you coming." Heavy and oppressive, the gravity of his statement lingered in the air, echoing the horror of what he had suffered.

Without hesitation, I strode forward, each step resolute, my voice cutting through the heavy tension as I addressed the Officer. "You better keep your hands and feet off of him," I warned, my tone sharp and unwavering, the gravity of my words resonating like a thunderclap. In that charged moment, a refreshing surge of strength surged through me, fueled by an unshakable conviction rooted deeply in my faith in God. It felt as though I spoke not just with my voice but with an authority that could command the cosmos to heed my declaration. I was acutely aware that my words had the potential to alter the unfolding drama around us, the energy crackling with the possibility of change as I stood my ground, a steadfast protector against the encroaching threat.

If my son were in trouble with the law, I would do everything I could to cooperate with the authorities. However, at that moment, as I stood there, my heart racing with concern, the officers around me exhibited an alarming level of unprofessionalism. They seemed unable—or unwilling—to provide any clear explanation for his arrest. Their vague responses and lack of transparency sent a chill down me, leading me to believe that their actions were driven by something far more sinister than a genuine pursuit of justice. The way they conducted themselves told me everything I needed to know about their intentions.

I refused to stand by and witness any madness unfold. At last, the truck containing Kris in the back began to reverse, turning down a narrow side street. I could hear Kris's frantic voice rise above the noise, pleading for them to stop kicking him. Adrenaline surged through me as I sprinted after the vehicle, my heart pounding. "You better stop kicking him!" I shouted, my voice straining with urgency. I quickly approached the supervisor, my tone sharp and unwavering, demanding that my son be taken immediately to jail—I would be right behind them. I made it clear that he had better not be harmed in any way.

Stacey pulled up in my truck, the engine rumbling as we arrived at the local jail. The gray cinder-block building loomed ahead, its barbed wire fence glinting under the harsh fluorescent lights. As we parked, I spotted Kris being escorted by officers, his hands cuffed behind his back, a look of defeat etched on his face.

Once the initial shock ebbed away, I felt an overwhelming sense of urgency: I had to find Jason. A knot tightened in my stomach as I pictured him making a beeline for my house, and I couldn't shake the feeling that time was slipping away. After an eternity on the road, filled with anxious thoughts and heavy silence, we finally pulled in front of the house.

As we stepped inside the softly lit living room, Jason stood. His posture was tense, and the flicker of worry in his eyes caught me off guard. Without hesitation, I rushed towards him, my heart pounding with relief and gratitude. I wrapped my arms around him, holding him as if to shield him from all the chaos outside. The warmth of his body and the steady beat of his heart reassured me that he was safe, and in that moment, everything else melted away.

He began to recount the harrowing events that had unfolded between him and his father.

They had strolled down the block to the corner store, a small convenience shop adorned with flickering neon lights, accompanied by their friend Frank, to grab a few cold drinks. As they wandered the aisles, laughter and chatter filled the air. Still, their lightheartedness quickly shifted when they noticed the unmistakable black vehicles of the Federales pulling up outside. Panic gripped them, and the instinct to flee kicked in. Frank, eyes wide with fear, bolted from the store, and the two boys instinctively ran after him.

As they raced through the dimly lit streets, their hearts pounded fiercely in their chests like war drums; the duo finally caught up to Frank, who stood at the corner, visibly shaken and gasping for breath. The shadows danced around him as he confessed, his voice trembling, that he had discarded his gun in a desperate bid to evade capture. Kris, fueled by a mix of anxiety and determination, pressed him for details. "Where did you throw the weapon?" he demanded, urgency lacing his words.

Frank's response was swallowed by silence, a heavy dread settling over him as the reality hit—law enforcement was close behind, and their presence felt like a dark cloud looming over them after witnessing their frantic escape from the store. The mounting tension crackled in the air, and before anyone could process it fully, Frank took off, his silhouette quickly swallowed by the night.

Fueled by adrenaline surging through their veins like wildfire, Kris and Jason followed suit, unsure why Frank had darted into the shadows. Jason felt an overwhelming urge pulling him in a different direction; he needed to reach me urgently. His feet pounded against the pavement as he sprinted toward my house, the familiar goal in his mind guiding his frantic race.

Upon reaching the metallic fence surrounding my yard, Jason paused momentarily. There was no time to lose; he had to get me to help his father. Without hesitating, he vaulted over the fence, landing softly on the other side, and veered sharply through the landscape of the nearby cemetery.

As he navigated the maze of shadowy paths lined with old gravestones, a wave of urgency collided with disorientation, a chaotic blend of fear and determination guiding him forward. He was aware of his odd appearance—one shoe missing, a stark reminder of his hasty departure—but the thought of my safety drove him onward. With each heartbeat echoing in his mind, he pressed forward, determined to reach the house where I waited. He was consumed by worry for his safety and the problem that loomed closer with every passing second.

Frank arrived at our home; his demeanor serious as he recounted his events. I instantly sensed the truth in his words; all the stories were aligned, like pieces of a puzzle coming together.

With a tone of urgency, Frank insisted that we needed to act quickly to get Kris out of jail. He warned us that Kris's being sent to Chapala would lead to problems, mainly because he was an American citizen. Frank explained the risky hierarchy of the Mexican legal system, emphasizing that Chapala would ultimately lead to Guadalajara, a place notorious for its harsh treatment of foreigners.

The Mexican authorities had a reputation for being especially unyielding when it came to dealing with U.S. citizens.

My granddaughter, America, held a respected place in our Pueblo community and was fluent in Spanish, so she took it upon herself to investigate our options. She rushed to the police station, only to find the office locked until morning, leaving us to endure the agonizing wait. Hours dragged on slowly, filled with uncertainty, but America refused to back down. When the doors finally opened, she strode inside the station, her heart racing as she learned Kris was scheduled to appear before a judge. Surprisingly, she discovered that the judge was her friend—a beacon of hope in our desperate situation.

Eager to help, she inquired about the charges against Kris. The judge informed her that he was being charged with trespassing. Confused, America pressed for clarification, leading the judge to explain that with a $35 fine, Kris would be free to go. Relief washed over her as the fine was promptly paid, and soon after, Kris returned to the safety of our home, exhausted but grateful.

Chapter Seventeen
Marie Arrives in Mexico May 19, 2020

Kris was apprehended on April 22nd, 2020, a day that sparked worry within me. His trusting nature often led him to see the best in everyone he encountered, and now that innocence felt like a potential target in a harsh world.

Meanwhile, Endora soared through the skies on her broomstick, leaving Mexico behind in a flurry of emotion and enchantment. The air was thick with the scent of adventure as she went, a bittersweet departure marked by frustration. Her connections with the local drug dealers had deepened, and the thought of returning to the States incited a fury within her. The vibrant, chaotic life she had crafted in Mexico was suddenly stripped away, leaving her with a sense of loss.

Back in the States, Kris found himself adjusting to a vibrant new way of getting around—a sleek, fiery red car that glimmered brilliantly under the golden sunlight. This compact vehicle allowed him to easily navigate the bustling city and helped reduce his gas expenses, offering him a sense of liberation and autonomy. Restless by nature, Kris thrived on the excitement of meeting new people and uncovering unique experiences. His days were intricately woven with a rich tapestry of diverse encounters, keeping him in constant motion and fully engaged with the vividness of life.

Thanks to his magnetic personality, Kris was frequently invited to various events, and he always took Jason along, cherishing their adventures together. One memorable occasion brought them to a sprawling ranch dotted with horses, where the air was filled with the earthy scent of hay and the sound of whinnying steeds. Kris felt excited about taking Jason horseback riding—an experience he knew would thrill his friend. Though Kris himself preferred to remain on the sidelines, he delighted in watching Jason, with his exuberant laughter and beaming smile, as he rode. Jason once confided in me that getting his dad on a horse was a rare feat; he could only coax him into the saddle for a few fleeting minutes before Kris would prefer to step back, allowing Jason to enjoy the ride.

After Kris's arrest, a palpable sense of terror consumed him, his unease gnawing at him like a relentless wave. Desperate for reassurance, he confided in Frank, expressing his desire to speak with a relative who held significant power in the local Cartel—an intimidating figure whose influence loomed large over the community. Kris sought to ensure our family's safety, believing that facing this daunting connection was preferable to hiding in fear. Summoning his courage, he stepped into the unknown to meet the man.

With its fierce reputation, the Cartel assured Kris that it harbored no ill will toward him. It pledged to protect him, promising to keep a watchful eye on our lives. Kris's apprehension eased as he was informed that he knew my school and vowed to shield it from potential threats. Their words, heavy with authority, lingered in the air, giving him a semblance of relief amid the chaos.

Yet, a deep-seated unease stirred me when Kris revealed his decision to approach such an influential figure. With pride and concern, he stated, "Mom, I made sure that nobody would mess with you or our family. The best way was to confront the man directly."

The weight of his words left me grateful for his bravery and anxious about the lengths he was willing to go to protect us.

Life took on an illusion of normalcy for a few weeks, a calm that briefly soothed my racing heart. Just as I began to find comfort in this newfound peace, Kris approached me again, his expression a blend of hope and uncertainty. He shared that he had been conversing with Marie, and they were considering mending their relationship for Jason's sake. The thought sent ripples of anxiety through me; the tensions in our lives were far from over.

I confided in Kris, voicing my deep-seated concerns about her trustworthiness. "Since when did she care about Jason?" I questioned, recalling how she had never really embraced the role of a mother throughout his life. Jason, with a hint of desperation in his voice, interjected, "Mom, she isn't using drugs or drinking anymore. She's been clean ever since our trip to Israel."

I remained skeptical, shaking my head as I replied, "I just can't believe she has truly changed." Undeterred, he insisted, "Mom, it's for real this time." Then he made an unexpected request: could Kris stay at our house for a few days while she finalized her plans to move to Mexico?

I considered the suggestion, and hope ignited within me. It could be an excellent opportunity to observe her firsthand and determine whether her behavior had changed. With family around, gauging her actions and attitudes would be easier. I firmly told Kris we would watch closely to see if she had turned over a new leaf. I made it clear that if I received any reports of her partying or slipping back into old habits, she would be out without hesitation.

Kris nodded in agreement, a gesture that initially brought me some comfort. However, I soon began to feel a sinking feeling in my gut as I realized one of the family members I had entrusted to watch over Marie was more loyal to Kris than to me. This individual shared a long-standing friendship with Kris and had even worked under him for years, making him acutely aware of Kris's desire for his marriage to flourish. Whenever I expressed my concerns about Marie's troubling behavior, he would dismiss my worries with an unsettling calm, offering nonchalant reassurances like, "I stay so busy I haven't noticed anything unusual." When I probed further, asking if Marie had been venturing out more frequently, he shrugged, downplaying my concerns with a vague response: she wasn't out any more than she typically was. This vagueness gnawed at me, leaving me feeling anxious and bewildered.

One afternoon, the phone's shrill ring jolted me from my thoughts. It was Phillipe on the line, his voice a curious blend of urgency and nonchalance as he relayed some alarming news: Marie had wrecked Kris's car. An icy wave of dread washed over me as I pressed for further information. "How did it happen?" I asked, heart racing. Despite my probing, Phillipe answered evasively, claiming he didn't know the specifics. He almost casually said, "It's just a small dent."

Yet, even as he attempted to minimize the situation, I felt a sense of foreboding. I needed to see the damage, so I instructed him to send me pictures.

When the images arrived, my concern morphed into a heavy weight in my chest. Although the car remained operable, the sight of the dent—a crumpled crease marring the once-pristine paint—was jarring. Kris had always been meticulous about his vehicles, treating them almost reverently as if they were cherished possessions. I could already envision the disappointment and frustration etched across his face when he eventually learned about the incident, and that image sent a fresh wave of unease.

Marie stepped off the bus in Mexico on May 19th, 2020, and an electrifying sense of anticipation filled the air, particularly for Kris, who was practically buzzing with energy. As her feet hit the ground, he wasted no time expressing his excitement, suggesting she stay at the school. He vividly imagined the two of them working side by side to prepare for its grand opening, an event they both had eagerly awaited.

Soon after, Kris and Jason made their way to my home, bringing an air of camaraderie that filled the living room as we sat together. The conversation naturally shifted to their living arrangements, prompting me to ask where they planned to stay. Kris responded calmly and assured me he and Jason would reside in my house. He hinted that he needed time to assess whether their circumstances would shift.

Establishing firm boundaries was essential. With conviction, I declared that I would not stand for any hint of the chaos I had experienced during my time in Israel. What else could I express? My daily immersion at the school was unwavering. I dedicated myself to overseeing operations meticulously, ensuring every detail perfectly aligned with our highly anticipated public debut.

However, just a few days later, tensions began to rise. I was repeatedly summoned to the school and thrust into the role of peacemaker as conflicts erupted between Kris and Jason. Each encounter weighed heavily on my shoulders, a palpable tension in the air as I hurried to diffuse their escalating frustrations and restore a sense of balance and tranquility.

About a month after she had departed for Mexico, I felt compelled to ask Paul to look into the room where she had been staying. I held my breath, hoping he might stumble upon something amiss. To my dismay, he uncovered a hidden stash of alcohol carefully concealed beneath the bed—a troubling discovery that ignited a flurry of questions and concerns within me.

Before the world came to a standstill due to the COVID-19 pandemic, several extended family members had managed to travel to Mexico, arriving just in time before the borders began to tighten. They sought refuge at the local school, which provided ample space to accommodate the growing number of guests during their unexpected stay. What was meant to be a joyful reunion filled with laughter and shared memories soon transformed into a confusing and tumultuous experience, as little did we know how quickly our carefully laid plans would begin to unravel.

In the days that followed, the promises of support and companionship from those around us slowly dwindled, leaving an aching sense of abandonment in their wake. Meanwhile, a noticeable shift occurred between Jason and me; he began spending more time with me than with his parents. This change didn't escape my notice. Despite his tender age of just 14, Jason carried himself with a remarkable maturity that defied his years. He navigated the upheaval with a steady composure, responding to the chaos around him in ways that made him seem wise beyond his age.

I had thought I had prepared for every conceivable scenario in this unfolding situation. Yet, I couldn't shake the feeling that more significant challenges loomed just out of sight, waiting for the right moment to emerge.

During Marie's nine days in Mexico, our interactions were fleeting and sparse, like wisps of smoke disappearing into the air. My mind was consumed with school responsibilities, leaving little room for anything else. Each time I tried to catch a moment with her, I found her locked in yet another heated argument with Kris, their voices rising and falling with the ebb and flow of their tumultuous exchanges. More often than not, I was jolted from my thoughts by frantic calls about the ongoing chaos unfolding just beyond my reach.

I sought clarity from the Staff, hoping for reassurance about the madness surrounding us. Yet, their responses felt like whispers against a raging storm; they insisted that Kris was immersed in festivities, socializing, and enjoying the vibrant energy of the local scene. But just as quickly, Marie would storm through the door, her face flushed with anger, her voice exploding into the room like a cracked dam, ready to unleash a flood of pent-up frustration directed at Kris. Caught in the eye of this emotional whirlwind, I felt helpless, swept along by forces that seemed entirely beyond my control.

On the warm, tranquil evening of May 28th, my late shift finally drew to a close. The school dimmed around me as the fluorescent lights flickered and buzzed, retreating one by one into darkness. As I gathered my belongings, a shadow caught my eye. Kris stood there, his expression grave yet earnest, an unusual seriousness etched into his features. He stepped closer, his voice trembling as he leaned in, "Mom, I am so sorry for all the heartache I have caused you. You never deserved the pain you've endured." At that moment, I could see the weight of his remorse reflected in his eyes, a powerful blend of sincerity and deep regret that pierced through the turmoil surrounding us.

Kris continued his voice steady yet laced with emotion, "I have always admired and respected who you are and what you stand for. You've poured your heart and soul into raising JD and me." His words hung in the air, heavy with a mix of regret and determination, like a weighty promise waiting to be fulfilled. "I want to be a changed man who loves and serves God. I know how you raised us, and you are my hero."

His heartfelt promise reverberated in my heart, echoing hope and commitment. "Starting tomorrow, Mom, I promise I will be different. I want to help you finish school, to show you that I will never be the same." The emotional sincerity in his voice brought tears to both our eyes, shining like tiny stars as they flowed down our cheeks, a testament to our vulnerability in that moment. It felt pivotal—a day that would forever be etched in my memory.

I gently took his hand in mine, feeling the warmth radiating between us, a tangible connection that spoke volumes as he shared his hopes and dreams for the future. That evening, as I enveloped him in a tight embrace, I whispered fervently in my heart, praying for his journey ahead, kissed him softly on the forehead, and breathed, "I know you can do anything you put your mind to." "I believe in you" were the last words I uttered that night, filled with hope and yearning that hung like a delicate promise.

After I returned home, the memory of our heartfelt conversation lingered in my thoughts. It was a sweet melody of words that resonated within me, providing comfort and a sense of eager anticipation for what was coming. Once again, I found myself on my knees in the quiet sanctuary of my room, praying for God to grant me the strength to fulfill the deep desires of my heart, my voice a soft murmur against the stillness of the night.

The following day, just as the soft tendrils of dawn began to stretch across my room, Stacey burst through the door, her expression a tumult of concern and urgency that was impossible to ignore. "There's a problem at the school," she declared, her voice barely a whisper yet charged with an electric tension that filled the air. "I have to go check it out."

I felt an undeniable urge to intervene before she could enter the morning light. "I'm coming with you," I asserted, my heart pounding in my chest as a knot of anxiety twisted in my stomach. The prospect of another confrontation loomed over me like a thundercloud, and the sheer thought sent waves of dread coursing through my veins. It baffled me how two people could muster the energy to argue. At the same time, I felt utterly drained—both physically and emotionally, as if my spirit had been siphoned away through sleepless nights.

We hurried into the cool morning air, the world around us still wrapped in an eerie, muted stillness. The day's freshness brushed against my skin, awakening my senses, but my mind was a frantic whirlwind of uncertainty. I turned to Stacey, the worry etched on my face more precise than words could convey. "I don't know what to do," I admitted, my voice shaky, feeling a heavy wave of helplessness over me. My feelings for Kris ran deep like a vast ocean; I loved him with every fiber of my being, and yet watching him suffer was a relentless source of heartache. The exhaustion I was burdened with was not merely from a lack of sleep but from the crushing weight of worry that clung to me like a thick, suffocating cloak, making it hard to breathe as I faced the chaos ahead.

We hurried up the staircase, our hearts pounding, only to find Kris helplessly bound at the ankles, his frantic screams echoing off the walls.

The scene before me was jarring; he had always had a flair for the dramatic, and now it was fully displayed. A wave of desperation surged as I dropped to my knees beside him. My fingers fumbled with the intricate knots that bound him; each twist and turn seemed more complex than the last. "Someone get me some scissors!" I shouted, my voice rising above the chaos, tinged with urgency and fear.

I wrapped my arms around him, trying to offer a small measure of comfort amid his palpable terror, which radiated from him like heat from flames. His eyes were wide, filled with raw panic, and I could feel the tremors of his body against me, each shudder echoing the desperation of the moment.

Casting a sharp, penetrating glare at Marie, who stood motionless in the doorway, I demanded, "What on earth is going on here?" Her silence was deafening, a striking contrast to the chaotic scene playing out around us. Her face was an unreadable mask, betraying none of the turmoil that swirled in the air as she observed us with an unsettling calm.

As we worked to untie the ropes that bound my son, my heart sank at the sight of bruises mottling his delicate skin. Anguish surged within me, igniting a desperate need to uncover who had inflicted such harm. Yet, Marie remained utterly mute; her lips pressed tightly together as if they were sealed.

Kris's words tumbled out in a disjointed rush, his voice trembling with emotion, but they barely registered in my mind. The incoherence of his speech struck me as a symptom of panic, and it took time for the weight of the situation to sink in, leaving me grappling with confusion and dread—only later would I come to understand the horrors that had unfolded.

With just a single glance into his eyes, a chilling realization washed over me: he was somewhere far away, disconnected from the world around him. I felt a surge of urgency and asked, "Kris, who am I?" Without a moment's pause, he responded with an enthusiasm that startled me, "The Last Prophet of the World."

I pressed further, "No, who am I?" His expression shifted to one of confusion, and then, in a soft yet relieved whisper, he murmured, "Mom."

A warmth spread through my chest as I replied, "Yes, baby, I love you." But then his demeanor shifted abruptly. Desperation crept into his voice as he cried, "Oh God, forgive me, help me." He sank back into the bed, and for a fleeting moment, I believed he was beginning to find his calm.

I turned sharply toward Marie, who lingered in the doorway, her expression unreadable. I stepped closer, the tension palpable in the air, and once again demanded, "What is going on?"

She then shouted, "Is he breathing?" My entire body felt like a heavy weight pressing down on me; I was in shock. In a daze, I dashed over to him and noticed his shirt had been removed. I quickly scanned his chest, my heart racing: was he breathing? There was no rise or fall; it was eerily still.

My staff members carefully turned him onto the bed, their expressions a mix of urgency and fear as they began administering CPR. The rhythm of their hands continued a desperate hope against the odds. Simultaneously, someone had called Julian, a person with training in medical emergencies whose expertise might be our lifeline.

Meanwhile, I could see my granddaughter on the phone, her face etched with worry as she desperately tried to reach 911, the emergency services in Mexico. With each ring that went unanswered, the tension in the room grew thicker.

I felt an overwhelming need to act. I refused to stand idly by while time slipped away. Determined, I sprinted down two flights of stairs, the distance feeling like a mile, and burst through the entrance gate that led to the school's exterior, my gaze scanning frantically for anyone who could help. I raised my arms, trying to flag down a passerby, desperate for assistance in this crisis.

My arms flailed wildly in a desperate attempt to attract attention, signaling for help. Two police cars zipped by, their flashing lights a blur, but neither vehicle stopped. Panic surged through me as I dashed back upstairs, my heart pounding. When I reached the room, I found Kris lying on the floor, his condition strikingly worse than before.

With fear etched on her face, my granddaughter informed me that she had called a friend whose father was a paramedic. As soon as he learned about the situation, he hastily approached us. I was told he was coming from Guadalajara, a daunting 30 miles away, but in my anxious mind, I could only hope he would arrive in time. When he finally walked through the door, a wave of relief washed over me; I could see the determination in his eyes. I knew then that there was still hope—that he could use a defibrillator to jolt Kris's heart back to life.

When the Paramedic finally arrived, I felt a wave of relief wash over me, but my heart sank as I noticed he wasn't using the defibrillator. I gathered the courage to ask whether they planned to use it, only to be informed with a hint of frustration that their ambulances were not equipped with such crucial equipment. Their primary mission was solely to transport emergencies to the hospitals in Guadalajara, leaving me feeling helpless.

As the Paramedic focused intently on his duties, the sound of rushing footsteps signaled the arrival of the Police. Their urgency was palpable as they began ushering us out of the room, clearly needing space to work on Kris. I wanted to protest, to stand my ground, but I was gently yet firmly guided out. I found myself lingering in the doorway, a painful knot tightening in my stomach as the reality of the situation hit me. I couldn't shake the thought: how would I possibly break the news to Jason that his dad was gone? The weight of that impending conversation loomed over me like a dark cloud, and I felt utterly lost at that moment.

I'm unsure who went to fetch Jason, but it might have been my granddaughters. Just moments later, I heard the unmistakable sound of a truck door slamming shut, followed by Jason's hurried footsteps as he raced up the stairs. Bursting through the door, he let out a primal scream that pierced through my heart: "DAD! NO DAD!"

In that instant, an overwhelming wave of anguish consumed me. My entire body trembled as the agony of losing my son washed over me like a relentless tide. I felt utterly helpless, unsure of how to provide any solace to my distraught grandson.

Frantically, Jason burst through the double doors of the building, his heart pounding as he raced toward the dimly lit exterior school restrooms. Each hurried step echoed the turbulence swirling within him, and I could almost feel the weight of his despair pressing down on my chest. Later, I would learn that he had thrown himself against the unforgiving brick wall, his fists pounding relentlessly as his anguished cries of "DAD!" rang out like a haunting symphony of grief, reverberating in the air long after the sound had dissipated, a painful reminder of his loss.

Once the officials had finally completed their solemn duties, I sank to my knees beside my son. Tears spilled down my cheeks as I sobbed inconsolably, each cry a desperate plea for comfort. "Oh God, please help me," I whimpered, the words tumbling from my lips like a prayer cast into a vast, empty void. Again and again, I repeated that heartfelt plea, clinging to the hope that, somehow, I could find the strength to face this unfathomable pain. I looked up into the heavens, my heart aching, and whispered, "God, I need you. I don't know how to handle this one."

After a little while, Jason's voice echoed from the dimly lit stairway, tinged with uncertainty as he called to Grandma, "Is it okay if I go home?" I nodded gently, reassuring him with a soft "Yes." He hesitated momentarily before asking, "Can someone take me home?" I replied warmly, "Yes, sweetheart, I promise someone will be there for you, so you won't have to face this alone." He sighed, his small shoulders drooping slightly, "I am just going to be in my room."

Noticing Jason's distress, Marie offered to accompany him back to the house, her presence a comforting promise that he wouldn't have to face his worries alone. I appreciated her kindness and took a deep breath, preparing to guide her through the necessary steps for handling the procedures in Mexico when a loved one passes away. It was a heavy topic, but I knew it was vital for her to understand the process ahead.

I remained curled up on the floor, my heart shattered as I wept uncontrollably, my eyes fixed on the stillness of my baby. The reality of his absence felt surreal, a heavy weight crushing my chest—I could hardly comprehend that he was truly gone.

As soon as the unimaginable occurred, I dialed JD's number, my hands trembling with grief. His voice was choked with sorrow when he answered; the bond between him and Kris was unbreakable, forged not just by blood but by years of laughter and countless shared moments. The loss weighed heavily on both our hearts.

Radiating determination and despair, Marie insisted she needed to be there for Jason, believing he needed her support in this difficult time. I understood the urgency in her eyes and reassured her it was important she take a moment for herself, but I urged her to return as swiftly as possible.

When Jason finally walked through the door, he seemed almost a shadow of himself, empty and distant. He retreated to his room in a heavy silence. Desperate to connect, Marie reached out to him, but he recoiled further into his shell, his voice icy as he declared he didn't want to see her.

As chaos enveloped the world outside, Stacey stood rigid, clutching the urgent instructions from the Police. Their demands for us to complete the necessary paperwork served as a chilling reminder of the grim reality we were facing—a reality that weighed heavily upon us as we confronted the unthinkable act of surrendering Kris's body. It was a thought so unbearable that we struggled to comprehend its finality.

Desperate to reach Marie, I grabbed my phone and dialed her number urgently. Each ring echoed my concern, but the call went unanswered. Frustration built within me as I continuously tried, my mind racing. Finally, I reached out to Samantha, urgently asking her to relay my message to Marie. We needed to focus and handle our affairs, no matter how daunting they felt.

Samantha's voice came back, laced with a hint of confusion. She informed me that Marie had left the house only moments after arriving, almost as if she were fleeing from the weight of the situation. My heart sank when I learned that Marie had chosen to walk away. "I thought maybe she was headed back to the school," Samantha speculated, her tone uncertain.

I turned to Stacey, my expression grave as I relayed the troubling news. "No one seems to know where she is," I said, the words heavy with concern. "She just walked out after she got there. Jason didn't want to see his mom, so she left." The uncertainty hung in the air, thick and oppressive, as we both grappled with the fact that Marie was now alone, her path unknown in a world suddenly filled with chaos.

In Mexico, specific protocols must be followed when a person passes away, especially as a United States citizen. The first step involves obtaining a doctor's verification indicating that death resulted from natural causes.

On that fateful day, we made frantic calls to various doctors' offices, desperate for assistance, but it was still too early for anyone to respond. The situation's urgency weighed heavily on us; the doctors needed to arrive at the school to ensure no foul play had occurred. The atmosphere was tense, and the presence of the Police only intensified the pressure, as they insisted we secure a doctor before they could take the body away. Their lack of empathy during such a traumatic moment was palpable, leaving us feeling even more alone in our grief.

As I sat in the sterile waiting area, the minutes dragged on like hours, stretching the very fabric of time. Every tick of the clock echoed in my mind, intensifying the weight of uncertainty. I glanced at Marie's vacant chair, feeling anxious that I could no longer postpone making decisions. A kind-hearted paramedic approached my granddaughter, his demeanor calm and reassuring. He knelt beside her, his voice gentle as he explained that it was time for us to head to the hospital. He shared that he knew the doctor on duty well and seemed confident we would receive the urgent help we desperately needed.

Hours had slipped away since Kris's sudden passing, and as dawn broke outside, the world began to awaken. Local businesses slowly lifted their shutters, their signs swaying gently in the morning breeze, an odd contrast to the turmoil that enveloped us. Just under three miles from the school, a small non-emergency clinic was gearing up to assist patients, offering a faint, flickering hope amid the chaos that had invaded our lives.

Entering the clinic, a wave of unfamiliarity washed over us. I was still trapped in a state of shock, my mind foggy, unable to process the reality of our situation fully. It felt like I was moving on autopilot, mechanically going through the motions without truly comprehending the gravity of the details unfolding around me. Beside me, Stacey remained steadfast, her presence a silent testament to our shared anguish. I could see her struggle reflected in her eyes, yet she persevered, navigating the turmoil with quiet determination.

Finally, we needed to find a doctor who could complete the necessary paperwork required by the Police. With that goal in mind, we made our way to the clinic's inner sanctum. When the Paramedic entered, he headed straight for the doctor's office, urging us to wait while he spoke with the physician.

We stood in anxious anticipation, the minutes dragging on as the Paramedic and doctor conferred behind closed doors for what felt like an eternity—twenty or thirty minutes stretched out, amplifying our apprehension. When the Paramedic finally emerged and beckoned us inside, I felt my heart race as I entered the doctor's office.

The atmosphere was clinical, the walls adorned with medical charts and diagrams. I was met with probing questions that intensified my grief. "What is your relationship with Kris?" the doctor inquired. "I am his mother," I replied, my voice barely a whisper, heavy with sorrow.

Then came the question I dreaded, "Is Kris married?" My heart sank further; his partner's whereabouts were unknown, lost in the day's chaos. I was handed a stack of paperwork, and with trembling hands, I was instructed to sign. Each stroke of my pen felt like a painful farewell, a chilling acknowledgment of the void now etched into my life.

CHAPTER EIGHTEEN
Kris was Murdered on May 28, 2020

The first step in preparing for Kris's burial was complete. We now needed to return to the school and provide the Police with the paperwork. Julian and Phillipe flew into Mexico and would arrive in Guadalajara in a few hours.

I wanted to stay with Kris as much as possible before we buried him. I kept sitting on the floor next to his body. In my spiritual position, God had allowed me to pray for those who were dead, and they came back to life. Now, here I sat beside the body of my son, asking God why he wouldn't allow me to bring him back.

I knew how much God loved me; he had always been at my side. I had seen God raise my husband from the dead and, several years later, tell me he was going to take him home. But God didn't prepare me for this one.

I never felt betrayed or that God let me down. All I could do was ask him why my baby. Later, the answer to that question would come, but not then.

Throughout the day, I tried to call Marie; I couldn't figure out what had happened to her.

I trained my Staff to provide incident reports on everything that transpired in my life when dealing with people. I only counseled people with witnesses present. This day would not be any different. All my senior Staff were there except Julian, who would soon be there.

I called Phillipe at 7:35 a.m. and told him that Kris was gone. Phillipe and Julian caught the next available flight out of DFW

International Airport at 10:50 a.m. and would arrive at 1:30 p.m. As the time approached to go to Guadalajara International Airport to pick Julian and Phillipe up, I called Jason. I asked if he wanted to ride to Guadalajara to pick them up. He said yes.

Stacey and I went by the house to pick up Jason, and right before we passed the school, I told Stacey to stop by first. I wanted to see what was going on.

When we were at the school, while the catastrophe was going on, I noticed how everything was a mess, with things scattered, broken, and destroyed. You could tell there was a fight, so I asked the team to try straightening things up. When I returned to the school, I saw the progress, and my granddaughter came out to the truck. She whispered something to Stacey, and when I said I was going upstairs, they told me that wasn't a good idea. I opened the truck door and went upstairs anyway.

When I went into the room where Kris's body lay, he hadn't been moved. Nothing, everything was just as it was when the Police were there. This time, what I saw was mindboggling: Kris was now lying in a pool of blood around his head. The Staff told me they didn't touch anything and found Kris when they gathered the cleaning supplies and returned to the room. Determined not to touch anything, they just closed the door.

I told them I was going to the airport to pick up the guys and would deal with this as soon as I returned. I had to think about what was going on. How could this be? Why was there now blood around Kris's head?

On our way back to Jocotepec, the guys listened to what had happened in the last six hours. I sat quietly, gathering my thoughts and trying to sort out the nightmare. I had to sort out what had happened when we arrived at the school. That's when I heard two individuals say that they had heard Marie say she didn't mean to hit him in the head twice. I stopped them and said, "What did you say?" Julian put on gloves and went into the body to take pictures, and we felt that we might need all the evidence we could gather.

I still had to make arrangements to bury my son. In Mexico, this is not an easy task, unlike in the United States, where you first contact a Funeral Home and then go to make the final arrangements, which can be challenging. In Mexico, I would need to find the cheapest wooden coffin, and we would have to dress him, place him in the coffin, sealing the coffin during the time that is being prepared; you have to get the death certificate from the doctor, register the death with the city officials find a burial plot and gravediggers.

We have Jewish burials, and that means there will not be any embalming.

I lived on a fixed income and had no idea how I was going to accomplish burying my son.

How would I be able to afford a place to bury him? I was told they don't sell plots in the area of Mexico we were in, and you can rent it by the year; after a set period, when the lease is up, they dispose of the bones and lease it out to another family. If you miss a payment, then the body is immediately exhumed and disposed of without any knowledge of where it will be taken. I called a friend of the family and asked him what to do. This amazing man and his wife told me that they had space in their family vault, and we could bury my son there. I asked him how much, and he said Your family is my family, no cost. I broke down in tears. He had met Kris and said that Kris was a fantastic man and very intelligent and that he and his wife wanted to do this for us.

I met this family through my mom when she lived in Mexico. The gentleman was her mechanic, and she had known them for years. Salvador and Rebecca loved my mom.

He had me go to their business, and when I arrived, I was given paperwork that allowed me to bury my son. Look how amazing God is. When the door was closed, he opened one I never expected. While I was getting the place to bury Kris, the Staff found a coffin and purchased it for me. Now Kris's death was registered, his wooden coffin was purchased, and a fantastic family provided his final resting place.

Julian and Phillipe would have the most challenging task. They were going to prepare Kris's body and place him in the coffin. I am curious to know how they did that. Phillipe was Kris's close friend when they were eight years old. Kris invited Phillipe to church and ensured that I picked him and his brother up every time they were allowed to attend church.

Now, thirty years later, he was helping me to prepare his body for burial. Julian had been there for Kris through tough times. Julian was like a son to me; now he is standing at my side again as I go through this horror.

While examining Kris's body, we saw what appeared to be wounds from a screwdriver, puncture wounds. Now, I will look around the room and try to summarize what happened that morning. Could this be the reason that Marie was gone? I don't recall which staff member took the pictures and pointed out the blood splatters around the room.

Then they found the hammer, and on the hammer was blood. Now, we knew this was no accident. It was murder. By this time, I was blowing up the phone, trying to call Marie, but she refused to answer.

We were in a foreign country and unable to contact the authorities. Calling the United States Embassy was impossible. The telephone would ring, but no one returned the calls. We were amid COVID-19. I told the Staff to take as many pictures as possible from every angle of the room, especially of Kris's wounds. One way or another, I would get justice for my son.

Kris had been dead for 24 hours. Things had been a whirlwind, everything flashing fast at me while I was trying to get my son buried.

Now, to reexamine what had just happened. The questions were rushing in like a flood. How did this happen? I looked at the pictures that were taken at the crime scene. Did Marie kill him? Then, as the reports came in about others being told by Marie that she didn't mean to hit him in the head with the hammer twice?

While the Staff was taking pictures, they discovered that there was a form of rat poison that was taken to get high, along with other drugs, paraphilia, and alcohol. We had no clue what we were looking for. They just took pictures, and then later, they searched on the internet to find out the details of what the side effects were when taking these drugs.

It is evident that Marie had fled the country and returned to the States. She knew that we would not rest until we knew what had happened.

Kris was killed on Thursday, May 28th, 2020, my birthday is May 31st

Chapter Nineteen
Justice for Kris

This book offers a stark and unsettling portrayal of Kris, yet it falls short of delving into the intricate layers of his character. In contrast, I explore those deeper complexities and untold stories in my work, Trapped in Another Dimension.

Kris's son, Jason, was in his room. I occasionally knocked on the door to check on him and see if he needed anything.

Ninety days after arriving in Mexico, my dear Kris is gone. On May 29th, 2020, I will take my final journey in this life with my son. I knew Friday, May 29th, would be the most challenging day for both of us.

I never had the chance to see Kris in the casket. After the guys finished preparing him, they sealed the casket without asking me, and it left me feeling powerless. The haunting image of my son on the floor, surrounded by blood, is something I'll never be able to forget.

I understand that Julian and Phillipe didn't intend to cause me further pain by sealing the casket. This tragedy has deeply affected them as well. Early that morning, I set out with the hope of seeing my son one last time, only to find that Julian and Phillipe had already closed the coffin.

Now, the final memory I hold of Kris is the heartbreaking sight of him lying on the floor.

Those moments will be imprinted in my mind, and I carry that weight daily.

I returned to the room where he was killed and then went to my office on the same floor.

Later today, the hearse will arrive to collect his body and transport it to the cemetery.

I brought him into the world, cradling the tiny, fragile being in my arms, and later bore witness to his departure from this dimension. I found myself unprepared to confront the tumultuous aftermath of what unfolded in that room; all I longed for was to accompany him on that final journey into the unknown. Years ago, I understood that God orchestrates everything intentionally, inflicting neither heartache nor pain. As the night unfurled, I settled into my recliner, the fabric worn and comforting against my back, and the haunting memories of Thursday replayed in my mind like a sad film that would not pause.

JD and his family were not here, and I didn't want him to witness what was happening. I knew how it would affect him; his rage would drive him to seek revenge, and I didn't need that right now. JD had expressed to me that losing his brother was the worst thing that could happen. He said, "Mom, before Dad died, he asked me to watch over my little brother and to take care of you." Then, JD added that he felt he had failed in both responsibilities. I told him that his Dad should never have put such a burden on him as a young boy, asking him to take care of us if something ever happened to him.

Questions raced through my mind. Although I wasn't prepared to see the pictures, I wanted to know what they had discovered. Once we confirmed that foul play had occurred in that room, the doors were closed, and nothing was disturbed to preserve potential evidence for the authorities. They had taken numerous photographs, and I needed to comprehend what had happened in that room.

Did Marie kill Kris? Is that why she fled the country and left her son, Jason, with me? I needed to gather all the evidence I could find.

If Marie were responsible for Kris's death, I would make sure she was prosecuted and sent to prison for murder.

As I waited at the school for the undertakers to bring the hearse, I felt my body weaken. Each step was challenging, and I kept looking up to the heavens, asking God for strength. In the past 24 hours, I have heard from a few friends in the States. I received a phone call from Betty and Omer Whayne. I had met them when I wrote my first book, "Be Ye Holy." Betty worked for the Pentecostal Publishing House, and they traveled from St. Louis to Dallas several times to visit us.

What Omer said on the phone had a significant impact on me. He expressed how much he loved Kris, especially when he struggled to perform in front of a crowd with his guitar and singing. Kris believed in Omer and recognized his talent, assuming the world needed to hear it. He encouraged Omer to confront his fears and stand for God.

What made this so remarkable was that Kris was a young man, while Omer was much older and felt it was too late for him to embrace his passion for singing country gospel. Omer told me that Kris's words profoundly changed him. He said that if it hadn't been for Kris, he wouldn't be singing for the Lord today.

I reflected on all the lives Kris touched. When I started the church, he was enthusiastic about getting everyone to attend Sunday School. When I purchased Kris and JD their first car, I remember Kris loading it up with as many street kids as possible and bringing them to church. He used scripture to persuade them to come.

At times, while in the pulpit, Kris would come through the front doors with six or more gang members, which was exciting. I don't know how he managed it, but those young men came in and were all very respectful.

Kris had a remarkable gift for persuasion and was loved by everyone he met.

Marie had not always been cruel. I immediately knew why my son loved her when I first met her. I recall the first time Kris spoke about her. He said, "Mom, I want to get married." I asked him when, and he said this weekend.

He wanted me to meet her and said, "Mom, prepare yourself. She has a few tattoos."

Then he followed up, but she was unique and kind. I thought, how bad can that be? I have never judged a book by its cover, not that of a person, without getting to know them.

I told Kris to bring her over to meet me. I was not prepared for the young woman who walked through my door. One look at her, and my first thought was my position and how people would view her. My preparation was then that I stepped back and looked at the person, not the artwork. That was a real test of character.

Marie walked through the door and looked like a mural, with tattoos covering her body. I am sure my shocked reaction must have been noticed. I stood looking at a young woman a few inches shorter than me, and I could see her sweet kindness in her eyes. At that point, I had forgotten the canvas that covered her body.

Kris and Marie were married within a week after I met her.

Stacey, along with several members of my staff, helped me put together a fantastic wedding. Since she had no money or a wedding dress, I allowed her to wear mine, which I wore when I married Robbie.

Marie had come from a terrible background. My Staff and I prepared everything for the wedding. Marie's mother had been invited to help us, but was far away. I had Marie go to the church to get dressed and prepare for the grand occasion in the back office.

My staff helped her with the festivities, and when I checked how things were going, she looked radiant. Marie asked me, "Is my mom here?" I told her, "No," and she said, "Can we wait before starting? I want my mom here." I told her no problem; we would wait. I want this day to be extraordinary.

After waiting over an hour, I told her that the guests were getting restless and that we needed to start. She said okay, and we started the music. At the beginning of the wedding, the church's front doors opened, and I saw a woman staggering down the aisle headed for the front. I watched to see what was going on.

It was her mother walking up to her at the altar. I stood there waiting for her mother to finish talking to Marie. Afterward, she took a seat, and the wedding continued.

When I started to get to know Marie, I found out what a terrible life she had lived. Her mother was never there, and Marie was not given any structure. When they could find a place to live, it was usually a vacant building with no walls or insulation. Marie wasn't provided for. She never had clothes and was raised on the streets. Marie's grandfather was the head of the drug cartel in Oak Cliff. I never met him, but I heard of some of the crimes he was a part of.

As I turned around to look out the window, my mind flashed to my precious grandson.

He was born because Adonai directed me to why Jason's mother couldn't have children.

Marie and Kris had wanted children, and when she got pregnant, she had a miscarriage.

After losing the first baby, Marie and Kris tried again unsuccessfully. That's when the Lord spoke to me and told me that Marie had a medical condition and what was going wrong.

I gave Marie the information, and she went to the doctor and told him what I had said. The doctor examined her and found out that I was correct. That is when surgery was performed to help her carry a baby. Not long after, Jason was conceived.

For the years I had been there for Kris and Marie, I knew her life story and had a great deal of compassion. I was not willing to believe that she intentionally murdered my son.

Now, as I sit in my office dealing with all of the emotions, not knowing where Marie is, I have to continue to take care of burying my son. I was now at the school, sitting upstairs in my office, waiting for Kris's final journey.

When Marie arrived in Mexico, the heat was unbearable, so I offered her my office, which had an air conditioner to keep her comfortable. As I looked around the room, memories flooded my mind, reminding me of my time with Marie.

I needed to understand what occurred at the school that led to this tragic murder. The young woman I met when Kris introduced us was not the same person she eventually became. I can only attribute this change to the party lifestyle filled with drugs and alcohol.

After Jason was born and the success of Kris's business flourished, everything changed.

Although Kris's family lived nearby, I seldom saw them. Marie became another person somewhere and at some time, and I know where things shifted. The book Trapped in Another Dimension addresses that.

For years, Marie had not been a mother to Jason; she wasn't nurturing or involved. Kris cared for his son when he was born, not Marie, and provided for his basic emotional needs.

Marie stayed messed up to the point that teaching Jason how to take care of himself or even sending him to school was not consistent.

When Marie would be abusive, I didn't hear about that until after Kris and Jason moved in with me, and sometimes Jason would tell me of things that happened. Jason loved his Dad and wanted to spend every minute of the day with him. It was beautiful to see how Kris took care of Jason. The love between the two of them was apparent. My son was an excellent father, taking care of every need.

Jason stayed at my house, waiting for the call to meet us outside the cemetery while I went to school.

I left my office and sat in my library, which had large windows facing the school's front entrance. I was frozen when I saw the hearse backing up from the front gate. I wanted to stop this nightmare and turn back the hands of time.

That's when someone came in to get me and told me the hearse was here, and my heart sank. I grabbed the table and slowly made my way down the stairs. When I got to the foot of the stairs, I watched them walk out of the school with my son's casket. I stood there shaking my head and saying God, please give me strength.

They put Kris's body up in the back of the vehicle and started pulling out of the driveway.

The cemetery was challenging to get to. It was located at the end of the block, and there was no parking. The predominant religion in Mexico is Catholic, and when someone from that area dies, their last rites are given in the large Catholic church, which is several blocks from the cemetery. Then, the family and friends walk behind the casket.

We parked the truck and waited a few minutes for the caretakers to prepare to carry Kris to the crypt. In Mexico, families have crypts where they bury their loved ones together.

Salvador and Rebecca had given me a place in their family crypt to bury Kris.

I had to hire workers to open the grave. Those men had shown up earlier to open the top of the vault. We followed the caretakers to the area where Kris would be buried. Men were waiting to position his coffin into the vault. That was very interesting. The vault was deep, and several other bodies were already in there. The men had to reposition those coffins to make room for Kris. That was a challenging task and took a while. Yet when we walked up to the vault, it was open. I would only leave Kris once he was sealed into the vault.

These vaults are unique, as they are viewed from the top. There is a concrete slab over the top with a small opening that looks like a door. Through that door, they lower the next coffin. I watched as they strapped the coffin to drop it into the hole. They were struggling to get Kriss's coffin in position, so Julian and Phillipe stood on top of the slab and helped lower him.

After Kris's body was in the vault, I stood there for a bit longer, and then Jason said Grandma, can we go home? I told him yes.

Later that day, I received a call and was told that Marie had just posted on social media that she was crossing the border and was glad to return to Texas. There was nothing about Kris dying. I knew she was on the run but had yet to learn where she would be headed. Until then, I had held back judgment, giving her every excuse or benefit of the doubt. Once I was told that and it was verified, I was determined to find out what had happened in that room.

At this moment, I am compelled to bring attention to the issue of Justice for Kris. It is important to emphasize that, throughout this distressing ordeal, there were only two genuinely innocent individuals: Jason and I. We have found ourselves caught in a devastating situation that has profoundly affected our lives, and the focus must remain on the real victims who deserve justice and understanding amidst the turmoil.

In the beginning, I wanted Marie incarcerated and sentenced to life without the possibility of parole. Now that I reflect on the story, both Kris and Marie were already sentenced to life.

They find themselves trapped in the sinister grasp of Satan and the evil schemes that have wreaked havoc on countless lives. Although I cannot bring Kris back into this world, I am determined to pursue justice, not directed at Marie alone, but at the higher echelons of those responsible.

The individuals who operate this evil empire, which has devastated countless families, should be held accountable for their actions. How can this be accomplished? First, through education, starting at kindergarten and continuing through higher education.

Let them face the consequences of their sinister plots by revealing the truth about the effects of drugs, alcohol, and smoking. We must continuously highlight the devastation and repercussions of today's party lifestyle.

It's impossible to watch any program without being subconsciously encouraged to engage in drinking and drug use. Once frowned upon, these activities are now glorified across all forms of media.

These harmful influences instill fear in many and ruin the lives of countless innocent people. It's time to expose their wrongdoings and seek justice for those whose lives have been shattered.

The education system needs to be restructured to teach children from early childhood about the consequences of engaging in a party lifestyle. Instead of promoting these images on social media, where people are constantly influenced to pursue harmful behaviors, we should educate them about the adverse effects of such choices.

The saddest part is that nothing will ever be done with the current upper echelon. They not only make money selling destruction but also continue to benefit when a person is incarcerated, making money on those in permanent lockdown.

Adonai gives everyone a choice to serve Him. However, Satan has clouded the minds of the world, so people are attracted to the end game.

Adonai is a just God who knows a man's heart, while I am limited to the depth of an individual's soul. From my viewpoint, Adonai will bring justice to every situation, including the loss of my son Kris. He is absent from me but forever present with God. To me, that is justice. Kris had been handed a life sentence from Satan through addictions, and Adonai set him free, giving him eternal life in the beauty of God's love.

I assembled my staff, and our investigation started. Samantha had already begun researching the pictures, looking up on the internet the side effects of the drugs found in the room. The one room that wasn't checked was my office, where Marie had stayed.

Somewhere in all the confusion, the journal was found. It belonged to Marie.

What was written was shocking. Marie had pictures and symbols, then a page where she wrote her plans to kill Kris, Jason, and me. The book didn't tell how she planned on doing this. I have always been well protected, so her getting to me would be impossible. With Jason staying with me, we had five watchdogs for our large house. The doors were metal, and the fence was built to separate our home from the neighbors. To get into my yard would be virtually impossible. The dogs were dangerous, and most of them were Rottweilers.

Sabbath had just begun. For at least twenty years, we have kept the Sabbath. We gathered at the school to have a service, and since I had touched a dead body, I couldn't teach, nor could my assistant, who had prepared the body. Everyone in the group was emotionally beaten. I decided to have time to share our memories; this would be the only funeral I would have for my son.

There are five stages to the mourning process in the Jewish Religion: 1) Aninut, pre-burial mourning. 2-3) Shivah, seven days following the burial; within the Shivah, the first three days are characterized by a more intense mourning. 4) Shloshim, the 30-day mourning period. 5) The First Year (observed only by the children of the deceased).

Attempting to follow this was impossible; I decided to use this period to find out if my son was murdered. I didn't want to falsely accuse anyone, especially Jason's Mom.

I called my staff and told them to bring all the pictures. I wanted to review what had been discovered. At that point, I told them I didn't want Jason to see the images or know what was happening. I wasn't going to say to him that I suspected his mom had killed his Dad. The only problem was that Jason was very observant, and I wasn't sure how to keep this from him. I had the staff transfer the pictures to me, and I put them on my private computer in my bedroom. Jason was never on that computer. He didn't have the password, so I felt confident he wouldn't have to deal with this. Little did I know that, eventually, he would go into my bedroom and find the pictures.

Within days, we knew for a fact that Marie had killed my son. Not only had she made the statement to two witnesses that she didn't mean to hit him twice in the head with a hammer, but she also had her handwritten plans to kill all three of us. There was one piece of the puzzle that I couldn't figure out. How was it when the Police were in the room with the paramedic, there wasn't a pool of blood around his head?

I knew that I had to get the death certificate changed. How was I going to do that?

Immediately, I went to Salvador and Rebecca. I knew they were related to the town president, but didn't consider that Salvador was going to their cousin, who was the municipal president of the town, to inquire how to change the death certificate. I wanted to know what it would require to ensure justice was served.

Salvador went to the municipal president and told him the situation. Salvador was told he could get it changed, but there would be massive consequences if he did. Then, he started to explain the procedure.

I was told we had to start with the doctor's statement, which would have to be corrected. When that happened, the doctor would be arrested and lose his license.

Then, everyone involved with his burial, along with all who were present at the school during that time, would be arrested.

No matter how much I wanted justice for my son. Marie had already caused a great deal of suffering. There was no way that I could allow innocent people to be incarcerated.

They would exhume the body and send it to Guadalajara to the medical examiner. At that point, I would never know what was done with the body. I could not have Kris cut up and disposed of.

When Salvador was told this, his cousin said, "You and your wife would also be arrested for providing a place to bury the young man."

The municipal president also told Salvador that the paramedic would be arrested.

That everyone would remain in jail until the murder was solved.

I had already sent an email to the US Embassy in Guadalajara, and according to the internet, they were closed due to COVID-19, and only the Embassy in Mexico City was working remotely.

After weeks, someone responded to my email and then called me. I explained the situation and told them that I needed to register my son's death with the State Department and was required to receive copies. They told me okay and later told me that Marie had contacted Social Security and filed for benefits for her and Jason. The crazy part about this, at this point, was that she had once again abandoned Jason, this time amid his Dad's death.

The only problem was that Jason had lived off and on between me and his Dad since he was nine. Kris had filed for a divorce. Marie signed the papers, but they weren't finalized, so technically, she was still married to Kris.

It had only been a few days when Marie called me and said Mom, I didn't kill Kris. I swear I didn't kill him. I said Why did you leave?

She then hung up the phone. That was the last time I heard from her. She never asked where Kris was buried or if I needed anything.

At that point, I knew she would try to get Jason for the Social Security money. I didn't know how she planned to do that since Jason had been with me for five years.

That was the least of my concerns. I had supported Jason in purchasing his clothes and paying for whatever he needed or wanted. I didn't consider this a burden. Jason was my miracle grandson sent by God.

Jason had gotten involved with working out and studying self-defense. One day, we were talking, and Jason asked me this question: Grandma, do you know what it is like to know that your mother has killed your father? I said no, I can't imagine. He then said I hate her and never want to see her again.

Realizing there was nothing I could do about Kris's murder, I focused my attention on remodeling the school. I was determined to open the facility as a way of connecting with Kris since the last thing we talked about the night before he was killed was opening the school for those in need.

Chapter Twenty
Does ObamaCare?

I am not a medical professional. The insights and opinions presented in my books are based on my experiences and understanding. A higher power inspires my insights, and I share these reflections to provide perspective rather than medical advice.

The topic of ObamaCare demands deeper exploration, especially regarding its societal implications.

It raises important questions about our values and attitudes when the act of murder is perceived as a matter of convenience. This situation prompts critical reflection on how healthcare decisions intersect with ethical considerations in our society.

Infanticide and abortion are complex and emotionally charged issues that raise significant ethical and moral questions. The argument often centers around a woman's right to choose.

While it's important to acknowledge this right, it is equally vital to consider the responsibilities that accompany such choices. Individuals should reflect on their lifestyles and the potential consequences of their actions, particularly regarding unplanned pregnancies and the decision to have children. Understanding these responsibilities can promote informed and thoughtful decision-making.

The institution of marriage is often associated with the significant responsibility of raising children, a rewarding and transformative task. Children are usually seen as a remarkable gift that brings new dynamics to family life, fostering deeper connections and offering lessons in partnership, love, and mutual respect. Each child is born with a unique potential, like a blank canvas, ready to engage with the world around them. How we nurture and guide these young individuals significantly influences their development and perception of life. Like older photographic techniques, where images take time to develop, children's lives evolve gradually, shaped by the actions, attitudes, and influences of those around them.

Research indicates that infants have a remarkable ability to sense and absorb their surroundings, including the emotions and behaviors of those around them, even before they can articulate their thoughts. This innate capacity highlights their inherent qualities of love and joy.

However, there is a growing concern that society often deviates from foundational principles and values, resulting in a focus on immediate and self-serving desires.

This disconnection from what may be seen as a higher purpose can manifest in various ways, including controversial legislation affecting the treatment of elderly and disabled individuals.

Such developments raise essential questions about societal values and priorities in caring for vulnerable populations.

In contemporary society, there is a diminishing respect for life. This concern is highlighted by the prevalent attitudes toward innocent lives and the treatment of older people, with calls to disregard them. Furthermore, one must consider the fate of young men sent off to war.

It is crucial to reflect on the long-term consequences of such attitudes and actions on our communities and the future of our society.

The question of when individuals worldwide contemplate Adonai's intentions for human existence is significant. Scripture explicitly states a commandment against killing, which raises important considerations about how nations rationalize their actions amidst moral scrutiny. This situation invites reflection on the responsibility of those who claim to love God and why there seems to be a lack of active opposition to the violence and disorder that permeate our societies.

How do we do that? By removing wicked politicians from office and making men accountable. If the United States is known as a Christian society and the Christians make up approximately 3 billion people, what is the excuse?

The separation of church and state raises an essential question about the role of religion in government. It suggests the idea of a nation that operates independently of religious influence. This principle aims to ensure that governmental decisions are made without the influence of religious doctrines, allowing for a diverse society where individuals can practice different faiths or none at all.

The separation of church and state has roots in early American history, with notable figures like Roger Williams and Thomas Jefferson playing critical roles in shaping the idea.

Roger Williams (1644):

•Founder of Rhode Island: He established the first Baptist church in America and founded the colony of Rhode Island, where religious freedom was a central principle.

•"Wall of Separation": He advocated for a "wall or hedge of separation" between the secular world and the church, believing that government involvement in religion would corrupt both.

Thomas Jefferson (1802):

•"Wall of Separation": In a letter to the Danbury Baptist Association, Jefferson described the First Amendment's Establishment Clause as a "wall of separation between church and state."

•Protection of Religious Liberty: He emphasized the importance of protecting religious liberty for all citizens, regardless of their faith or lack thereof.

Key Influences:

•Puritan Era: The Puritan colonies in New England had a strong connection between church and state, which led to intolerance and persecution of dissenting religious views.

•Enlightenment Philosophy: Thinkers like John Locke emphasized individual liberty and the separation of powers, influencing the American founders' thinking.

Modern Interpretations:

The separation of church and state has evolved, with various interpretations and debates.

While the exact meaning of the phrase is subject to ongoing legal and political discussions, it generally refers to the principle that the government should not establish a state religion or favor one religion over another. It also implies that the government should not interfere with the religious practices of individuals or religious institutions as long as they do not violate the law.

A world without the influence of Adonai is nothing but a prison. Where are those who live and serve God? Are they hiding in the background, afraid of being noticed?

Regarding ObamaCare, the nation was sidelined in the decision-making process regarding international health care; only politicians were consulted.

In 2020, a single individual emerged as a pivotal figure, leading to a significant halt in activities across an entire nation. The global atmosphere was dominated by a pervasive fear of death, prompting individuals to reflect on their existence and mortality. This fear raised profound questions about humanity's relationship with life and the potential encounter with a higher power.

Did the health directives that originated with ObamaCare evolve into the guidelines that shaped our response to the COVID-19 pandemic?

The first confirmed case of COVID-19 in the United States was reported on January 20th, 2020.

In the United States, the first coronavirus-related activity restrictions were issued on March 12th, 2020, when a community within New Rochelle, New York, was declared a "containment area." A traditional quarantine order would require individuals presumed to be exposed to stay at home. This containment order was not intended to limit individual movement.

Instead, it mandated closing schools and prominent gathering places within the zone, including religious buildings.

Residents could enter and leave the containment zone but not gather in large groups within the designated geographic area.

On March 16th, 2020, a "shelter-in-place" order was issued for six San Francisco Bay Area counties. Shelter in place was a term many Californians were familiar with due to its use during wildfires and other natural disasters, active shooter drills, and other short-term emergencies. In those contexts, "shelter in place" means "stay where you are," but that was not what the COVID-19 orders asked residents to do. The order did not require individuals to stay where they happened to be located when the order was released. Residents were allowed to leave home for essential purposes, including food, medical care, and outdoor exercise, and people working at businesses deemed to be "essential"—such as grocery stores, hospitals, pharmacies, veterinary clinics, utilities, hardware stores, auto repair shops, funeral homes, and warehouses and distribution facilities—were allowed to continue onsite work.

Obamacare (the Affordable Care Act) was not connected to the COVID-19 pandemic. It was a healthcare reform law passed in 2010, long before the emergence of COVID-19.

My dear and thoughtful husband, Karlton, once said, "If you truly wish to understand the motivations behind something, look closely at where the money leads."

However, the Affordable Care Act did play a role in the response to the pandemic in the following ways:

•Increased Health Insurance Coverage: The ACA expanded health insurance coverage to millions of Americans, which helped ensure more people had access to healthcare, including testing and treatment for COVID-19.

•Protection for Pre-Existing Conditions: The ACA prohibited health insurers from denying coverage or charging higher premiums based on pre-existing conditions. This was particularly important for people with underlying health conditions, which made them more vulnerable to severe COVID-19 illness.

•Expanded Medicaid: The ACA expanded Medicaid eligibility, providing health insurance coverage to low-income individuals and families and increasing access to care during the pandemic.

Therefore, while the Affordable Care Act was not the cause of the pandemic, it did play a role in mitigating its impact on the U.S. healthcare system.

The Affordable Care Act, often called ObamaCare, was designed to tackle various challenges in the U.S. healthcare system. One ongoing discussion regarding its implementation involves strategies for controlling costs.

Some critics argue that specific measures could disproportionately impact the elderly population. This concern arises from the belief that older generations have different perspectives on societal values and norms compared to the changing dynamics of contemporary culture.

Who benefited from the pandemic financially? The medical profession

While the medical profession certainly played a crucial role in responding to the pandemic, it's not the only sector that saw financial gains. Here are some of the key beneficiaries:

•Big Tech Companies: Companies like Amazon, Microsoft, Apple, and Zoom saw significant growth as people shifted to remote work and online shopping.

•Pharmaceutical Companies: Companies developing and producing vaccines and treatments for COVID-19 experienced substantial financial benefits.

•E-commerce: Online retailers benefited from increased demand as physical stores were closed or had limited capacity.

•Streaming Services: With people spending more time at home, streaming services like Netflix and Disney+ saw a surge in subscribers.

•Grocery Stores: Essential businesses like grocery stores remained open and saw increased demand for food and household supplies.

It's important to note that the pandemic also devastated many individuals and businesses, leading to job losses, economic hardship, and increased inequality.

Here are some statements involving ObamaCare.

In the spring of 2008, news broke about a new healthcare act affecting those on Medicare and Medicaid. At first, I disregarded the conspiracy theories that the new plan had not come into effect and had not passed Congress. Congress comprises the Senate and the House of Representatives for those not from the United States.

For any new legislation to be active, it must pass both government bodies.

Most of the time, laws are passed, and the general public only learns what is happening once the President signs them. Still, the news is biased, so many details are not included.

Obamacare, aka the Affordable Care Act, I took a personal interest in since this was a form of mercy killing or euthanasia. When the bill passed, I had already researched the topic, and from everything I could find, this would be another way of killing without conscience. The United States had legalized abortion, and everyone's tax dollars paid for this horrible crime without a choice. Now, there is a discussion about killing senior citizens in the bill promoting end-of-life care.

While writing this section, I again reviewed the facts and found this article.

10 Frequently Asked Questions: Medicare's Role in End-of-Life Care Published: September 26th, 2016

About eight of 10 of the 2.6 million people who died in the U.S. in 2014 were people on Medicare, making Medicare the largest insurer of health care provided during the last year of life. Roughly one-quarter of traditional Medicare spending is for services provided to Medicare beneficiaries in their last year of life, and this proportion has remained steady for decades. The high overall cost of health care received in the previous year of life is not surprising, given that many who die have multiple severe and complex conditions.

Aside from cost, several other factors contribute to difficult clinical and policy discussions about whether patients are getting the care they want or need as they approach the end of their lives. Research has found, for example, that most adults (90 percent) say they would prefer to receive end-of-life care in their home if they were terminally ill. Yet, data show that only about one-third of Medicare beneficiaries (age 65 and older) died at home.

In 2016, Medicare began covering advance care planning—discussions that physicians and other health professionals have with their patients regarding end-of-life care and patient preferences—as a separate and billable service. The following 10 Frequently Asked Questions explain Medicare's role in end-of-life care and advance care planning. In addition to defining relevant terms and explaining Medicare's current and future coverage for end-of-life care, these Frequently Asked Questions also describe recent relevant rules released by the Administration and additional proposals from Congress regarding advance care planning and care for people with severe and terminal illnesses.

Question 1: What is "end-of-life care," and does Medicare cover it?

Answer: End-of-life care encompasses all health care provided to someone in the days or years before death, whether the cause of death is sudden or a result of a terminal illness that runs a much longer course. For people ages 65 and over, the most common causes of death include cancer, cardiovascular disease, and chronic respiratory diseases. Medicare covers a comprehensive set of healthcare services that beneficiaries can receive until death. These services include care in hospitals and several other settings, home health care, physician services, diagnostic tests, and prescription drug coverage through a separate Medicare benefit. Many of these Medicare-covered services may be used for curative or palliative (symptom relief) purposes. Medicare beneficiaries with a terminal illness are eligible for the Medicare hospice benefit that includes additional services, not otherwise covered under traditional Medicare, such as bereavement services. The Medicare hospice benefit is discussed in more detail in Question 5.

Question 2: What is "advance care planning," and does Medicare cover it?

Answer: Advance care planning involves multiple steps designed to help individuals. a) learn about the health care options available for end-of-life care, b) determine which types of care best fit their wishes, and c) share their wishes with family, friends, and physicians. Sometimes, patients considering their options may need only one advance care planning conversation with their physician. However, experts state that beneficiaries frequently require a series of discussions with their physician or other health professionals to clearly understand and define their end-of-life wishes.

Starting January 1st, 2016, Medicare began covering advance care planning as a separate service provided by physicians and other health professionals (such as nurse practitioners who bill Medicare using the physician fee schedule). Medicare now covers advance care planning provided in medical offices and facility settings, including hospitals.

As with most other physician services, beneficiaries are subject to cost sharing for advance care planning provided by their physician or health professional. If Medicare beneficiaries desire advance care planning during their annual wellness visit, physicians and other health professionals may provide it during the visit and bill Medicare separately for it. However, beneficiaries will have no cost-sharing liability for advance care planning provided in conjunction with their annual wellness visits.

The Centers for Medicare & Medicaid Services (CMS) is a federal agency within the U.S. Department of Health and Human Services. It administers Medicare and works with state governments to administer Medicaid, the Children's Health Insurance Program (CHIP), and other healthcare programs.

Critical functions of CMS:

•Medicare: This agency oversees the Medicare program, which provides health insurance for people 65 and older and younger people with disabilities.

•Medicaid: Works with states to administer Medicaid, a joint federal-state program that provides health coverage to low-income individuals and families.

•CHIP: Administers the Children's Health Insurance Program, which provides low-cost health coverage to children in families that earn too much to qualify for Medicaid.

•Health Insurance Marketplaces: Oversees the Health Insurance Marketplaces, where individuals and families can purchase health insurance plans.

•Health Information Technology: Promotes the adoption and use of health information technology to improve the quality and efficiency of healthcare.

•Quality Improvement: Works to improve healthcare services provided to Medicare and Medicaid beneficiaries.

Question 3: Are policymakers, such as CMS or Congress, considering changes in Medicare's coverage of advance care planning?

Answer: Yes. In the fall of 2015, the agency that runs the Centers for Medicare and Medicaid Services (CMS) finalized regulations allowing Medicare to pay physicians and other qualified healthcare professionals to plan advanced care.

Specifically, in a proposed regulation released on July 8th, 2015, CMS introduced two new billing codes—previously recommended by the American Medical Association—for advance care planning provided to Medicare beneficiaries. On October 30th, 2015, CMS finalized these proposed provisions, allowing physicians and other health professionals to bill Medicare for advance care planning as a separate service, starting January 1st, 2016. Previous Medicare coverage rules only allowed reimbursement for advance care planning under minimal circumstances.

In Congress, before this new CMS regulation on advance care planning, two bipartisan bills on advance directives and end-of-life care were introduced—one in the Senate and one in the House. Senator Mark Warner and Senator Johnny Isakson introduced the Care Planning Act of 2015 (S.1549) with other cosponsors in the Senate. This legislation included coverage under Medicare for advanced illness planning and care coordination services, including structured discussions about treatment options and patient preferences, for Medicare beneficiaries with a severe progressive or life-threatening illness. Representative Earl Blumenauer and 59 cosponsors introduced the Personalize Your Care Act 2013 (H.R. 1173). This legislation included Medicare and Medicaid coverage for advance care planning consultations between patients, doctors, and other health care professionals.

Question 4: What are "advance directives"? Are healthcare facilities, such as hospitals or skilled nursing facilities, required to keep records of Medicare patients' advance directives?

Answer: Advance directives are written instructions intended to reflect a patient's wishes for health care and guide medical decision-making if they cannot speak for themselves. They typically result from advanced care planning and often take the form of a living will, which defines the medical treatment patients prefer if incapacitated, or the designation of a specific person as a medical power of attorney. Advance directives fall under state regulation, and the required forms for formal advance directives vary from state to state.

Studies have found that about 4 in 10 Americans ages 65 and older still need to have advance directives or write down their wishes for end-of-life medical treatment.

Additionally, demographic differences play a role in the likelihood of having advance directives. Specifically, African Americans and Hispanics have advance directives at lower rates compared to whites, as do people with lower incomes and lower levels of completed education. Researchers have identified several factors contributing to these differences, including cultural and religious differences, communication challenges between patients and medical Staff, distrust of medical care systems, and awareness of advance directive options.

The Patient Self-Determination Act, which took effect in 1991, included a list of Medicare requirements for healthcare facilities regarding advance directives. Under this law, hospitals and skilled nursing facilities must ask each patient if they have an advance directive and record its existence in the patient's file upon admission.

Facilities cannot require patients to create an advance directive before providing treatment or care. Likewise, Medicare patients are not required to have an advance directive before they receive care. Recent surveys show that among long-term care patients, those receiving care in a facility (such as a nursing home or hospice facility) are more likely to have advance directives in place.

Question 5: Does Medicare cover hospice care? How many Medicare beneficiaries use hospice?

Answer: Yes. For terminally ill Medicare beneficiaries who do not want to pursue curative treatment, Medicare offers a comprehensive hospice benefit covering an array of services, including nursing care, counseling, comforting medications, and up to five days of respite care to assist family caregivers. Hospice care is most often provided in patients' homes. For most hospice services, 19 Medicare patients who elect the hospice benefit have minimal cost-sharing liabilities. To qualify for hospice coverage under Medicare, a physician must confirm that the patient is expected to die within six months if the illness is typical. If the Medicare patient lives longer than six months, hospice coverage may continue if the physician and the hospice team re-certify the eligibility criteria.

Of all Medicare beneficiaries who died in 2014, 46 percent used hospice—a rate that has more than doubled since 2000 (21 percent). The rate of hospice use increases with age, with the highest rate existing among decedents ages 85 and over. Hospice use is also higher among women than men and among white beneficiaries than beneficiaries of other races and ethnicities.

Hospice care accounts for about 10 percent of traditional Medicare spending in beneficiaries' last year of life. Medicare Advantage plans do not cover hospice care; therefore, when a Medicare Advantage enrollee receives hospice care, their hospice coverage falls under traditional Medicare (Parts A and B).

While many researchers, policymakers, and patient advocates cite the numerous benefits of hospice care in providing appropriate end-of-life care to Medicare patients, questions have been raised about the growth in for-profit hospice agencies, citing differences in the average care needs of the patients they serve compared with those served by non-profit agencies.

Question 6: What is "palliative care," and does Medicare cover it?

Answer: Palliative care can be integral to end-of-life care because it generally focuses on managing symptoms and comforting patients and their families. While palliative care is common among people receiving end-of-life care, it is not necessarily restricted to people with terminal illnesses. The Center for Advanced Palliative Care emphasizes that palliative care is commonly used among people living with serious, complex, and chronic illnesses, including cancer, heart disease, general pain, or depression. Approximately half (45 percent) of all Medicare beneficiaries have four or more chronic conditions for which palliative care services may be clinically indicated to alleviate symptoms, either in combination with or in addition to curative treatment. The Medicare hospice benefit (described in Question 7) also covers palliative care for beneficiaries with terminal illnesses.

Question 7: How much does Medicare spend on end-of-life care, and for which services?

Answer: Among seniors in traditional Medicare who died in 2014, Medicare spending averaged $34,529 per beneficiary – almost four times higher than the average cost per capita for seniors who did not die during the year. Other research shows that over the past several decades, roughly one-quarter of traditional Medicare spending for health care is for services provided to beneficiaries aged 65 and older in their last year of life.

Medicare spending during the year of death decreases with age after age 73 (Figure 1), suggesting that patients, families, and providers may be opting for less intensive and less costly end-of-life interventions for beneficiaries as they grow older. Specifically, per capita Medicare spending among decedents in 2014 peaked at age 73 ($43,353) and decreased by almost half ($23,181) by age 95. Approximately half of the total Medicare spending for people who died in a given year goes toward hospital inpatient expenses. At the same time, hospice and skilled nursing services accounted for about 10 percent of Medicare spending.

Hospice is a group that is encouraged when preparing for the end of life.

Read the list of drugs that are given.

The information I am providing is found on the Internet. I am not a doctor; this information is only a place for you to start investigating the sinister behavior behind the laws.

The problem with our health is that our food is poisoned. Food needs to give us the nutrients necessary to live healthy lives.

If the health care system cares about humanity, then why don't they invest their money in ways to harvest our food without pesticides and preservatives? Instead of supporting Big Pharma to keep people captive or enslaved to prescriptions. I am not advising you to stop taking your medication. Just find out what you have been prescribed and research the side effects. If a medication says it may cause something, you can guarantee that it will cause it.

The list of medicines usually given by Hospice: Acetaminophen suppository- Placed in the rectum to relieve mild pain or fever. Haloperidol (Haldol) liquid- swallowed to relieve restlessness or confusion. Atropine liquid- given under the tongue to dry secretions in the mouth and throat. Lorazepam (Ativan) liquid is swallowed to alleviate anxiety, restlessness, or trouble sleeping. Morphine (Roxanol) liquid is swallowed to relieve pain or shortness of breath. Prochlorperazine (Compazine) suppository- Placed in the rectum to alleviate nausea or vomiting, Bisacodyl (Dulcolax) suppository- Placed in the rectum to relieve constipation.

In my book "Dream Come True, I addressed the issues I faced when dealing with my husband Karlton's health, specifically kidney failure.

The COVID-19 pandemic created unprecedented challenges across the globe, dramatically altering daily life and travel. As the situation unfolded, I felt a sense of urgency that prompted me to act. I received a solid instinct to inform my family about the impending crisis and urged them to travel to Mexico before any travel restrictions were imposed. It was a race against time, and I experienced a mix of anxiety and determination as I wanted to ensure their safety.

By March 30th, 2020, after weeks of careful planning and consideration, the last members of my family successfully arrived in Mexico. Little did we know that this country would become our temporary refuge as the pandemic continued to escalate and international borders were closed across many nations.

Now that we were all together, my focus shifted towards the future. I had plans to invest my funds into repairing and remodeling an existing building to transform it into a nurturing educational environment. I envisioned opening a school providing a haven for learning during such turbulent times. However, with the borders closed due to the pandemic, my family and Staff found themselves in a challenging situation, navigating life in Mexico while adapting to the new normal brought on by COVID-19.

In light of the ongoing healthcare challenges faced by the United States, one must consider whether deeper, perhaps more concerning motives are at play. Amidst these complexities, individuals must prioritize their family's well-being and safety, especially when time is of the essence.

Over the years, we have made several trips from Dallas/Fort Worth to Mexico, moving equipment to the Lake Chapala area to facilitate the opening of a community school.

However, additional funding was required to complete the project. Before departing for Israel, I had allocated $30,000 for this endeavor; upon my return to the United States, I was surprised to find that I had only spent a few thousand dollars.

Using the remaining funds from my trip to Israel, I planned to remodel the building designated for the community school.

After Kris's passing, I was responsible for organizing everything stored in the building while working on the remodel necessary to open the school. I sought guidance and support to complete the renovation and establish the school for the lakeside community. The night before his death, Kris had expressed a strong commitment to assisting me in any way possible to see this project come to fruition.

CHAPTER TWENTY-ONE
Dream School

For three decades, I have dedicated my career to education. Educators teach, inform, or inspire others, encompassing roles such as teachers, professors, lecturers, tutors, and anyone facilitating learning. They serve a vital societal function by imparting knowledge, skills, and values to future generations. Through their guidance, educators help individuals realize their potential and become well-rounded citizens.

Opening a business in Mexico can present several challenges, particularly the initial expense of hiring a reliable individual to manage the paperwork required for business registration.

After approximately six months of traveling back and forth, I was determined to establish an educational facility. I gained valuable insights into successfully navigating this process through research and preparation.

A clear plan and the necessary steps often become apparent by listening and adhering to Adonai's direction.

My journey to Mexico was motivated by two primary objectives. First, I wanted to protect my family from the implications of ObamaCare. Second, I aimed to create an educational facility based on a successful model I had previously implemented in my private school in Texas. This dual focus underscores the intertwining personal and professional motivations for launching a business in a foreign country.

When I filed for approval for the school's name, the Mexican Government allowed me to select several names, and then they would choose the final legal name. Lake Chapala Research Center was the name the Mexican government decided for us, but to me, it was misleading, so we changed all advertisements to read AT Life Center.

Since 2008, I have been taking equipment down to Lake Chapala. We would pull a trailer with a utility van for at least two days, which took a while because I was working with limited funds. It cost me over $2000 each time I brought supplies to the area.

I would provide the community with the best education center I could. I wanted the school to be unique, affordable, and a place the community could be proud of. The subjects that would be taught would be set up differently.

AT Life Center was starting to take shape. Looking back through the years, I noticed that the school system was failing drastically. The young people needed to be educated, and it was the same old environment. At Life Center, it would be different, creative, and unique. The school would differ from any other school in the area or country.

First, I want to explain how the classes would be designed. The classes would be sectioned off according to grade, from the first to the age of nine. We would teach the basics of reading, writing, math, and languages, specifically English and Spanish. We would have tables and chairs in that area, each seating four students. We would encourage teamwork and studying together, preparing them for being in a work environment.

We lived at the Lakeside, the area they call the communities along Lake Chapala. This region catered to expats, so dual language skills were essential.

When I first came to the region, I couldn't figure out what an expat was. Eventually, I learned that an expatriate is an individual born and raised in a different country from the one they live in.

The United States and Mexico school systems must be updated and more effective.

There were more high school dropouts annually. The standards were unrealistic, and the teachers were only interested in teaching the students to pass tests.

Our school would not have homework, tests, or awards for those who excelled; we needed to prepare them for the real world. Teaching the students to accomplish their goals through guidance and instruction would establish a feeling of accomplishment and success. We would teach them to have confidence.

In this educational model, students are first provided with a solid structural foundation and an understanding of the school's operations.

Progression to the next grade level is based on students' progression and learning engagement rather than age or traditional academic timelines. This system supports personalized advancement, allowing students to move to higher grades at a pace that suits them. By facilitating this flexibility, the approach helps prevent boredom and frustration among students, particularly those who may learn more slowly. This method is designed to help all students reach their full potential according to their unique capabilities.

Establishing the students' aptitude would be necessary when enrolling in the Life Center.

Aptitude refers to a natural ability or talent for a specific task or skill. It's the innate potential to learn and perform a particular activity, whether physical or mental.

Here are some critical points about aptitude:

•Innate potential: Aptitude is often considered a natural ability, meaning you're born with it.

•Aptitudes are specific to tasks: Aptitudes are specific to functions, particular tasks, or skills. For example, someone might have a natural aptitude for math, music, or sports.

•Can be developed: While aptitude is innate, it can be developed and honed through practice and experience.

•Related to intelligence: Aptitude is related to intelligence, but it's different. Intelligence is a broader concept that encompasses various cognitive abilities, while aptitude is more specific.

Aptitude tests are often used to assess a person's potential for a particular job or academic program. These tests measure various cognitive abilities, such as verbal, numerical, and spatial reasoning.

Once the level was set, we moved on to assigning placements. We aimed to ensure students felt confident and capable, never belittled or discouraged.

Students aged 4 to 6 were placed in a designated section to foster teamwork and social interaction. After completing the entry-level requirements, they progressed to the second level.

In the second level, the student would move from a desk to an armchair, creating a relaxed learning environment. I had remarkable armchairs made in graduated sizes. The chairs accommodated different leg lengths according to height, allowing the students' feet to be flat on the floor. They were also given small tables with adjustable legs.

Students would start to become familiar with an office environment by not sitting at a hard desk all day, feeling frustrated and restless to be in a soft, cushioned armchair.

Each educational level would be designed with a unique framework and consistent theme. While students must be able to follow instructions to attend, there would be no specific age requirement for enrollment.

Students must conduct themselves appropriately in a group environment, ensuring they do not disrupt their peers. Each educational level would also have scheduled access to the computer lab. The curriculum would focus on fundamental classes emphasizing essential life skills and preparing students for practical, everyday challenges.

This school aimed to produce entrepreneurs, self-starters, and those who wanted to pursue a dream but could not otherwise do so. The tuition would be cheap. Each student would only pay $50.00 a month. If they could not pay, they would be allowed to work at the school in exchange for their education. Not only would they get paid as personal income, but they would also have enough money to pay their tuition. It would be a win-win situation.

Because of economics, I wanted all students to be included. If they had a desire to learn, then we would teach them everything that we could. While preparing to open this school, I realized internet access would be virtually impossible. So, I prepared over 500 computer classes that taught all phases of technology. From beginner to advanced, they would receive certifications at the end of the courses. If they wanted to be certified with Microsoft or another company like Adobe, they would be shown how to accomplish that.

I am self-taught. I graduated from high school a year early and only attended college once I was in my 40s. I thought I had missed out for years by not graduating from college, only to discover that it was also a money-making joke. I went to college to learn how to build computers for a project I was working on. I can recall being in class when the professor walked in, put the desktop pieces on the professor's desk, and told us what each part was, yet didn't describe their function. The professor said you put all this inside a computer case and have a computer. Wow,

Realizing they would not teach me what I needed to learn to build a studio, I left the school and launched independently. During that time, I learned how to assemble and troubleshoot desktop computers. Before I was 60, I had been certified in 137 computer programs. I felt well qualified to teach young people how to pursue a career accommodating this generation.

The school had some unique functions, for one. Students were not required to spend 8 hours in an educational setting. They would come in, do their required work, and study. When they had completed the objective for the day, they would be allowed to leave the school.

When my oldest son graduated from sixth grade and transitioned to high school, he encountered unexpected challenges that he was unprepared for. My son, JD, had overheard discussions about possibly homeschooling him and his brother, but I lacked the confidence and felt ill-equipped to handle such an endeavor. Despite my unfamiliarity with homeschooling, a pivotal moment occurred one day when I went to pick up JD from school. I noticed that he appeared deeply upset. When I inquired about what was troubling him, he was unwilling to share his feelings.

The boys had been through so much with the murder of their Dad, I had to provide some form of mental stability. That's when I decided to step out on faith and homeschool the boys. Once different church members heard that I would do this, requests started for me to teach other children. What had I just done? I wasn't prepared or equipped to open a private school, but I did.

I learned what worked at schools and what didn't since I had volunteered at various times when my boys were in public school. I structured my private school according to what I felt worked and avoided what I felt was a downfall for students.

I used this method when I first started my private school in Texas. I never could understand how the education system would shove a minimum of six courses in our faces daily. We would spend approximately 45 minutes in class and instruction, but we must learn something. The courses we were given would not apply to daily life or our future. It was simply a waste of time.

When in high school, we were given a course of study. To this day, I have never used anything but essential reading, writing, and arithmetic. In 2024, we see that most people use their phones for math, and they speak on their cell phones and apps to write their text. Forget reading and following instructions. That will not happen. This generation wants everything done for them. We have lost essential communication and social skills that are quickly and easily accessible. The younger generations didn't know how to problem-solve.

I realized that specific skills were needed to sharpen one's mental abilities, so I provided various jigsaw puzzles. Jigsaw puzzles taught several skills and required concentration.

Over the years, those skills have been removed from public schools, stifling individuals who want to excel in knowledge.

AT Life Center would not be like any other school. The students would be given plenty of opportunities to excel, depending on whether they were better at visual or auditory learning. The classes would be structured for each personality so that the individual could progress.

The area of Mexico that we lived in was very depressed. There were only two opportunities for employment. Unfortunately, one of those was working for the drug cartel, and the other was a general laborer.

Children had been robbed of a future, one with hopes and dreams. I wanted to inspire children, young people, and adults of all ages to become the best for their families and community.

The school had to be the talk of the Lakeside, so every detail had to be met with perfection. We painted the bookcases yellow, which helped in the dimly lit rooms when evening came. It was attention-grabbing. We then made giant books. On the front, we had titles with the authors' names. Some of those were the books that I was in the process of writing, which are now included in this series.

Book designs were everywhere in the computer lab. On the desks, there were giant books. I wanted to promote reading subconsciously. There were reading areas with private meeting rooms.

The teachers would be called instructors, eliminating the stereotypes associated with negative past experiences. They would serve as supervisors, guiding and directing. If there were questions, the students could ask them. Researching the answers to questions was a critical part of life skills. Comprehending what was read would set the students apart from the average person.

The term "woke" originated in African American Vernacular English (AAVE) as a synonym for "aware" or "well-informed." It describes someone conscious of social and political issues, particularly racial injustice.

The term in question can be understood in various ways, highlighting its positive and negative dimensions.

On the positive side, being socially aware refers to being conscious of and engaged with social and political issues, particularly race, gender, and inequality. This awareness often leads to advocacy for social justice and equitable treatment.

Conversely, negative aspects associated with this term can include excessive preoccupation with political correctness, which can lead to an individual who may be easily offended.

Additionally, some individuals may exhibit judgmental tendencies, quickly forming opinions about others based on differing beliefs or actions. There is also a potential for elitism, where a person perceives their viewpoints as superior to those of others, which can create barriers to open dialogue and understanding.

The negative connotations of "woke" are often used by those who oppose social justice movements or progressive ideologies. They may use the term to dismiss or criticize those who advocate for change.

It's important to note that the meaning of "woke" can vary depending on the context and the individual using the term.

In today's society, young people must develop resilience in the face of rejection and criticism. Rather than concentrating on public opinion, emphasis should be placed on cultivating strong character.

Promoting positive character traits is vital for personal growth and success, making it one of the primary goals and objectives in guiding the current generation.

Three months have elapsed since the tragic murder of Kris, and significant progress has been made in various initiatives. Notably, a group of women and their children have come together to construct an impressive structure, showcasing their resilience and determination.

When my mother discovered the building, our need for a secure location was urgent. The site needed to be close to town and accessible via bus. Despite the known limitations, I was determined to use our resources best. In retrospect, the transformation of the building from when my mom found it to its current state was remarkable, surprising everyone involved. The renovation process required significant financial investment, which at the time was a challenge given my limited resources.

Walking through the building, I saw it would take a lot of money to bring it up to a standard that was conducive to my dream. We would have to replace all the bathroom facilities, which would be a massive problem if many people came to the school. Since the internet was fragile, I decided to record classes beforehand so the students could continue their training.

The building needed substantial parking for those driving to the location, which would create another issue. Fortunately, it was on the bus route, so those who decided to take the bus from any part around Lakeside would find it easy to get to the school, as the bus started right in front of the school.

Once they realized my vision for the school, my staff quickly joined the party. No group could match their creativity and teamwork.

The team was pulling together, hoping that we could open the school in November 2020. Jason was more settled. He was laughing and horsing around with everyone. I felt a sense of relief that the chaos that his parents had brought into his life was no longer present. I knew he loved his Dad. He loved him with everything in him. He protected him daily and watched after him, which seemed strange when it should have been the other way round.

Before we went to Israel, I needed the funds to work on my schoolwork. Now, I still had the majority of funds from the trip and was ready to put everything into the school.

The building had been used more as a storage facility and a small private school for our children, who were with us on the journey. The inside appearance was very rustic. Now, I wanted to create an environment that would foster creative learning.

Between July 2014 and January 2017, Phillipe went to Mexico to help at the school. I had to travel back and forth due to my husband suffering kidney failure and being on dialysis. I relied on Phillipe to get things started. The only problem was that I needed to figure out where to start. I wanted to get the Library set up first. So, the team asked around to find someone to build the bookshelves. Stacey and I went to the man's home, where he showed us some of his work. What I wanted him to make was very easy. I described the bookshelves and sketched out a drawing. The plan was for the man to build the first one for my approval. It took about two weeks before I received the phone call that said he was ready for me to take a look at the bookshelves.

Finally, getting the bookshelves made was exciting. We could get the books organized and put up properly. We went and saw the bookshelves. There was only one change that I needed to make: the shelves had to be adjustable. I explained to the gentleman that I showed that holes had to be made about every 2 inches in my diagram. That way, book size wouldn't be an issue. Now, with these adjustments going to be made, I knew we would need at least ten, if not more. After all, there were over 5,000 books that had to be put on shelves.

Within days, I was called again to see if the bookshelves were made according to my specifications. This time, the ones I saw were perfect. I paid for them, and we took them back to the school.

When we were going to the States, I left everything in Philippe's capable hands. The only problem I should have realized was that he was absent from the meeting when I set the final plans for the shelves in motion. I told Phillipe I had ordered 10 to 12 bookshelves and would send him the money each time he was ready to pick them up.

Then, before the order for the bookshelves was completed, I had to take Karlton back to the United States. While I was attempting to gather the furniture to build the school, Karlton was on home dialysis, which required 24-hour care. I am incredibly blessed to have a fantastic team that rotated around the clock for his care.

We had brought his special fluid via trailer to continue his care while in Mexico. It was amazing how much Karlton improved medically while in Mexico. Every four to six weeks, I had to take my husband back to the United States for follow-up doctor appointments.

The doctor noticed that Karl's blood work was excellent when we were in Mexico. When asked what I was doing differently, I told the doctor that my husband eats organic food in Mexico without preservatives. In the United States, we eat the same things, but the blood work returns negative for the pesticides and chemicals in the food.

I have provided some information on his treatment. Here is a general term that encompasses two specific types of dialysis that can be performed at home:

1. Home Hemodialysis (HHD):

•It uses a machine to filter your blood.

•Typically, it requires a care partner to assist with the process.

•It offers more flexibility in scheduling treatments and can be done more frequently than in-center dialysis.

2. Peritoneal Dialysis (PD):

•This procedure uses the lining of your abdomen (peritoneum) as a natural filter.

•It involves filling your abdomen with a special fluid (dialysate), leaving it there for a period, and then draining it.

•It can be done manually (continuous ambulatory peritoneal dialysis, or CAPD) or automatically (automated peritoneal dialysis, or APD).

The information presented here summarizes my personal experiences establishing a school and should not be interpreted as medical advice.

Since Karl improved while we were in Mexico, we needed to continue traveling for his health. Getting his treatment in Mexico required us to transport the solution in our trailer.

In December 2017, my sweet Karlton left this life for his new home with the Lord.

Now, here we are three years later, and I walk in to look at how we will organize the books, only to discover that all the shelves but two need to be corrected. Not wanting to waste more time, I would buy tools at the hardware store in Guadalajara. We would not let anything stop us.

Now, picture this: it is June, and only the women and children are in Mexico, and the flights are restricted due to the COVID-19 pandemic. I wasn't going to let that stop me from helping the community.

I had always taken pride in constructing various structures, whether temporary sets for productions or more permanent installations. I once held a workshop where I shared my knowledge with some of the team, guiding them through the intricate process of building our production sets from the ground up. We had worked tirelessly, and the satisfaction of bringing our creative visions to life was unparalleled. Reflecting on those days, I realized that we had achieved remarkable feats together, and I felt a renewed confidence that we could replicate that success again.

However, I noticed a significant shift from the past years, and I was now much older, bringing the skills I had honed and a wealth of experience that shaped my approach to every project.

I asked the ladies if they wanted to remodel the building so we could open the school. Everyone agreed to take on the challenge.

At the outset of this project, six women and our children were available to contribute their time and energy. At that time, the only members in Mexico were dedicated to demonstrating remarkable resilience. This group is determined to learn how to effectively use hand tools to complete the school and open its doors successfully.

The ladies were extraordinary. Every day, they went to the school and worked to rebuild the bookshelves. It took several weeks to accomplish this task. Yet, the teamwork was incredible as each shelf was completed, the books were entered again into the computer, and they were put in alphabetical order. Organizing 5,000-plus books is a challenging task; it took some time.

I wanted to make the school colorful and creative. My fantastic staff worked tirelessly with me. They were all creative geniuses. Samantha taught herself to use a Dremel, a hand tool that allows perfect design cuts. One of the lady's designs was the game of "Life" with large cut-out wooden pieces. Then, they created the scene from "Around the World in 80 Days."

Each section in the school represented a country.

Determining how many supplies we would need was impossible, so Stacey and I picked up supplies every few days. The school was coming together, and we had an open house in October for the community to see what we were doing. This school became the talk of the town.

From June until November, we worked daily at the school, with only a few days off. Jason went to the school to help wherever he was needed.

Losing Kris wasn't easy, so I tried to stay as busy as possible, hoping each day would be less complicated with time. Jason was still living with me, and he reminded me so much of his Dad, both in how he walked and his mannerisms. This fact was a great deal of comfort to me. Being with Jason, I had a part of Kris, who was still living. I never pried into Jason's business or told him he couldn't call his mom. There were times Jason made known his feelings about the murder and said he never wanted to see or talk to her again. He blocked all communication with her.

With everyone involved in remodeling the building to open the school, I let Jason know he was welcome to help. Jason started taking self-defense classes in Ajijic, a nearby town, working hard to lift weights and exercise. Eventually, Jason asked if his instructor could come to the school and teach him. He said he wanted me to see how well he was doing. I thought it was a great idea, and he asked if we could look for some mats to put down at the school. I told him we could go to Guadalajara and see if we could find equipment. It took some time, and we couldn't find a gym mat, but I found large foam squares used in schools. Jason said Grandma, that will work. It doesn't have to be precisely the same as they have in gyms.

July was going to be hard on Jason. It would be his first birthday without his Dad. I asked him what he wanted to do, and he couldn't figure it out. One of his cousins suggested that we go camping. I asked Jason if he thought he might like to do that. He said, "Sure, that would be interesting."

One of my granddaughter's friends owned a place outside Mazamitla where they had cabins. Close to that was an outdoor recreation park with a zip line and a paintball area where you fired paintballs at each other.

When I told Jason about going there for his birthday, he said that would be great, but is it alright if I get a tent and sleep outside? I told him it was his birthday, and we would celebrate with our family. We rented a large cabin, thinking it would shelter the ladies, but we did not realize there was no air conditioning and that it was sweltering hot in July.

All the young people decided to get tents and sleep outside. That was better for them at night.

On the first night, everyone was getting settled in. My bedroom window faced the front of the house, where the young people pitched their tents. My room might have been outside. I had brought my laptop, and it was working, but that was cut short. Every bug and crawling creature loved the light from my computer. I tried to put a jacket over the screen and type with my head under that, but I quickly gave up. My room was crawling with little creatures.

I had to make sure that all the lights were off, and that being said, there were other little creatures like giant spiders and field mice. I would have gone to the tent if there had been enough room, but I needed to be strong; this was for Jason, not me. The next day, we headed to the recreation park. Jason wanted to ride the zipline; almost everyone did, except for me and a few others. I enjoyed watching the expressions as each descended the mountain on the zipline.

Years ago, Kris asked me to promise to take care of his son if anything happened to him.

He said Marie was not fit to do it, so I made him that promise, never realizing that I would one day try to do what I promised him.

We planned to spend at least four days in the cabin. The recreation park had been fun, so now we would return to the cabin to get cleaned up, and everyone but me would go on a hike.

From my bedroom window, I could see the beautiful mountains. The cabin was on a hill, and looking out gave me time to meditate on God and reflect on what had happened. I spent much time on that mountainside praying, watching the butterflies, and listening to the birds.

The clouds were rolling in, and the beauty of waking up and seeing the clouds at ground level fascinated me. I thought about how happy

Kris must be now with his Dad, grandma, and stepdad. How could I be selfish and wish him back to a harsh, cruel world? Naturally, I would have given anything to change the events on May 28th.

My only consolation was knowing that the God I served knew the future and took him home. When Kris's Dad was murdered, it was devastating for Kris, JD, and me. Kris was only ten years old when we found out that a Texas highway patrolman killed his Dad in mistaken identity; it was devastating for the boys and me. I cover this story in "Wounded Soldier-Victorious Book 03." When Kris learned that the Lord had spoken to me and Robbie was in heaven with God, Kris immediately hugged me and said Who said life didn't have happiness ever after, Momma? We will be with Daddy again and have a family again, this time forever.

During the time after Kris was killed, I thought how excited Kris must have been to step into the other dimension and see his Dad. The beauty of that reunion would be spectacular. Now, he was with those who loved him. He would not be abused by this world, and just like King David said about his son, he can't come back to me, but I can go to him. One day, my tears would be dried by the creator I served. My family was taking that journey to be with God.

It was now the second night camping, and the weather started changing. We wouldn't throw in the towel and head back to Jocotepec, but we would wait and see if the rain would keep us inside. We bought a cake with beautiful fruit to celebrate Jason's birthday. Jason wasn't fond of sweets; he wanted to stay in shape.

We made it through the second night.

The next day, Jason approached me and asked if we could go home. I asked him if he was sure that was what he wanted to do, and he said, "Yes, I need to get some sleep."

At this point, I knew that our camping experience was over. We packed up the trucks and headed back to town. It had been an exhausting few days.

I told the team, "Let's go home, get some rest, and we will start fresh tomorrow." It would take a little while to return to the Pueblo, where we lived.

When we got to the house, everyone unpacked, and some of the group decided to go to school and work.

Kris's murder had been devastating for everyone. The work at the school seemed to keep us focused and working through the horrific event.

Chapter Twenty-Two
One Big Swoosh

Labor Day is September 7th, 2020, in the United States. It is a three-day holiday, and most businesses are closed. It is considered the last break before children return to school. During this time frame, I would lose my family in one swoosh.

I received a phone call from JD. We had talked numerous times since Kris died, and he was taking the murder hard. He regretted not being in Mexico for me, yet I kept telling him I didn't want him here to see or experience what we had been going through.

JD was enveloped in a darkness of despair that offered no solace. Kris wasn't just his brother. He was his best friend, the kind of companion who understood the essence of JD's soul. They had forged a dynamic partnership in their business ventures, celebrating successes together and navigating challenges. Their connection transcended the ordinary; it was a deep-rooted camaraderie, often leading them to embark on spontaneous adventures, sharing laughter and excitement in a world that usually felt too serious. The bond they shared was unbreakable, woven with threads of love that held them steadfast through the trials of life.

It had been just over 90 days, and now I was faced with another tragedy. JD called, his voice heavy with emotion. This time, it wasn't about delivering justice for Jason or Kris. It felt as if he was carrying the weight of past battles and unspoken burdens. The air was thick with a sense of urgency, suggesting something had changed beneath the surface. I braced myself for the news he was about to share.

JD was grappling with a profound personal tragedy: his wife, LeAnn, had left him. The weight of her absence bore heavily on him, and he felt compelled to share the painful details of what had transpired. LeAnn had been excited about attending a family get-together that day to reconnect with relatives and enjoy the familiar chaos of family reunions. She had urged JD to join her, but being surrounded by a crowd made him uneasy. With a conflicted heart, he replied, "Let me think about it."

"I'm going to pick a few things up from the store first," LeAnn had said before walking out the door. "Then I'll give you a call. If you decide to come, I can pick you up." Her tone had been light, but JD often detected an urgency in her voice—a drive that seemed to push him toward social interactions he would rather avoid.

After some time spent in contemplation, JD had a change of heart. He shot it and called LeAnn, eager to tell her he would join her. But to his dismay, she didn't answer. He waited a few moments, hoping she was busy or had entered a store. But when minutes turned to an hour, he felt an unsettling knot form in his stomach. He tried calling her repeatedly, but still, there was no response.

A sense of dread began to seep into his thoughts, wrapping around him like a cold fog. He glanced at the clock for the umpteenth time, its ticking sound becoming more pronounced in the room's stillness. "Maybe she just lost her phone," he mused, trying to rationalize the overwhelming anxiety gripping him. LeAnn had a well-documented tendency to misplace her belongings—keys, sunglasses, even her purse on occasion. "Perhaps she's just lost track of time while shopping," he told himself, forcing a deep breath that barely assuaged the rising tide of worry within him.

But as the minutes turned into hours, the silence that enveloped him morphed into an oppressive weight, and his tiny flickers of hope dwindled into shadows. Each passing moment heightened his concern, drawing his thoughts to darker possibilities. A gnawing anxiety led him to consider reaching out to her family; perhaps they had heard from her or could offer some insight into her whereabouts. His fingers trembled as he dialed their numbers, the anticipation building like a storm in his chest.

Disappointment settled in when each call was silent, and he could not hear a voice on the other end to soothe his growing fears.

Desperation clawed at his insides, vivid and merciless. His mind raced, spiraling through a cascade of horrifying scenarios that played out like a nightmare: what if LeAnn had suffered an accident on the road? What if she were trapped somewhere, unable to call for help? Each thought was a jagged shard, puncturing his composure further. Unable to remain still any longer, he picked up the phone again, this time dialing the local hospitals, his heart hammering against his ribcage like a caged bird. With each ring, his anxiety tightened its grip, leaving him breathless.

Finally, feeling cornered and frantic, he picked up the phone a third time, calling the police department. As he nervously explained LeAnn's absence, he could hear his voice tremor, a mixture of fear and frustration. Anger surged within him, directed not only at LeAnn for her reckless carelessness but also at himself for being unable to reach out to protect her. The weight of the unknown loomed before him, making each breath harder to take as he waited, hoping for a glimmer of reassurance.

With each passing minute, the lack of information transformed his worry into a tumultuous storm of emotions. His mind darted from anxiety to aggravation, the fight against the tide of panic now waged in earnest. JD knew that LeAnn tended to be scatterbrained, and now, in this moment of uncertainty, that trait gnawed at him. She needed to be more mindful, he thought. The clock continued to tick, and the void of her absence felt as oppressive as ever.

The hours drifted by in a haze, the weight of uncertainty pressing down on him. Unable to shake off the troubling thoughts, he finally checked their safe, a small metal box that had once been a symbol of security. The familiar sight greeted him as he opened it, but today, it felt different. Inside lay a stash of approximately $10,000, neatly bundled in crisp notes, alongside his prized possession—a golden collector's gun, a relic of days long past, cherished for its craftsmanship and rarity. But as he rummaged through the safe, an unsettling realization struck him: the cash and the gun had vanished.

In a cruel twist of fate, LeAnn had taken their daughter with her when she left, and now waves of emotion crashed over him. Confusion, anger, and profound sadness swirled together as he grappled with the situation. I tuned in with concern and curiosity when he called LeAnn, hoping for clarity. Despite having only a few details, I kept my perspective neutral, although I couldn't help but be intrigued by the unfolding drama.

Within two days, after an eternity of anxious waiting, he received the call that would change everything. During this call, the harrowing truth emerged: LeAnn was leaving him. The revelation hit him like a punch to the gut, and in that moment, the reality of his situation settled in, heavy and unyielding.

JD had been grieving a lot for Kris, and when he tried to talk to LeAnn, she would tell him to get over it, that he was gone. That didn't seem surprising since she was good friends with Marie. In years gone by, they would go out, and both gravitated to each other. The only times I saw my daughters-in-law contact me were when they wanted me to buy something for their families.

Of course, I would, and after all that had recently been discovered, I wouldn't say I liked the fact that I was being used. Marie knew how much I loved my grandchildren, and if they wanted me to pick them up, they would call and tell me that they needed clothes, things for their rooms, etc. I would immediately not question but tell them I would pick them up, and we would go shopping.

I had noticed since Kris's murder that I had not heard from my granddaughters or even LeAnn asking if I needed anything or just to check on me. It was as if I ceased to exist when Kris was dead.

I was deeply involved in opening the school and couldn't leave Mexico to go to the United States. The only solution was for JD and Michael to come to Mexico. JD asked what he should do with their household items. I told him to call LeAnn, be cordial, and tell her he was moving out of the house and, if she wanted anything, to come and get it before it went to storage. She told him she didn't have a place then and just put everything in storage.

JD hoped LeAnn would snap out of it before everything was in storage and come home. That never happened. JD and Michael were headed to the airport to board the plane to Mexico. He had Michael help him put his belongings into storage, and both of them got on the plane and headed to Mexico.

When he arrived, his emotions were horrible. Both of us had lost Kris, and now we were losing the rest of the family with one swoosh.

The first few days after JD arrived, I stayed at the house and didn't go to school. At first, I couldn't figure out what happened. JD wouldn't tell me; finally, he started opening up about the mystery man. During our conversations, I found out that both JD and LeAnn had been drinking and using drugs. Both had become abusive while using and had attacked each other physically. LeAnn had been raised with boys and knew how to be equally as a man, never wasting time to make her position known.

LeAnn had pretended to be a Christian when she was around me, and she took on a completely different persona the minute she was away. Listening to what I was being told and knowing from first-hand experience dealing with LeAnn, I didn't question what I was being told. There was a time when she worked at one of the local music stores, and she called me to say they had taken her to the hospital for a drug overdose.

She didn't want JD to find out that not only was she in the hospital for this, but that she had wrecked their car. She wanted me to intervene and be the buffer for JD, who was angry about what was happening.

At first, he didn't know she had run off with a man. He thought it was because he didn't want to attend the party, and the dirty laundry would be aired through social media. She had run off with a married tattoo artist with four children.

All of a sudden, it hit me that this is the reason you couldn't go to Israel with us. She would blame JD's drinking when the facts were discovered that it wasn't half of the issue. She used drugs and drank alcohol, and when both of them were doing this, the household was explosive. The abuse was happening in both parts.

I was completely unaware of the abuse until this event happened.

They had been married for 18 years, and that story is complicated in itself.

All of a sudden, it hit me that this was the reason why Adonai told me that she couldn't go to Israel with us. She would blame JD's drinking when the facts were discovered that it wasn't half of the issue. She used drugs and drank alcohol, and when both of them were doing this, the household was explosive. The abuse was happening in both parts.

People use social media to expose their darkest secrets and brag about their lives. Eventually, I would find out that she had been seeing the other man for 9 to 10 months when she posted that she was celebrating her first anniversary with her King, who treated her like a Queen. She was finally becoming who she wanted to be without restrictions. Her boyfriend covered her with tattoos, used filters, and changed her look.

Ultimately, I was finally made aware of all the difficulties that both families had been living with. They all became chameleons, changing when they came around me.

I am sure you are asking if I am the anointed of Adonai; why didn't I do anything if I saw what was happening? God never forces his will upon man; they can serve him or walk away. I serve God not because I want to receive blessings or self-gain, but because I love him. I wouldn't force anyone to serve the Lord, not my family.

I am the anointed, not a psychic. My children and grandchildren didn't come and spend time with me. They only came around when I offered to buy lunch or dinner. Or I would see them on special occasions like birthdays, Thanksgiving, or Hanukkah. I was busy helping put the event together during those times, so they weren't included in the conversations. My daughters-in-law did very little, if anything, to assist in the cooking, cleaning, or preparation of events.

My presence made the evil spirits uncomfortable, so the family stayed briefly and left. An important note is that I didn't talk with them about their lives and serving God. They knew what I believed and how I felt about God.

During a challenging period, I dedicated considerable time to comforting my son as he navigated his emotions. Despite this extended commitment, I recognized the importance of returning to the school to assist with ongoing projects. To facilitate this, JD, Michael, and Jason volunteered to help with the remodeling efforts. My goal was to keep them engaged in productive activities to prevent them from focusing on family difficulties. The trio concentrated on tasks such as installing new bathroom fixtures, ceiling fans, and lighting, as well as constructing large books, which allowed the women to focus on the finer aspects of the artistic designs.

This ugly building was turning out to be a fabulous work of art. We could finally hold an open house for the community to see what had been done.

To secure the necessary support from the city government, we arranged a meeting with the President, whose role is comparable to that of a city mayor in the United States.

In our recent discussion, we outlined our current initiatives related to the educational facility. I invited city officials for a guided tour of the facility to enhance their understanding of our efforts.

Additionally, the President facilitated a connection with the regional head of education, and I expressed interest in arranging a personal tour of the site for her.

Unfortunately, the COVID-19 pandemic significantly impacted our plans, leading to delays as people were instructed to remain indoors and limit activities. When the head of education was finally able to visit, she was impressed by what she observed. She took several photographs and expressed her amazement at the school's uniqueness, noting that there had never been a project like this in the region. Her encouraging feedback was invaluable, as she assured us of the city government's full support for our initiative.

November was just a few days away, and I wanted to dedicate the school to the Lord on November 16th and then open the doors to the public. After long, exhausting hours and years of struggle, we would now present the city with a fantastic school.

He arrived on the day of the building's dedication. Walking through the building with community members, I was thankful that God had provided the funds, the strength, and a fantastic Staff.

With the community's excitement, we knew the school would be a success. Although we hadn't officially opened the school, the language classes had already begun.

The downstairs at the school was complete, but there was still work to complete upstairs. I was setting up a private research area where people interested in current events and ancient history could investigate topics.

I have been an investigative researcher for over 35 years, and my private Library in the United States and Mexico has at least 80,000 books, including periodicals and printed material.

When I discovered that the enemy's sinister evil plan was to destroy all faith on earth, I was driven to expose every possible lie. How did we fail God? When this was revealed to me, I felt it was my duty and responsibility to God to share my knowledge.

When I first started moving some of my books to Mexico, I brought only a few thousand on various topics, with a large number of ex-pats in the area who knew the depths of the Illuminati and the New World Order. I knew they would be interested in the books that I had.

Over the years, I have watched numerous books become available in libraries and bookstores and disappear. Could this process be a genius scheme, and is the truth lost forever through this process?

I was upstairs working in my office, setting up a system and organizing research books so I could open up phase three of this project.

After several weeks of operation, we received a phone call from Julia, Mr. Lopez's daughter. She expressed a keen interest in visiting the school for a personal tour. This visit is particularly significant for Julia, as it will be her first time returning to the building since her father's passing over five years ago. Currently living in Guadalajara, Julia has decided to travel to Jocotepec for this tour of the school.

When the owner's daughter arrived on November 20th, she was extremely excited and said she wanted to discuss the rental agreement for the building that functioned as a community school. I told her that her father, Mr. Lopez, and my Mom had a long-standing rental arrangement, and her father reassured my Mom that the rent would never change due to the school's significance to the local community. Julia reassured me that she knew about the agreement, but since both her father and my Mom were deceased, we needed to update the contract.

During our discussions about the property, it became clear that Julia was focused on the financial aspects of the building purchase, which was priced at $250,000. I expressed my concerns regarding the acquisition, emphasizing that this building did not align with our objectives due to strategic issues, specifically the school's critical need for high-speed internet access. After consulting with internet providers, I learned that there were no forthcoming plans to extend services to that location.

In response to these concerns, Julia said she would consider raising the rent. I mentioned that I would be open to paying a higher rent once the school began receiving funding, primarily since I had already invested a considerable amount in necessary repairs for the building.

The situation involved a property that had undergone significant renovations to prepare for opening. Upon observing the completed work, the property owner wanted to increase the rent immediately. I acknowledged her request but emphasized establishing a steady income first. She then proposed that I purchase the property. I explained that all my financial resources had been invested in renovating, including upgrading bathrooms and fixtures, remodeling, and ensuring the building met safety codes.

I took the initiative to cover all the renovation expenses, amounting to $20,000, without seeking reimbursement from her or her family.

Several critical repairs, particularly the roof and walls, were essential due to the building's vulnerability to flooding during the rainy season. This area of Mexico typically experiences regular rainfall from June to November, highlighting the urgency of resolving these structural issues.

Julia was unresponsive to my concerns and insisted that purchasing the building was essential; otherwise, she would increase the rent significantly. She then requested that I sign a new contract, which would take effect in four days.

In our conversation, I clarified that our parents had reached an agreement regarding the estate. However, she maintained that they were both deceased and that she was in control as the estate executor. Her responsibilities included collecting rental income and distributing the funds among the family members. She pointed out that her father had five children, so the rental income generated from the property was limited once it was divided among them.

I wondered if Julia knew the agreement, so I reviewed the details with her. I clarified that the contract stipulated her father would support establishing a school for the community, with the condition that he would not raise the rent at any time. As long as there was a school, the rent would remain unchanged. I had the paperwork to back up this agreement. Julia acknowledged its validity but mentioned she was there to discuss making changes.

I didn't sign a new agreement, but told her we would start looking for a new location. Then, I told her I needed a few months to accomplish this enormous task.

Julia packed her briefcase, and her body language suggested she was unhappy with my decision to look for another building. She seemed intent on convincing me to purchase a property that was over 40 years old. I viewed that as something other than a wise investment, especially since I didn't have the necessary funds or credit. So, we had come to a mutual understanding when she left.

On November 27th, a large crowd gathered at the school in the late afternoon. A staff member informed me that Julia had arrived, prompting me to go downstairs to greet her. At that moment, I was unaware that we would face significant challenges.

Julia and her uncle, who turned out to be the current property owner, approached the patio. A judge from Chapala joined them, and there was a significant presence of federal police, commonly referred to as Federales, and at least twenty other individuals. The sudden arrival of this large group was unexpected and raised concerns among our team regarding the situation's circumstances.

Julia informed me that we hadn't paid the rent for several months and had just two hours to vacate the building. I immediately called Samantha, the financial director, to request the records and asked both ladies to review the bank statements, showing that the rent had been paid and nothing was due until December 1st.

Samantha logged in to the bank records, which confirmed that rent payments had been made consistently. The documents indicated that Julia had transferred the funds into her account. When we presented this evidence to the concerned parties, they declined to view or acknowledge any records. Julia had been receiving the money and was supposed to give it to her uncle; instead, she kept it for herself.

In the beginning, I faced challenges in understanding the conversation due to my limited proficiency in Spanish. My granddaughters, America and Joi, who are both fluent in the language, helped me by translating during our discussions. However, they needed help persuading Julia and the Judge to review the bank records. To enhance communication and achieve our goals, I recommended that they contact their father, Julian, for additional support.

Julian was called to negotiate with the group about an ongoing issue. When the call was passed to me, Julian explained that they insisted we did not pay the rent. I informed him that we attempted to present our online bank records as proof of payment, but they declined to review them. Julian requested a few more days in the current month that were already paid, allowing us time to secure a new location for the school; however, the group needed to be more forthcoming in their response.

After excusing myself, I entered the school and found JD and Jason in the Library, examining some books. When JD inquired about the situation, I explained that efforts were being made to remove me from the property. This revelation sparked a strong feeling of anger within the guys.

JD said, "Mom, I have some money. I will help you." I told him no, this wasn't what this was about. It is evident that since I refused to purchase a building that we could not utilize due to massive issues, I wouldn't be forced to pay $250,000.

When I find myself in this "zone," the atmosphere transforms; a sense of palpable fear washes over those who witness it. My mind clears, and all doubts dissipate as I call upon the Lord, connecting deeply with the spiritual realm.

With renewed confidence, I strode out of the school, my arm extended like a conductor leading an orchestra, ready to pronounce judgment on the woman who stood in my path and the property surrounding her.

It was as though the air around us crackled with energy, a powerful force surging through me like a laser beam of divine authority. As I began to speak in another language, I knew that no one could understand but God.

As I opened my mouth to speak, the words that emerged sent waves of astonishment rippling through the room, leaving an indelible mark on everyone present. With unwavering certainty, I delivered a declaration of judgment upon the nefarious individuals behind this heinous act. The weight of my words hung thick in the air, freezing everyone in their place, their eyes wide with a blend of terror and disbelief. It was as if time itself had come to a standstill, a collective breath held as all were drawn into the magnetic force of the moment, captivated by the intensity of the confrontation unfolding before them.

How convenient that these wicked people had come to take over the building and take what I had. Instead, they got a bargain of a lifetime.

I started down the steps and saw this woman's uncle. That is when I realized the woman controlling everything wasn't the owner; her uncle was. I found this out when I stepped over to him and said, "We have paid everything and owe nothing."

The uncle told everyone to stop and went to his niece. He told her it was a mistake, and she said, "No, uncle, they haven't paid anything in months." They are lying once again. We tried to present the papers, and they were refused.

I discovered that the niece was responsible for collecting the money from us and was supposed to give it to her uncle. Instead, she kept the money for herself and told her siblings we were not paying for the building.

Everything was fabricated for her financial gain.

It is important to insert here that when I stretched my arm out, I cursed the property and said, "Let no man purchase this place." Four years later, the building still needs to be sold or rented.

I looked and told Stacey I needed to find a place for us to move this stuff.

As JD, Jason, and I headed to JD's car to secure another location, several people told me they didn't want to do this. I know they felt God's presence come into the zone when I stepped into it.

The head of the Federal Police approached me with a concerned expression and said, "We don't want to proceed with this operation. I will do my utmost to hold my officers back as long as possible." However, later, I learned that he had instructed his officers to help us save as much of the school as possible. They began gathering items from the school and transporting them to the edge of the property to assist us in our efforts.

Meanwhile, news of the situation quickly spread through the community, drawing others not directly involved in the ordeal to lend a hand. Seeing neighbors and residents coming together was heartening, galvanized by a shared sense of urgency and solidarity. The support we received from the community was overwhelming, as more people arrived to help salvage what they could, ensuring that amidst the chaos, there was also an outpouring of kindness and cooperation.

During the event, some passersby inquired if the furniture and equipment were for sale. In response, one of our team members explained the situation to the community. Volunteers stepped in to help safeguard our equipment.

With all of the community, including the police, helping us, Julia was forced to keep the gates open until midnight instead of closing them in two hours.

The property housed two specialized trailers engineered explicitly to transport materials across the border between the United States and Mexico. These trailers were meticulously loaded with a comprehensive assortment of tools and equipment vital for remodeling and refurbishing the building. The contents included everything from power tools, saws, and hammers to various paints and safety gear, ensuring that the renovation could proceed without significant delays.

However, access to these trailers was tightly controlled, with only a few individuals permitted. This restriction heightened tensions, particularly as Julia plotted to steal our trailers. Her intentions were clear, and we were acutely aware of the potential ramifications of such an act.

In light of this threat, we remained grateful for our two trucks, which offered us a practical alternative for transporting the school equipment housed on our property. Although using the trucks for this purpose would require more time and effort, we were resolute in preserving as much school equipment as possible. Each piece was crucial for the ongoing projects and the community that depended on them. Our commitment to safeguarding these resources remained unwavering, even in the face of challenges.

When I thought I couldn't possibly be hit with any more tragedies, I am now facing the heartbreak of watching my dreams be demolished. All the years and hard work were thrown on the side of the street.

Later, I was told that when some of the officers who were present to experience God's presence found out where we were going, they showed up, offering hot coffee and helping unload some of the furniture.

CHAPTER TWENTY-THREE
The Exodus Escape

In the pursuit of finding a suitable location to move the contents of our school, I was inspired to turn to our landlord, the owner of our current rental. He might connect us with someone who has a building that could perfectly accommodate our needs, guiding us toward a safe and efficient storage solution.

When I found Jose, I told him what had happened at the school. He said he didn't know anyone who might have a building, but to check with Javier, he is better connected to the people in town.

Javier was JD's landlord, and I told JD, "Let's talk to Javier; he may know someone who can help us." We found Javier at his home and quickly shared our situation. He was genuinely concerned and said, "I have a building; let's look and see if it meets your needs."

As Javier leaned forward in the car, giving JD detailed directions, I felt a sense of anticipation about our destination. Glancing out the window at the passing scenery, I tried to piece together the clues from his directions, mentally mapping out where this elusive building might be hidden among the bustling streets. The excitement of the unknown journey filled me with a sense of adventure.

When we parked the car, we started walking toward the plaza. That's when my mind flashed back to where I felt the school needed to be when we first came to Jocotepec.

A Mexican plaza, also known as a "plaza" or "zocalo," is a central public square in many Mexican towns and cities. It typically serves as the heart of the community and hosts a variety of activities and events.

Key features of a Mexican plaza: •**Central location:** Plazas are usually in the center of the city or town, often surrounded by important buildings like the city hall, cathedral, or government offices. •**Open space:** The plaza is a spacious, vibrant area designed for gathering and socializing. •**Surrounding architecture:** Plazas are often framed by beautiful colonial-era buildings with colorful facades and balconies. •**Cultural significance:** They play a vital role in Mexican culture, hosting festivals, celebrations, markets, and political gatherings. •**Community hub:** Plazas are places where people come together to relax, socialize, and enjoy the local atmosphere.

Mexican plazas are more than just public spaces; they are symbols of Mexican identity and culture, reflecting the country's rich history and vibrant spirit.

If the school is situated near the plaza, it will provide greater exposure to the community and facilitate easier access for students, allowing them to walk to school more conveniently.

Javier's building was only a few buildings down from the government buildings. When we went in to see the size, I knew it would need to be bigger, and we would pay twice the rent. In my heart, that was ok. We only had a little time to waste if we were going to save the school.

The school's exodus started at 2 p.m. on Friday, November 27th, and ended after 7 p.m. on Sunday, November 29th. For over 48 hours, no one rested but worked steadily. Julian caught a plane from Dallas and flew in to help us.

After I had finally secured the building, JD and Stacey sat down to discuss my involvement. They both agreed that, considering everything I had endured over the past several months, it would be in my best interest to remain at home for the time being. I attempted to voice my disagreement and push back against their decision, but deep down, I knew it was a futile effort. At 66 years old, I felt the weight of emotional exhaustion from the trials and tribulations that had recently unfolded. The thought of staying home felt overwhelming, yet I couldn't deny the truth in their concern for my well-being.

It wasn't right for everyone to work and stay up for 48 hours. I stayed awake, praying, and only dozed off for about an hour. If they were going to suffer, I could at least pray for their strength and call to check on them every few hours.

As I sat in the house, contemplation washed over me like a heavy tide, forcing me to reflect on the overwhelming events unfolding in six months. It felt surreal to think that I had lost Kris, my beloved son, in a senseless act of violence—his life extinguished far too soon. JD, my oldest son, was left shattered, having lost his entire family through a pending divorce.

In that moment, it felt like I, too, had lost my entire family, save for the steadfast support of JD and Jason. Each day seemed to unravel another thread of stability in my life, and now, with the loss of the school, the final anchor had slipped away. I often asked myself, "What else could go wrong?"—a thought I realized was not just a passing whim but a dark invitation for fate to intervene, with the grim certainty that something else would come crashing down.

The new building turned out to be significantly smaller than anticipated, making it inadequate for holding classes. Due to this unexpected limitation, we had no choice but to relocate some of the school's resources to my house. Consequently, the new building and my home began to resemble cluttered storage units filled with various educational materials, furniture, and supplies. The once spacious rooms in my house became crammed with stacks of books, boxes of supplies, and scattered classroom items, creating a chaotic environment that felt far from conducive to learning. The entire situation was overwhelming as we struggled to find a solution for the lack of space and the pressing need for an organized educational setting.

The team spent the next few months trying to clear some space for the language classes and possibly to hold church services.

Things had been so hectic that no one had time to settle down and deal with the issues of Kris's death. This murder didn't just impact JD, Jason, and me, but also my staff and their families.

When someone you love is brutally killed, you see the aftermath. The mind can't comprehend what has been seen.

The term for this condition is PTSD. This information is intended for educational purposes only. For medical advice or diagnosis, consult a qualified professional.

PTSD stands for Post-Traumatic Stress Disorder. It is a mental health condition that can develop after experiencing or witnessing a traumatic event. This event could be life-threatening or significantly threaten your physical, emotional, or spiritual well-being.

Some common examples of traumatic events that can lead to PTSD include: •Natural disasters (earthquakes, hurricanes, floods) •Accidents (car crashes, fires) •Physical or sexual assault •Combat or military service •Witnessing violence or death.

People with PTSD often experience a range of symptoms, which can be grouped into four main categories: 1.Intrusive memories: These include flashbacks, nightmares, and unwanted thoughts about the traumatic event. 2.Avoidance involves avoiding situations, places, or people that remind the person of the trauma. 3.Adverse changes in thinking and mood can include guilt, shame, or detachment from others. 4.Changes in physical and emotional reactions can include hypervigilance, irritability, and difficulty sleeping.

Find someone you honor and respect if you or a loved one faces difficult situations and needs someone to talk to. Share your thoughts and emotions with them, and never be afraid to shed tears or express to a loved one that you are having a hard day.

I have trusted God for over 50 years, and He has always been my confidant, counselor, and Waymaker. Throughout every traumatic event, my focus has been on Him and not the circumstances.

The team had organized everything as best it could under the circumstances, and we started having church inside the building. I knew that JD and Jason, along with Michael, were having a difficult time coping with the losses; however, I wasn't aware that JD had started hitting the alcohol hard. That, once again, was kept from me.

When I sought clarity from the JD about Jason's situation, I was met with deceitful responses. Deep down, I understood that Jason required a sense of stability in his life, especially in the wake of recent events. After JD arrived in Mexico, Jason strongly desired to move in with his uncle. This revelation filled me with concern. While I knew that JD cared deeply for his nephew, I couldn't shake the feeling that he was so caught up in his grief over their shared loss that he failed to recognize the significant impact of his emotional state on Jason. I worried that Jason, in his vulnerable state, might become overwhelmed by the situation and lose the support he truly needed during such a tumultuous time.

On April 4th, 2021, JD called me, sounding frantic. He told me that Jason was missing. I asked him to explain what he meant. JD said Jason had gone to the corner store to buy milk but had yet to return. He had spent the last few hours searching the lakeside, trying to find him.

I knew that Kris had brought this son around some shady characters while they were in Mexico, and I wasn't prepared to cope with another loss.

Our extended family rallied together, tirelessly searching for Jason through day and night, scouring every nook and cranny of the lakeside area and even venturing into the bustling streets of Guadalajara. We printed countless flyers, each adorned with Jason's smiling face, and designed matching shirts emblazoned with his image, hoping to spread awareness in our desperate search. Weeks passed with little hope, and the only tangible lead we received was a fleeting sighting: someone reported seeing him board a bus alongside a woman, a potential threat that we clung to with apprehension and hope. Every moment felt like an eternity as we continued our quest for answers, fueled by love and determination.

When we talked, we knew Jason didn't have a girlfriend, and he had made it a point to say he never wanted to see his mom again. Then the question came: Had he been harmed?

For weeks, we searched, even reporting him missing to the Polly Klass Foundation, Amber alert, and reporting him to every organization we could think of.

I knew how much Jason loved me and swore never to leave me, but he was gone. I told the team that if Jason didn't show up soon, I would go to the avocado farms and ask the cartel where my grandson was.

I had heard that the cartel takes young people to their avocado farms and works them like slaves. The cartel didn't like dealing with Americans and kept their distance, but how would these evil men know that Jason was an American citizen? Jason was half-white American and half-Mexican.

Finally, after about six weeks, JD came to me and said he read online that Jason was with his mom in Texas. That was the worst blow I could have dealt with. Kris had told me that if anything happened to him, I should take care of Jason, and now I feel like a complete failure.

Jason was gone. How could this be?

Daily, I prayed for Jason and cried a million tears. The only part of Kris I had left was Jason. He walked like his Dad and had his Dad's gestures.

Since April 4th, 2021, I have been yearning to hear from Jason to know if he was ok. It felt like an eternity since our last meaningful conversation. We were so close and shared some fantastic times. We never had a crossword, and Jason was always respectful to me. I left numerous messages on Facebook telling him I loved him or wished him a happy birthday.

At one point, we set up a GoFundMe account to cover advertising expenses, and LeAnn posted on my page that I was a liar and a scam artist and that Jason wasn't missing.

I wondered: What did she know? How and why did my ex-daughter-in-law make that claim?

If Marie wasn't guilty, why didn't she contact me and tell me that she wanted to come to Mexico and pick up Jason? I never told Jason he couldn't see or talk to his mom.

Then, on November 14th, 2024, everything changed. As I glanced down at my phone to see if JD had texted, my heart skipped a beat when I saw a message from Jason.

His words were filled with emotion: "Grandma, I am so sorry for how I left. Will you please forgive me?" He explained that he had been in a dark place following his father's death and needed to return to the States to find himself. Reading his message, a wave of relief washed over me. I quickly responded, "Yes, I forgive you absolutely," and followed up by telling him I had prayed for him daily, hoping he would find his way back to us.

That day marked a turning point as Jason reached out to his uncle. They had never argued, and Jason hated conflict. There wasn't any disagreement when Jason vanished.

Then, my grandson told me he was now in the Army. The door to rekindling our love swung wide open, filling me with a renewed sense of connection and hope for the future.

Chapter Twenty-Four
Miracle in the Plaza

After spending over a year at the Plaza, we have faced significant challenges in progressing towards the school's reopening. Some individuals have suggested that, from a natural perspective, these obstacles may indicate that they are not aligned with divine intentions.

I want to address the idea that sometimes there are hindrances to distract the true objective, and sometimes we have reached adversity to train us for the end game.

The attack on this team was not a sign of Adonai raising His hand against us. In this story, you will see how a disaster transformed into a miraculous event.

At the end of January 2022, I felt compelled to open the school doors and reach out to the community. I called Julian and told him that I wanted to open the school on or around February 12th to bring the presence of the Lord to the people.

I wondered how I would accomplish this; however, I knew that Adonai's presence was unrestricted by buildings or locations I had seen throughout the years.

Throughout the years, numerous accounts report that my encounters with the divine coincide with my entry into a particular spiritual zone. In these moments, it is as though God's presence becomes palpable, manifesting in ways that deeply resonate with those present. It is remarkable to witness individuals from diverse backgrounds and locations around the globe experiencing this profound connection simultaneously. This phenomenon transcends physical boundaries, as hearts and souls align in unison, drawing everyone into a shared, transformative experience of God's actual presence.

The atmosphere becomes charged with overwhelming peace, joy, and awe, leaving participants with a lasting impression of the divine interaction.

Many have shared that their experience during the services or classes has been phenomenal. Over the years, there have been times when God's presence felt incredibly strong. I would often ask those entering the building if they could feel God's presence outside, and in every case, the answer was a resounding "Absolutely."

I have witnessed God's miraculous acts countless times, and each event uniquely differs from the last. God continues to amaze me.

Ministers have claimed that God was present in their services when, in fact, he wasn't. Adonai would never be present where pagan practices were taking place, nor would He violate His Commandments concerning no other gods. I was ignorant of this in my earlier years of attending various church services.

For as long as I can remember, I sensed a more profound truth waiting to be uncovered. It took me over 20 years to start piecing together the fragments, but it wasn't until recently, during my time in Jerusalem, that the complete picture finally came into focus. The past few years have been a profound journey of revelation, illuminating the intricate tapestry of my understanding.

When I attended Christian Churches, I couldn't understand how God could be present, and there was no evidence. When I inquired about this, I was told that Jesus was present because they used these scriptures.

Matthew 18:19-20 New King James Version: *"Again I say to you that if two of you agree on earth concerning anything that they ask, it will be done for them by My Father in heaven. "For where two or three are gathered together in My name, I am there in the midst of them."*

Then, I was told we have to accept this by faith.

I could never quite grasp the depth of it all. Adonai was a God of profound emotions, and His essence seemed to resonate in every aspect of our lives. How did I come to this understanding? It was rooted in the belief that we were created in His image and likeness, suggesting that the traits we hold dear—love, compassion, kindness—reflect His divine nature. This profound connection made me realize that Adonai's love and compassion transcended our earthly experiences, reaching a level of understanding and empathy beyond our comprehension. It filled me with awe to think that while we grapple with our limited notions of affection, divine love is immeasurable and everlasting, illuminating our existence in ways we cannot fully articulate.

As a servant of Adonai, my life reflects His divine nature, and through all my experiences, I understand the journey we all have traveled. Some of us choose righteousness, while others choose destruction.

Living a life centered on serving Adonai involves a commitment to spiritual principles and practices. Negative influences, often attributed to Satan, can lead individuals to experience doubt and question their faith. Additionally, it is noteworthy that God allows specific challenges, such as the emergence of institutions that may promote harmful ideologies, often facilitated by individuals' deceitful actions.

Life presents a series of challenges and obstacles rather than a continuous stream of successes. Engaging in a spiritual journey, particularly involving a relationship with God, can foster personal growth in wisdom and knowledge. This growth equips individuals to navigate difficulties effectively and empowers them to guide others in overcoming their struggles and achieving victory.

Some people believe that if a school initiative were part of God's divine plan, there would be no resistance or opposition. However, I hold a different viewpoint. The reality is often quite the opposite. We genuinely felt we were acting within God's will, yet it became clear that there was significant opposition from Satan, who sought to prevent us from establishing the school. Nevertheless, we held onto our faith, trusting that God would ultimately pave the way for us. Through perseverance and prayer, we uncovered the true purpose behind this endeavor and witnessed the unfolding of God's plan in our lives.

I was confident that the Plaza was where we were supposed to be. I wasn't sure why, but I'd had the strongest feeling that this was God's plan. So, I wouldn't murmur, gripe, or complain, but I would repeatedly question why things happened the way they did. I never knew that there was a more excellent picture that eventually would be opened up to me.

I asked Julian to fly down and join me as I opened the doors to the small building to usher in the presence of the Lord. I had always been extremely private about my relationship with the Lord and didn't want to draw attention to myself.

The long-anticipated day arrived, and with a sense of excitement and reverence, I instructed the team to open the doors. As we began to sing and worship the Lord, a wave of spiritual energy enveloped us, lifting our voices and hearts in unison. Yet, amid this sacred moment, I realized I had not yet stepped outside to allow the community to witness the source of this movement – to see who we were, what we stood for, and the vibrant spirit unfolding within our walls.

Reports soon reached me that individuals had gathered just outside our entrance. They stood on the steps, watching intently, drawn to the atmosphere of worship. Inching closer with a palpable sense of curiosity and respect, they were careful not to disrupt the sacred gathering.

While I could sense that God was indeed moving among us, I felt a deep conviction that we had not yet reached the pivotal moment we needed to connect fully with those outside. So, on the following day, I made an intentional decision. I planned to emerge onto the steps, allowing the community to see me, to bridge the gap between our worship and their curiosity, and to invite them into this transformative experience.

I wasn't accustomed to stepping outside in public and allowing others to see who I was, but I couldn't let anything hold me back.

The following day, we went outside, and although nothing seemed to be happening, I knew that God was present. I asked Him what I was doing wrong, and He responded, "You can't rely on what you see; you must trust in what you cannot see. The people are inside the buildings, watching and listening."

Now, more determined than ever, I knew that day three would be filled with confidence. I had heard from the Lord and understood what was occurring behind the scenes.

As we gathered outside on the steps, excitement filled the air. We sang with open hearts and raised voices, praising God in joyful worship. The moment felt alive as if all of heaven joined our celebration.

At that moment, I felt a shift within me; it was as if I had crossed a threshold into a sacred space. I stepped into the zone where distractions slipped away and focused my full attention on God, immersing myself in the worship.

As the atmosphere grew more charged with spiritual energy, I noticed people moving toward Julian, their faces etched with hope and longing. They approached him one by one, seeking prayer and guidance. The sight of individuals stepping forward ignited a fire within me; their urgency and faith bolstered my spirit even more. I could feel my energy surging, and I redirected my focus solely on God, determined to be a vessel for His love.

Julian quickly grabbed a notepad from a nearby table during this profound moment. With a steady hand, he began jotting down the names and prayer requests of those approaching him. His calm demeanor reassured them that he would be their liaison, promising to promptly relay their requests to me as soon as I was available. In that busy yet sacred exchange, I could sense the collective faith surrounding us, fueling our worship and deepening our connection with God.

A woman approached Julian in desperation, seeking prayer for her daughter. When Adonai began to fill the area with His presence, she asked if I would pray for her daughter. I paused everything to pray.

The power of God flowed through the phone so remarkably that when I handed the phone back to the mother, her daughter exclaimed, "Mom, please take me to see the lady. I know I have to see her."

Stacey told me the mother asked if I would meet with her daughter, and I said absolutely. I didn't know they wanted to see me right then and there.

As I was heading to the back room to change my clothes, Stacey hurried up to tell me that the mother and her children were in the building. I stopped and turned around to greet the family.

A divider separated the congregation from the view of the street, and when I rounded the corner, I saw a sweet young lady in a wheelchair talking with my granddaughters.

Julian was talking with the mother.

I walked in and sat in a chair close to the young woman, and for her privacy, I will refer to her as Gabby.

Joi and America were a tremendous help during our conversations with Gabby. Their willingness to translate made connecting so much easier, especially when Gabby's mother was speaking, Julian would translate.

Their support impacted our communication, and I greatly appreciated it.

I remember one of Gabby's questions: If I knew what heaven was like, she said she would not live much longer and was afraid she wouldn't go to heaven.

I told her that I had seen heaven twice in two different visions. She asked me what it was like, and while I explained that it was so beautiful, words could not fully describe it. I will convey my experience.

In the first vision, I found myself in a stunning heavenly place. A horse and carriage pulled up, and I was so fascinated by what I saw that I ignored who was inside the carriage. When the carriage stopped, the door opened, and I looked up to see God with His hand outstretched to me. As I began to step onto the carriage, I suddenly woke up.

There was a time when I missed my husband so much that I had a vision of him. I was lying on my bed and dozed off. When I opened my eyes, I found myself in his arms. I could smell the beautiful flowers and hear the soothing sounds surrounding me. Being in his embrace filled me with warmth. I told him I wanted to stay with him forever, and he responded that my work on earth was not yet done, but he would be waiting for me. I felt an overwhelming presence of love and peace in that moment.

After I shared with Gabby how incredible I believed the afterlife to be, she confided in me her deep fear of dying. I reassured her, telling her not to be afraid, as I had experienced death myself. I began to recount the remarkable events that unfolded during that time.

It happened during a prayer meeting at our church. We were all deep in prayer, seeking comfort and guidance, when suddenly, I felt a strange sensation wash over me. In an instant, I had an out-of-body experience.

As I floated above my lifeless form, I could see the concerned faces of my friends and fellow congregants below. They were in a state of panic, frantically trying to revive me. I kept reassuring them that I was okay, to let them know I was right there with them, but no one could hear me.

Despite my attempts to communicate, I was no longer connected to my body. In a surreal moment, I was aware of everything happening around me. When I finally returned to my body, I learned that Gayla was the first to notice something was wrong.

She had seen me slumped over and realized I had stopped breathing. Trained in CPR, Julian quickly jumped into action to check for signs of life.

To everyone's horror, I wasn't breathing; I had technically died. It was at that moment that the atmosphere in the room shifted dramatically. Sensing the urgency and gravity of the situation, my friends began to pray fervently for my revival, pouring their hearts and souls into their pleas. The intensity of their prayers filled the room, creating a powerful sense of hope and faith. Little did they know their collective prayers would soon bring me back.

I told Gabby I knew what was happening around me and felt no pain, only total peace. That there is nothing to be afraid of when you die.

I was able to answer every question Gabby asked through personal experience.

Gabby told us what she was facing. She had brain cancer and had been ongoing chemotherapy, but the results had not been successful, and she only had a very short time to live.

Gabby asked me if she would live, and my reply was yes. Although the doctors told her no, she would only live a few more weeks. Adonai showed me she would live.

Gabby asked me if she would ever walk again, and I said yes. Then she asked about her hair returning, and again, I told her it would regrow.

The more profound experience happened that day, and those gathered, including me, were shocked.

Gabby looked at me and asked if I would ask God if he would hug me.

Wow, I had never been asked that before and didn't know how to answer, so I bowed my head and asked God how I would fulfill that request. I waited for Adonai's direction.

Then he said, "Tell her that when you hug her, I will hug her through you."

I looked up at Gabby and relayed the message from God. Then I stood up, walked over to her wheelchair, wrapped my arms around her, and started praying. That's when an unexplained energy force came down and encapsulated both of us. God hugged Gabby, and everyone in the room had the same experience.

The look on everyone's face revealed the miraculous presence of Adonai, and when Gabby started to leave, she asked if I had a picture of myself that she could put in her room.

My granddaughter, Joi, maintained an excellent connection with Gabby throughout an incredibly challenging time. Over the next several months, after countless treatments and unwavering support from loved ones, Gabby received the joyous news that she was cancer-free. It was a pivotal moment for her, beginning her entire recovery journey.

Gabby often shared with Joi how much the picture of the remarkable woman who prayed for her meant to her; she would gaze at it daily. It served as a source of strength and encouragement, reminding her of the hope and love surrounding her during her most challenging moments. Gabby's resilience and the power of prayer truly inspired Joi and everyone around them.

Lives were changed at the Plaza that day, and miracles happened. If you ask me whether it was worth losing my school, my answer would be a resounding yes.

Witnessing Adonai's impact on people's lives will always be my dream.

That day marked the end of outdoor service on the patio for us. The following week, Julian brought a team to the RV to repair my deck in front of the house. I found myself chatting with a neighbor lady near my towering palm trees, their fronds swaying gently in the breeze. As I stepped back, my heel unexpectedly caught on a large, rough volcanic rock hidden among the soft, sun-warmed grass. I lost my balance and fell backward, the impact jolting me as my head struck the ground with a bone-rattling thud.

I remember the moment vividly; the neighbor's horrified scream pierced the air, shouting, "She hit her head!" Panic struck as the men rushed over, their faces etched with concern, and they quickly helped me off the ground. I was carefully guided into my RV, the world spinning around me.

In that instant, I had a sense that I had flirted with death, but it became clear to me that Adonai had other plans for me that day.

For the next few months, I would be struggling with massive pain, which was limiting my movement. There were times when I felt that I had a concussion. Not only had I hit my head, but I didn't realize that I had also hurt my back.

Once again, the information provided is not intended to be used as professional medical advice but only as a physical description of what I was going through.

A concussion is a type of traumatic brain injury (TBI) that occurs when a bump, blow, or jolt to the head or a hit to the body causes the head and brain to move back and forth.

This sudden movement can cause the brain to bounce around or twist inside the skull, stretching and damaging brain cells and leading to chemical changes in the brain.

Symptoms of a concussion can vary widely and may include: •Headache •Dizziness •Nausea or vomiting •Blurred vision •Sensitivity to light or sound •Difficulty concentrating •Memory problems •Fatigue •Changes in mood or behavior •Sleep disturbances.

It's essential to seek medical attention if you suspect you or someone else may have a concussion. Early diagnosis and treatment can help reduce the risk of complications and promote recovery.

Here are some tips for preventing concussions: •Wear a helmet when participating in sports or activities with a head injury risk. •Use seat belts and child safety seats in cars. •Be aware of your surroundings and take steps to avoid falls. •Encourage safe play and discourage roughhousing.

I lived in Mexico and didn't seek medical advice; instead, I rested and tried to become stronger. There hadn't been much improvement when I realized that I had Medicare and could seek treatment.

One day, when I left my RV and headed to the house where I used to live, I told Stacey to check on flights back to the United States. I needed to figure out what I did when I fell.

Stacey called the airlines and scheduled a flight for May 19th. We were headed back to Dallas.

CHAPTER TWENTY-FIVE
Medical Emergency

When we left Jocotepec, I wondered what would become of my mission there. Little did I know at the time that I would spend the next year undergoing multiple surgeries.

The COVID-19 restrictions were now lifted, and I was ready to address all of my medical issues that seemed to show up rather quickly.

Once we returned to Dallas, Stacey took the initiative to research and find the top specialist in the area for my back issues. After a thorough search, she discovered Dr. Craig C. Callewart, MD, PA, renowned for his spinal care expertise within the Dallas-Fort Worth metroplex. I was scheduled for my first appointment, filled with a mix of hope and anxiety.

When I arrived for the consultation on June 4th with Dr. Callewart, he greeted us warmly, instantly putting me at ease. He began with a comprehensive examination, taking the time to listen to my concerns and understand the details of my fall. His attentive approach made it clear that he genuinely cared about my well-being. He shared with me his trust in God, and that is all it took to convince me that God would guide the doctor's hands so that I wouldn't be permanently disabled.

Dr. Callewart then outlined a detailed treatment plan designed to address the damage and alleviate my persistent back pain. His clear explanations about the necessary procedures and recovery process gave me hope for a return to a pain-free life. With a solid plan and Dr. Callewart's expertise, I felt more confident about tackling my recovery journey.

After being examined by Dr. Callewart, I needed to obtain clearance for surgery, a process I initially thought would be straightforward. However, it turned out to be more complicated. I was referred to a general practitioner for blood work and additional tests to fulfill the pre-op requirements.

On June 17th, 2022, I was referred to a Primary Care Doctor who was out of the office, so her nurse practitioner filled in for her. Her name was Susanne Robinson. When we first met, she asked me why I was referred to her, and I told her that I had to have pre-op tests. I told her that I was a diabetic and had not had my A1C test for years, so I wasn't sure how that was going.

When my A1C was performed, it showed that my diabetes was out of control, which would delay the surgery for at least 60 days. Wanting to get the pain behind me, I immediately returned to the low glycemic diet, and within a week, everything was under control; however, the surgeon still refused to operate until the 60 days had passed. As a diabetic, I have successfully managed my condition through a low-glycemic index diet.

However, following my accident, maintaining this regimen became challenging due to the pain and stress I experienced. It's important to note that trauma can significantly affect blood sugar levels, often leading to fluctuations that complicate diabetic management.

A1C is a blood test that shows your average blood sugar level for the past 2-3 months.

It's used to diagnose prediabetes and type 2 diabetes and to monitor how well you're managing diabetes if you already have it.

The next time I went to my appointment with Susanne, I was delivered some very disappointing news: my A1C was high, and the surgery was bound to be delayed.

When I received the news, I expressed my disappointment, and Susanne asked me why this news was so upsetting. I explained to her that I had to go to Israel and that I needed to leave as soon as possible.

Susanne asked about what I did for a living. I told her that I had been a pastor for over 30 years. When I started sharing with her all that Adonai had done during the conversation, the presence of God filled the room.

Before I left that day, Susanne asked if we could have a word of prayer that God would guide her in her profession. I prayed, and once again, His presence permeated the room.

It would be necessary for me to see Susanne several more times before finally being released for surgery, and each time, she asked if we could pray. I remember she was training a new employee on the last visit, and when I started to leave, Susanne asked if we could pray. This time, it was different. She turned to the young woman and said You must hear her pray; the atmosphere changes when she prays. Once again, the presence of the Lord came in.

The day finally came for the report of my A1C to be sent to my surgeon, and this time, when I went to see Dr. Callewart, the diabetes was under control.

Although it only took a week once I returned to the low glycemic diet to take control, the surgeon wanted to make sure there were no possible complications.

I appreciated his professionalism and genuine concern. Most physicians would ignore the dangers, but I would not. After expressing why he had to wait, I told him I respected him and would comply.

On August 23rd, the back surgery took place. If you remember, I had lost all of my children and grandchildren, so if it had not been for my amazing adopted family, I would have faced the surgery alone. Adonai had put Stacey and my senior staff in my life. With the date now set for the surgery, Ali would be flying in from Mexico on August 26th to help with my care.

Now that the back surgery was behind me, I had to address a few more issues. The fall I had in February was not my first one. The first one took place in 2020 when we first arrived in Jocotepec. I tripped over a strap from my backpack and fell, this time catching my fall with my left hand.

In my experience with health issues, I encountered significant problems following several falls that resulted in the development of trigger finger. When I saw a physician, I was concerned that my other hand had started developing the same problem. I was right; I would need surgeries on both hands.

Additionally, years prior, I had cataract surgery. Still, I was unaware that a complication known as posterior capsule opacification can develop several years after the procedure, leading to cloudiness in vision. As a result, I needed to undergo surgery on both eyes to address this issue.

The surgeries for the right eye were on January 12th, and the left on February 16th.

Reading this chapter may seem like a class in medicine, but by the end of the book, you will discover why I am sharing this information.

Once again, this is for informational purposes only. For medical advice or diagnosis, consult a professional.

When I faced these issues in one year, some would say it was time to call it quits and grow old. Not me. I am just getting an overhaul to live 70 more years.

Posterior capsule opacification (PCO), often referred to as a secondary cataract, is a prevalent complication that may arise following cataract surgery. This condition occurs when a layer of cloudy scar tissue forms behind the intraocular lens (IOL) implanted during the procedure. Patients experiencing PCO may notice symptoms such as blurred or hazy vision and increased sensitivity to glare.

PCO develops from the proliferation of cells originating from the lens capsule, the delicate membrane surrounding the IOL. These cells can migrate and multiply over time, creating a cloudy layer that obstructs light from reaching the retina.

PCO typically emerges gradually over several months or even years after cataract surgery. The intensity of PCO can range from mild to severe; in milder cases, patients might not observe any symptoms, whereas in severe cases, it can lead to significant visual impairment.

Fortunately, PCO can be effectively treated with a straightforward laser procedure called YAG laser capsulotomy. This procedure involves using a laser to make a small opening in the opaque capsule, facilitating improved light passage and vision enhancement. The YAG laser capsulotomy is swift, typically painless, and can be conducted in an outpatient setting.

If you notice blurred or hazy vision following cataract surgery, consult your eye care professional to determine whether PCO is the cause.

Timely diagnosis and intervention can be essential in preventing potential vision loss associated with this condition.

During that particular year, I had a total of five surgeries. I viewed this series of procedures as an opportunity for a comprehensive health overhaul, preparing myself for a healthier future over the next 70 years.

After a few months, I was anxious to be released. It was then that I was told that the journey for total recovery for an individual in my age bracket would be a minimum of two years.

That was not what I wanted to hear. I had to get back on my feet fast; however, there were still more medical issues that I would have to deal with.

In March 2023, I was finally given the release from my surgeon, and I had to return to Mexico.

Before I faced the medical issues, I knew it wasn't time to retire, for I had heard the voice of God. Adonai asked me, "Do you think I gave you my anointing to bring to Mexico or the United States?" Then Adonai said, "Take my Spirit back to Jerusalem."

Before the surgeries, I knew what Adonai wanted me to do. I am His servant and the last prophetess of the world. The urgency to recover was constantly before me.

Now you will find out why I had to open the school at the first location.

A young doctor came to our language classes. She was a geneticist, and my granddaughter Joi was her language teacher. I was curious about what type of medicine she practiced, and when COVID-19 hit the world hard, I had my family go to her office and receive treatment as a preventative measure to protect us from COVID-19. No one in the family was ever sick two years after our treatment.

A geneticist is a scientist who studies genetics, the science of genes, heredity, and organismal variation. They explore how traits are inherited from parents to offspring and how genetic variations influence an individual's characteristics and disease susceptibility.

Geneticists can work in various fields, including: •Research: They conduct experiments to understand fundamental genetic processes, identify genes associated with specific traits or diseases, and develop new genetic technologies. •Medical Genetics: They diagnose and treat genetic disorders, provide genetic counseling to individuals and families, and conduct research to improve the understanding and management of genetic diseases. •Agricultural Genetics involves developing improved crop varieties with higher yields, disease resistance, and better nutritional value, and breeding animals with desirable traits. •Forensic Genetics: They analyze DNA evidence to identify individuals, determine parentage, and solve crimes.

Geneticists are crucial in advancing our understanding of genetics and its applications in various fields, contributing to improvements in healthcare, agriculture, and other areas. I had to make at least one more trip to Mexico.

Once I was released, Joi contacted Dr. Ada and told her what I had been through medically, and she said I needed to see your grandmother immediately. Her body has taken a beating with all the surgeries we need to prepare her for the mission. Ada set an appointment for the day after I arrived back in Mexico. She administered the cells necessary to rebuild my body.

I was in Mexico for a month, packing my RV and preparing to move. It was a very emotional time for me. My son was buried in Jocotepec, and we had spent years traveling back and forth.

One day, while heading from the RV to the house, I came down over the mountainside and realized I wouldn't be living here again, and my heart was saddened. I shed my tears and then thought of what I had to do, and that was to get to Israel.

Our flight left for Israel on April 28th, 2023.

CHAPTER TWENTY-SIX
Critical Mission

When Adonai told me to return to Israel, I understood that my primary purpose was to bring His Spirit to the world. I was incredibly excited to fulfill that mission. However, I just realized I needed to learn more about the Jewish faith and how the monotheistic religions were interconnected.

Team Israel comprised Julian, Stacey, Ali, Joi, and me. When we arrived, I was eager to begin the work I had been sent to Israel, but things didn't unfold as expected.

Instead, Adonai guided us to the Vatican in Rome and Athens, Greece. I was meant to see where things had gone wrong and how people had been misled.

As I mentioned earlier in this book, I learned I was Jewish by ancestry; however, I was unaware of the historical context.

During my trip to Israel, I delved into the history and origins of Jewish culture. This research was enlightening and significantly enhanced my understanding of the Jewish faith.

After completing my studies on monotheistic religions, I am confident I can share my knowledge with you.

Deep within every human being lies a strong desire to connect with the Creator of the universe, Adonai. The challenge is that many throughout history have been unaware of what has separated them from God.

Billions have never experienced the miraculous physical presence of Adonai, while I have been incredibly blessed to encounter this phenomenon for over twenty years. At first, I believed many others like me, but I discovered this was not the case.

I am Adonai's anointed Servant. It is time for my critical mission: to bring His Spirit to the world.

We spent several months in Israel and traveled to other countries to investigate the causes of spiritual blindness. I was ready to accomplish the mission, but Adonai instructed me to wait.

Through several dreams, He revealed to me what I needed to do. First, He showed me that a war would commence on October 7th at 7 a.m. The fighting would be swift and take place by the sea. I was instructed to stay in Jerusalem to protect the city. He assured me that when the military arrived, I would have the power to speak to the enemy and that their weapons would be neutralized.

I shared this revelation with my team. When I awoke on October 7th, Stacey asked if I had heard the sirens. I replied that I hadn't, as I sleep with earplugs to block out external noise. Stacey was shocked to inform me that rockets were being fired at Israel. I responded, "I told you that was going to happen."

I was conscious of the time and remembered that I needed to be in Jerusalem. The war continued for months, and one evening, as sirens sounded again, I shut the windows to protect my research materials in case shrapnel started flying. I went to inform the others to ensure the windows were closed, only to find all three standing on the balcony.

We could hear the blasts from the rockets as we looked out from the balcony. Two missiles were headed in our direction: one toward the building across the street and another straight toward us. I stood there, waiting for the Iron Dome or military defense to intercept the rockets, but nothing happened. I stepped forward into the danger zone, extended my hand, and said "No" while pointing at the missile approaching the building across the street. Immediately, I moved my hand to the next rocket headed straight for us, repeated the word "No," and watched as it exploded. Both missiles were neutralized, and then I turned toward the old city and prayed, "Please protect your city." That night, over eight rockets targeted Jerusalem, but no one was harmed. After the intense attack, Stacey turned to me and said What took you so long? I responded that I was waiting on the Iron Dome to take care of the threat, and when I didn't see that happening, I responded.

Then came the second part of the dream, where I lifted my arm, pointed, and spoke, destroying the weapons.

I understood that I could not let myself be exposed; I needed to remain hidden. What Israel didn't realize was that Adonai had sent me, His anointed Servant, to Israel months before this attack. I was there while Israel prayed for the Messiah.

The next rocket attack was even more significant, and this time, I stood on the balcony with both hands raised. I faced the rockets, repositioning myself to pray in multiple directions once again to protect the city.

Yet, Adonai did not permit me to come forward, so I asked Him why. He replied, "For your protection. I didn't bring you to Israel to die. I brought you to lead the people and teach them how to love, honor, and serve me."

When November came, the Lord told me to write this book so the people could understand how much Adonai loved them and that He sent His prophetess, His Servant.

This book was almost finished when Adonai gave me the next set of instructions: to write an instructional manual titled "Be Ye Holy" to educate the people on what symbols and actions had taken them captive and bring back His Commandments.

The world will never find the Ark of the Covenant, for Adonai placed that inside me.

Adonai conveyed that people must learn about His divine plan once His Spirit is revealed. Then, individuals worldwide would comprehend who He is and how deeply He loves those who honor Him.

For the first time in thousands of years, Adonai sent His anointed Servant to teach people how to serve Him.

World Peace Plan

Adonai's Servant has a guaranteed World Peace Plan that is, without question, one that will change the reign of terror. If the 4 billion individuals who are Christian, Muslim, and Jewish live what they profess, action can quickly be implemented. Invasion of countries for personal wealth must end. Men and women are called on to fight the battles. At the same time, politicians sit in their ivory towers, demanding the human sacrifice of the innocent while war never touches their families. Only wicked demon-possessed animals hide behind their security fences, hearing the praises of others who are just as evil. Their egos fuel their continued wealth and secure agenda. Mothers and fathers who grieve the loss of their children can NEVER be comforted by the words.

"Thank you for your service (sacrifice) while handing a flag. Words cannot bring back the military injured or killed. The homes that have been stripped of their loved ones are all lost for political gain.

Presenting parents, wives, or children with money is total insanity. Money can't restore precious loved ones or families. Countries are fighting each other in a state of hostility, impacting the world, and no one is addressing the real issues. Politicians have an agenda to appease the money-hungry idiots. Money is the goal behind every insane agenda. They are not concerned about the people. They are living in luxury while innocent people have seen their homes destroyed, loved ones crippled or killed. Hostility is running amok with no plan of action. I challenge heads of state: if you believe in taking over countries, then arm yourself and your families and march off to face your enemies. The terrorist that you fear with every breath is the one that stares back at you every morning in the mirror. Not one of you evil demons is a God-fearing man or woman. We don't see you praying before your meetings as you plot the course of action taken. Time to fall on your face before HaShem Adonai (God) and repent, begging forgiveness for violating His precious command ***Exodus 20:13 NLT: "You must not murder. (Kill)***

Look at current world statistics. There are 8 billion people on the planet, of whom approximately half are monotheistic, believing in one God.

The monotheistic religions are Christianity—2.38 billion, Islam—1.91 billion, and Judaism—14.6 million. Together, they make up almost half of the world's Population.

After that, you will find the following five religions' total estimated Population for 2020: Hinduism—1.16 billion, Buddhism—507 million, Folk Religions—430 million, Other Religions—61 million, and Unaffiliated—1.19 billion.

Looking closer at each monotheistic group's core beliefs, all three believe in prayer. Prayer is defined as a spiritual communion with God or an object of worship, such as supplication, thanksgiving, adoration, or confession.

Most Muslims pray five times a day, with their prayers being known as Fajr (before dawn), Dhuhr (noon), Asr (late afternoon), Maghrib (at sunset), and Isha (nighttime), always facing towards the Kaaba. Some Muslims pray three times a day. The direction of prayer is called the qibla; the early Muslims initially prayed in the direction of Jerusalem before this was changed to Mecca in 624 CE, about a year after Muhammad migrated to Medina. Therefore, it is easy to say that in a year, each individual prays to Allah (God) approximately 1,825 times a week, or 35 times. It would appear that with this much prayer, Muslims would be on a higher spiritual plane.

Christians do not have a set prayer schedule. Each denomination may incorporate different forms of prayer, but that is up to the group.

Understanding the Jewish faith, we see different forms of prayer at various times of the year.

Traditionally, three prayer services are recited daily: •Morning prayer: Shacharit or Shaharit ("of the dawn") •Afternoon prayer: Mincha or Minha, named for the flour offering that accompanied sacrifices at the Temple in Jerusalem, •Evening prayer:[4] Arvit ("of the evening") or Maariv ("bringing on night")

Two additional services are recited on Shabbat and holidays: •Musaf ("additional") is recited by Orthodox and Conservative congregations on Shabbat, major Jewish holidays (including Chol HaMoed), and Rosh Chodesh. •Ne'ila ("closing") is recited only on Yom Kippur.

A distinction is made between individual and communal prayer, requiring a quorum known as a minyan. Community prayer is preferable as it permits the inclusion of prayers that otherwise would be omitted.

For this section, it is easy to say that the Jewish people pray three times a day, at least 1,095 times a year, not including the special times of the year, and 21 times a week.

With all this praying going on, can anyone tell me what the countries are fighting about? And who are they praying to? What are they praying about? More importantly, to whom are they praying?

I know that they are not praying to the Creator of the universe, or their attitudes would be different. People would treat each other with kindness, love, and respect.

It is time to reevaluate, seek God's wisdom, and reflect on His nature.

www.ingramcontent.com/pod-product-compliance
Lightning Source LLC
Chambersburg PA
CBHW071647090426
42738CB00009B/1447